CONTENTS

BOOK I

YOUTH

CHAPTER   PAGE

I. THE CHILD 9

II. THE ABBEY-IN-THE-FIELDS 16

III. COUSIN VITART 29

IV. UZÈS 38

V. THE FOUR FRIENDS 46

BOOK II

THE THEATRE

I. THE BREACH WITH MOLIÈRE 55

II. THE BREACH WITH PORT-ROYAL 66

III. " ANDROMAQUE " 74

IV. " LES PLAIDEURS " AND " BRITANNICUS " . . . 83

V. " BÉRÉNICE " 91

VI. " BAJAZET " AND " MITHRIDATE " 103

VII. " IPHIGÉNIE " AND " PHÈDRE " 114

BOOK III

THE PRODIGAL'S RETURN

CHAPTER   PAGE

I. MARRIAGE AND A NEW START IN LIFE . . . 130

II. PORT-ROYAL REVISITED 136

III. POETS ON A BATTLEFIELD 144

IV. THE GREAT POISON CASE 149

V. THE DEATH OF CORNEILLE 160

VI. RACINE AND BOILEAU 167

BOOK IV

THE POET OF THE BIBLE

I. " ESTHER " AT SAINT-CYR 176

II. " ATHALIE " 192

III. A HISTORIAN AT COURT 202

IV. THE FATHER OF A FAMILY 215

V. LAST DAYS 231

EPILOGUE 240

PRINCIPAL WORKS CONSULTED 249

ANALYTICAL INDEX 251

THE LIFE OF RACINE

BOOK I

YOUTH

τό σοφόν δ' όύ σοφία·
τὸ τε μὴ θνατὰ φρονεῖν
βραχύς ἀιών.   EURIPIDES: *Bacchæ*.

'Tis wiser not to be too wise ;
To think no more than mortal thoughts :
Brief are our destinies.

CHAPTER I

THE CHILD

EARLY in the seventeenth century there lived in the little town of La Ferté-Milon a respectable and pious family called Desmoulins. They were Jansenists. Religion, in France—recovering from the new ideas of the Renaissance—had divided into two channels : there were the Jesuits, who attempted a compromise with the strange disconcerting relativities of science ; and there were the Jansenists, plain and dour sticklers for Bible truth, believers in predestination and in grace, whom we may call the Calvinists of French Catholicism. The hotbed of their doctrine was a convent in a secluded valley —the Abbey-in-the-Fields—Port-Royal-des-Champs, near Paris.

La Ferté-Milon is a picturesque little place, on the edge of the Valois country, towards the southern limit of the department of the Aisne. The landscape, wooded and hilly, is fertile enough to-day ; three hundred years ago it was marred by moss and marsh. The Ourcq, now so leisurely in its course, was then too often a rapid dangerous stream. The forests crept close to the streets of the little

town, isolating from the outer world a small but
locally important centre, where families lived and
spread from generation to generation, branching
out into innumerable cousinships.   As in all such
places in France, then as now, the townspeople
were divided into two categories : those who buy
and sell over a counter, or practise some modest
craft, and those, again, who are Civil Servants,
Registrars, Tax-collectors, Agents for the various
State properties, Inspectors of Rivers and Forests,
Clerks of the Inland Revenue ; persons more or less
in contact with the Law, with Medicine, with the
Church and the University. The Desmoulins belonged to this upper stratum of the middle class,
and   married   their   daughters   into   it.   Marie
Desmoulins became the wife of one, Jean Racine,
clerk in the Salt Office ; another sister married a
M. Vitart, a lawyer, also employed in the Salt Office ;
while a third, early a widow, became a nun at
Port-Royal-des-Champs, Sœur Suzanne, the cellaress.

As time went on, Jean Racine became a man of
note in his native town, Comptroller of the Salt
Office ; he was enobled by the King, and bore arms,
of which he was proud : a rat and a swan (*Rat-
Cygne*), a punning allusion to his name which, fifty
years later, will distress his fastidious grandson,
anxious to let the rat drop out of the family
scutcheon, retaining only the musical, the melancholy bird. But to return to this first Jean Racine :
he had eight children by his wife, Marie Desmoulins,
of whom only two have left a trace in our remembrance : the eldest, Jean Racine the younger,
because he was destined to become the father of
our poet ; and a daughter named Agnès, who,

entering Port-Royal-des-Champs as a schoolgirl at the age of twelve, never left the Abbey, becoming in course of time Prioress and Abbess. She was to play an essential part in the life of her immortal nephew, the third Jean Racine.

It was natural that the Jansenist Desmoulins should send their children to school at the convent, which was in their eyes a sort of second Bethlehem, where religion was re-born—where also one of the sisters Desmoulins had taken the veil. Not only Agnès Racine, but her first cousin Nicolas Vitart was educated at the Abbey-in-the-Fields. In 1638, when the little girl was about thirteen, the boy perhaps fourteen years of age, the ties were drawn still closer that bound La Ferté to Port-Royal. The Jansenist community, already regarded with suspicion by Church and State as a nest of semi-heretics and quasi-rebels, entered then on an era of serious persecution. By Royal mandate, the schools were dissolved, and, while the nuns were permitted to remain in their cells, the Solitaries of Port-Royal were dismissed and dispersed. These " Gentlemen of the Abbey," these " Messieurs de Port-Royal " were men of name and fame, celebrated in Paris, who had left the world, and given their fortunes to the poor, in order to live, as hermits, a life of penitence and prayer in the huts they built for themselves in the Abbey grounds. When, in July 1638, little Nicolas Vitart returned to La Ferté-Milon for those long holidays which were enforced by Royal order, he brought with him to his father's house three of these exiled Solitaries : M. Lancelot, the learned Hellenist ; M. Lemaistre, the great lawyer and Latinist ; and his brother, M. de

Séricourt. They remained for more than a year
under the roof of M. and Mme. Vitart, leading exactly
the same austere and penitent life as in their hermitages of Port-Royal. At first they were rarely seen
by the townspeople, for they left the house only
on Sundays and feast-days to attend Mass at the
Parish Church ; but during the summer evenings of
1639 they relaxed to some extent the rigour of their
rule and might be remarked after supper, always
accompanied by M. Vitart, as they took the air on
a little hill outside the town.

We had to pass through more than one street in order to
reach it [wrote one day M. Lemaistre], but we kept our habit of
silence as we went, and, on our return, about nine o'clock at
night, we walked through the streets in single file, one after the
other, telling our beads as we went. The townspeople, seated
at their doors, as is their wont of a summer's evening, would
stand up as we passed by in silence, out of respect to the
Gentlemen of Port-Royal.

During that year of the hermits' visit to La
Ferté-Milon, the eldest son of Jean Racine and
Marie Desmoulins married Jeanne Sconin, whose
father was an important personage in those parts :
Royal Commissioner, Crown Attorney, President of
the Salt Office, and so on. In later days our poet
did not love his mother's people. They were all
(he wrote to a friend) mere country bumpkins—
" ce sont tous de francs rustres "—all, at least, save
one, his Uncle the Canon : " he alone among the
lot of them has a tender and a generous soul." Was
Madame Jean Racine, the younger, " une âme
tèndre et généreuse," like her brother, the Canon ?
We cannot say ; we know very little about her.
Only that she gave birth to her first child, the poet,
about the 22nd of December, 1639, when she was
twenty-six years old and her husband three years
younger ; the child was baptized Jean Racine, like

his father and his grandfather before him ; and in
January 1641, at the birth of her little girl, the
young woman died and left two babies motherless.

While these events were happening the ban was
removed from Port-Royal. The Solitaries left La
Ferté-Milon and returned to their hermitages at the
Abbey, accompanied by M. and Mme. Vitart and
their five children. They took with them Agnès
Racine, who entered the convent as a postulate.
The Vitarts were lodged in a small building just
within the Abbey gates, where M. Vitart, who had
some legal training, exercised the profession of steward
and land-agent to the Community of Port-Royal.

The Racines remained at La Ferté-Milon, except
the girl Agnès. But Jean Racine, the poet's father,
died in 1643, barely twenty-eight years old. The
two grandfathers then divided the babies : the
prosperous Sconins taking the little girl, the old
Racines bringing up the heir to their name and
arms. Probably the children did not see much of
each other—the Jansenist Racines and the worldly
Sconins were not made to mix. I imagine the
orphans like those children of divorced parents,
distributed in different households, who, when they
meet, contemplate each other in silence with a
curious and wistful stare.

Then old Racine, in his turn, died in 1649, and a
comfortable home was broken up. The Racines (at
least this branch of them) disappeared from La
Ferté-Milon. The widow, Marie Desmoulins, drawn
as by a magnet to Port-Royal, found there two
sisters, a daughter, nephews and nieces, but M. Vitart
had died two years after his arrival at the Abbey.

Madame Racine lived there quietly enough, helping
her sister the cellaress in her household duties, a

kind, gentle, melancholy woman, the servant of the saints. But she seems to have missed the home in which she had brought up her eight children, where she had lived of late years between her husband and the little grandson who had been the last of her brood, and who was very tenderly attached to her. "La pauvre Madame Racine!" writes the Mother-Abbess a few years later to M. Lemaistre (that year-long guest of the Vitart's), "she tells me you have been good enough to have some conversation with her, and she is quite consoled. C'est une très-bonne femme, vous le verrez."

Meanwhile Jean Racine, in his eleventh year, was sent to Beauvais, where there was a large grammar school of Jansenist sympathies. He had no longer a home of his own. All the circumstances of what had seemed a safe and solid existence had vanished at a blow : the quiet old house, the important master of it, the tender grandmother, the nurse Marguerite (whom the poet never forgot, and to whom, in his sixtieth year, he still gave a yearly allowance). That wrench from a soft nest to a public school and the rough promiscuity of comrades, often violent or harsh, may account in some degree for certain defects of character noticeable in our poet's earlier life. The beautiful, delicate, imaginative boy, cut off from all his natural surroundings and associations, learned at Beauvais how to protect a tender nature by an armour of sarcasm and biting wit ; he acquired at the same time an oversensitive reserve, a restive independence, a certain selfishness, too, an Ishmael-like resolve to fight for his own hand. Racine remained six years at Beauvais—years of which we know nothing, but which assuredly he never forgot. In the first as in the last of his tragedies the central figure is a little orphan boy : the child Astyanax, in *Andromaque*—an exile in an enemy's country—

> Un enfant malheureux qui ne sait pas encor
> Que Pyrrhus est son maître et qu'il est fils d'Hector ;

and, in *Athalie*, the child Joas, miraculously snatched from the slaughter and nourished, safe at last, in the inmost sanctuary of the Temple, as Racine himself, in his sixteenth year, will be saved and cherished at the Abbey-in-the-Fields.

Those six years spent by Jean Racine in the College of Beauvais were momentous for France. They were the years of the Fronde. The King—a boy one year older than our poet—was a child of eleven when the conjoined revolts of the princes and the Parliament broke out, a lad of sixteen when they ended. The weak point of a hereditary monarchy is always the risk of a Regency. Mazarin ruled both France and the Queen-Mother. The child-king seemed of little importance, while the struggle went on between two different ideals : a constitutional monarchy or an absolute autocracy. It seemed as if the wars of religion might break out again. The Sorbonne and the Jesuits backed an infallible Crown, while Jansenists, Protestants, Gallicans, princes and Parliament clamoured for a constitution. These Liberals were defeated at last in 1653. The power of Mazarin, and after his death the authority of the young King, were acknowledged to be complete, unquestioned, unrestrained ; and Louis Quatorze was the more jealous of his supremacy, because his youth had experienced a long and deep humiliation.

THE ABBEY-IN-THE-FIELDS

I N the beautiful neighbourhood of Chevreuse the Abbey of Port-Royal stands in a steep-banked and humid valley harmonious by the lie of the land, sad by association and because the few buildings that remain there are ruins. Three hundred years ago the valley seemed deeper and darker because of the woods that fringed the heights above ; there were pools and marshy lands in the bottom ; it was a misty dell, a moist and feverish refuge—"Une profonde vallée, une demeure triste et affreuse" (wrote one of the nuns, in 1616), "mais le ciel y était plus screin qu'ailleurs." Nowhere else did the sky appear so serene ! About the time, when Sœur Anne-Eugénie composed this description, an outbreak of malaria drove the community to a convent in Paris, purchased for them by a wealthy Jansenist lady, Madame Arnauld, the mother of the Abbess and of Sœur Anne-Eugénie herself. The nuns remained in Paris for twenty years. During their absence M. Antoine Lemaistre and the earliest of the Solitaries took up their abode in the abandoned Abbey, to lead the hermit's life of meditation, prayer, and manual toil. They drained the marshy fields, they sowed and planted ; when the nuns returned to inhabit the Abbey they found their deserted gardens salubrious and fragrant, full of plants and trees. The Solitaries who had reclaimed, as well as their own souls, the marshy meadows of Port-Royal ; the Abbess, Mère Angélique, who had reformed the Order ; no less than Mère Agnès and Sœur Anne-Eugénie—indeed most of the saints and the scholars of Port-Royal—belonged to one eloquent and pious family : the Arnaulds. They may call themselves d'Andilly, de Séricourt, Lemaistre, de Sacy, de Luzance, or Pomponne. They are all Arnaulds on the father's or on the mother's side. It was the habit in those days, among the landed gentry, for the elder son alone to keep the family name ; the younger brothers took the title of some fief or farm : thus, M. Antoine Lemaistre (our friend of La Ferté-Milon), whose mother was an Arnauld, called himself M. Lemaistre ; but his brothers are M. de Saint-Elme, M. de Séricourt, M. de Sacy, M. de Vallemont. It is as well, early in this history, to familiarize ourselves with a confusing custom, or we shall never understand with whom we are dealing.

The Solitaries, even before the nuns' return, had begun to establish a school in the farms and granges of Port-Royal, where Nicolas Vitart was among their earliest pupils. And it was to this school that in October 1665 young Racine was admitted by an unexampled favour, although he had long passed the age (he was sixteen), since the Gentlemen of the Abbey believed in taking their scholars young, at eight or nine years old, without relinquishing their hold upon them until their schooldays were completed.

Let us imagine young Racine, one autumn afternoon of 1655, approaching Port-Royal from the rising ground above : what a prospect is spread out before him ! The buildings of the Abbey are clustered round its church, whose tall spire rises from the very heart of them. Beyond the stables and the forge, a low tenement is reserved for some of the Solitaries ; but here and there (dotted among the orchards and the kitchen gardens, built against the barns, sheltering under the wall of the Abbey itself) are strange little structures, where other of the hermits have a lonelier abode : great soldiers, great lawyers, great scholars, suddenly converted, live silent and contented in these meagre shanties. Perhaps the watcher on the hill may see them working on the land, hoeing the vineyard, pruning the orchard, digging the deep ditches that drain the marshy hollow, mute as phantoms, yet busily cultivating the fruit and vegetables which not only supply the convent and the school, but are sold in the neighbouring markets to increase the slender resources of the Abbey ; or they are employed on other forms of labour, some of them making shoes, others sawing logs, others, again, translating Greek or Latin texts to be sold for the advantage of the community. They work in silence and apart, each in his solitary sphere, meeting rarely, save to discuss the general interest, or in the Abbey Church. Nothing is too hard for them, nothing too mean ; and he who is cooking the meals or washing up the pots and pans of the day labourers, was yesterday, perhaps, the glory of Paris and the idol of his hour.

From his station on the hill, looking down into the hollow, the boy can see in a sequestered part of the Abbey grounds, quite separate from the market-garden of the Solitaries, a Calvary built in the shade of the trees. Seated in a circle on low wooden benches, before the crucifix, are some twenty women dressed in a beautiful religious habit, a wide loose garment of creamy white wool, a black veil; a long and large cross of scarlet cloth is sown upon the breast. Most of them are spinning, some are busy with needlework, one reads aloud, while the others listen.

But most of all the youth would fix his eyes on that farm of *Les Granges*, which houses the scholars of Port-Royal, for it is there that he will take his envied, his enviable place. The Solitaries will be his teachers; his schoolfellows are chosen among the first families of France. The terms of the school were high: five hundred livres; but a few scholars are accepted free of cost, and Racine, I fancy, is among these, partly, doubtless, on account of his own abilities, but chiefly because of the merit of his kinswomen.

The scholars of Port-Royal were a weapon in the Abbey's Holy War against the Jesuits—a war which was to last for more than sixty years—they were a bomb (shall we say?) calculated to explode a decade or so ahead when a generation, prepared in secret, should burst upon the world in all the vigour of its powers, a Chosen Few, a sacred remnant, bent to an ideal, trained in a spirit, which the redoubtable seductions of the Jesuits could never penetrate, envelop or waylay. Here the Jansenists were poaching upon their adversaries' manor. Were not the Jesuit colleges bringing up the finest flower of the French nobility and gentry? Bringing them up, too, by a method far superior to any which had until then prevailed? Facile, chivalrous, playful, indulgent, the Jesuits have always understood the soul of children. There reigned in their classes an animation, an elasticity, a romantic outlook, which made learning a pleasure. They produced gentlemen and (to a certain extent) scholars, not pedants. But something was lacking, a grit, a zest, a fibre. What was it ? Perhaps a deep sincerity ! At least it is certain that they bred neither a Pascal nor a Racine. Their very perfumes stank in the nostrils of Port-Royal ! Yet the Solitaries borrowed something of their methods : constant but cheerful employment, a tolerant attitude towards the natural exuberance of childhood, a watchful superintendence never relaxed, but full of an affectionate cordiality, approaching comradeship. " I can stand the children's tempers and humours," said Antoine Arnauld, " if they are continually occupied with something or other." Work or play. The great invention of Port-Royal was to give the lessons in French, and not in Latin, as hitherto had been the habit and the rule. Their little scholars were obliged to understand, and then, by all sorts of devices, encouraged to remember. The learned scholars of the Abbey arranged a sort of game, a string of semi-nonsense verses whose lilt and whose rhyme preserved, like flies in amber, a quantity of incoherent facts : notions, Greek words with their meaning explained, which, later on, the children could apply, as we all use words and notions picked up haphazard in our infancy. The rest was chiefly a question of atmosphere and influence : an ambient enthusiasm which penetrated everything, a certain austere amenity, a sacred charm, which emanated from the convent wall behind which moved, prayed, watched, fasted, those sacred vestals who had renounced their humanity on Earth, those white-robed beings with the scarlet cross, whose conversation was in Heaven.

Racine looked at the Abbey which sheltered, among those glorious souls, the gentle old grandmother who had brought him up, his two great-aunts, and an energetic young aunt, rising thirty, whose missionary zeal had sought him out, eager to impress on the schoolboy the sense of sin and the necessity of Grace. " She it was who taught me to know God in my childhood," the poet will write, forty years later, in a letter to Madame de Maintenon.

What a change from Beauvais ! A change not only to tenderness and piety, but to loveliness and loneliness, after the rough bustle of a country grammar school. Jean Racine had barely been for six months a scholar at Port-Royal-des-Champs when the schools again were dissolved, the Solitaries again dispersed, under the ban of Royal and ecclesiastical displeasure. Two relicts lingered on : M. Hamon, who, being not only a hermit but physician to the ladies of the Abbey, was permitted to remain ; and Jean Racine, a hobble-de-hoy, not quite a pupil, and homeless, the kinsman of so many pious women. Since he had nowhere else to go, he was permitted to stay on and finished his education in conditions very different from the constant supervision, application, companionship in which he had begun his indentures to Port-Royal. He picked up a vast deal of Greek and Latin from his old masters, whose " underground " visits to the Abbey seem to have been frequent, especially those of M. Antoine Lemaistre, with whom Mazarin soon made his peace. M. Lemaistre, once the most brilliant barrister in Paris, who gave the lonely boy lessons in diction, taught him how to recite and read aloud in a manner which, one day, far ahead, will make his fortune at Court (such are Time's revenges), and help him to form the two finest tragic actresses of the French stage. Could M. Lemaistre have foreseen the result of his instruction, doubtless he would not have despaired, for he had been a man of the world himself, but would have concluded that the other lessons of Port-Royal would also come to their harvest in due time.

Long days spent wandering in the woods or reading *Euripides* by the pool, they also were a liberal education, and taught the solitary lad that love of Nature which was to mark him all his life. " Il aimait extrêmement les jardins, les fleurs, les ombrages " —he loved exceedingly a garden, flowers, the shade of trees—so his distant connection, La Fontaine, will write of him one day. The trees were his friends, and he loved to talk with them : " Il aimait se promener dans les jardins et *converser* avec les arbres et les fontaines," and these rural passions, adds the Fabulist, filled his heart with tender feeling : " ces passions, lui remplissaient le cœur d'une certaine tendresse."

There still remained one man of learning in permanence at the Abbey, M. Hamon, the doctor, an excellent scholar in the classics, and it was to him that Racine owed the chief of his finishing. A saint, this M. Hamon, but nothing much to look at beside the humorous, pensive, powerful face of Antoine Arnauld, the eloquent outgoing personality of M. Lemaistre. M. Hamon was small, insignificant and sickly as to his outward man. Unspeakably shabby, sometimes in rags, see him seated on a donkey as unkempt as himself, as he goes to visit some sick farmer who feels himself by far the better man of the two ; or look at him again, on his return, munching his daily dinner, a dog-biscuit and a cup of cold water, taken standing from a shelf in the passage. Doubtless young Racine, who in later years admired his rare and mystic spirit, had many a schoolboy laugh at the expense of the man whose remembrance will none the less console his dying hours, at whose feet he will ask to be buried. Yet for a lonely youth, imaginative, self-willed and passionate, the sole companionship of this gentle and saintly eccentric was not perhaps sufficient. Racine's personality expanded unimpeded. Under a strong master, an Antoine Arnauld, an Antoine Lemaistre, his nascent egoism might have been more effectually checked.

We possess one letter that M. Lemaistre wrote to the lad from his hiding-place, dated on the 21st of March, 1656.

My Son,
Send me I beg you as soon as you can the *Apologie des Saints Pères* which belongs to me. It is the first edition, in quarto, bound in marbled calf. The five volumes of the *Conciles* have come to hand ; you packed them famously, and I thank you for all your care of them. Let me know if the books I left at the Château de Vaumurier are neatly arranged on shelves, and if my eleven volumes of Saint-Chrysostome are among them. Dust them all from time to time and set some saucers filled with water at the foot of the book cases (so that the mice may not gnaw the bindings). Give my regards to Madame Racine as well as to your excellent Aunt, and follow their advice in everything. Remember that youth must be led and should not strive to emancipate itself too soon. Perhaps God will let us return where you are. Meanwhile we must try to profit by

this persecution, which should teach us to disengage ourselves from the bonds of this world, so dangerous to a pious soul. Good bye, my dear son. Do not forget to love your Papa as he loves you. Write to me from time to time, and send me my in-folio *Tacitus*.

And the dear bookworm, Racine's " Papa," inscribes his letter : " Pour le petit Racine, à Port-Royal."

Racine was happy at the Abbey. He owed to his kind instructors a solid foundation in the classics and in theology, an intimate knowledge of the best ancient poetry, and, above all, the practice of that Spartan rule, Μηδὲν ἄγαν : Nothing too much ! which in the years to come will regulate all his poetry, giving a decent garment to the most sensitive and lacerated of souls, and imposing, on a psychology which tolerates the monstrous, an exquisite intellectual order and an æsthetic harmony. Yet perhaps in his boyish heart (for who so critical as a boy ? And Racine had a mocking wit) he may sometimes have thought his wise preceptors a little mad. Was M. Hamon, whom he loved, quite sane ? Or that long-nosed, loose-lipped young man with the splendid eyes and a look which varied from solemn brooding to passionate appeal—was M. Pascal, the great mathematician, quite " all there," as he stands broom in hand, lost in a brown study, while he forgets to sweep out his hut in the garden ?—was M. Pascal in his right mind ? Or Mère Angélique, the Abbess, for that matter, who feeds the stranger within her gates with food from a different loaf and wine from a different flagon, according as his sympathies be Jesuit or Jansenist ? All these good people, undoubtedly eccentric, with their incomprehensible grown-up enthusiasms, affront something in the heart of their pupil, cause him to murmur more deeply Μηδὲν ἄγαν, inflame him, by reaction, with a young desire for poetry and splendour and pre-dominance in a free, an unsectarian sphere. And thus explain, it may be, that period of ingratitude and apostasy which, in later days, Jean Racine will expiate with tears and redeem by an undaunted championship of his dear, odd, holy, persecuted saints.

All that lies far ahead. Racine, in those three years of his sojourn at Port-Royal, was, first of all, deeply imbued by the zeal of his Aunt, Mère Agnès, by the goodness of M. Hamon, by the beauty of the valley, by that incomparable atmosphere of peace, of prayer, of piety, of recollection that still penetrates the seven little Odes, first essays of his Muse, which he wrote in his schooldays and collected, later, under the title: *Le Paysage, ou Promenades de Port-Royal-des-Champs*—and in which we see, at strife in a young heart, an instinctive love of free Nature unadorned, and a spiritual enthusiasm for Grace and Discipline.

> La Nature est inimitable
> Et, quand elle est en liberté,
> Elle brille d'une clarté
> Aussi douce que véritable.[1]

And yet there is something else at Port-Royal besides the ancient kingdom of the woods, besides the doe bounding beneath the bright shade of the holly, besides the flowering linden and the oak, giants with a hundred arms, that stand reflected in the shining waters of the pool.

[1] Nature can never be imitated. Left to herself, she shines with a light as soft as it is true.

Je vois aussi leurs grands rameaux
Si bien tracer dedans les eaux
   Leur mobile peinture,
Qu'on ne sait si l'onde, en tremblant,
   Fait trembler leur verdure,
Ou plutôt l'air même et le vent.[1]

The sound of a hymn, wafted across the garden, or a mere sight of the Abbey wall, warns the young poet that there is another ideal than Beauty, Freedom, or Nature to guide our human life :

Je vois ce cloître vénérable,
   Ces beaux lieux du Ciel bien aimés
   Qui de cent temples animés
Cachent la richesse adorable.
C'est dans ce chaste paradis
Que règne en un trône de lis
   La virginité sainte.[2]

. . . Sacrés palais de l'Innocence,
   Astres vivants, chœurs glorieux,
   Qui faîtes voir de nouveaux cieux
Dans ces demeures de silence.[3]

These verses, still so childish—a world away from the choirs of *Athalie*—attack already a theme which will haunt Racine until his dying day : the double character of our humanity.

[1] I see their great boughs trace so plain in the water their shifting image, that it is hard to say whether the rippling wave displace their foliage reflected, or the wind in the branch above.

[2] I look on the time-honoured Close,—
   Fair scene, and well-belov'd of Heaven,
   Which, like a worshipped treasure, hides,
A hundred animated fanes.
There, in this purest Paradise,
Set on a throne of lilies, reigns
   Sacred Virginity ! . . .

[3] O palaces of Innocence !
   O living stars ! O choir of Saints !
   You a new Heaven build and grace,
In this your silent dwelling-place !

Mon Dieu, quelle guerre cruelle !
Je trouve deux hommes en moi.[1]

So he will sing in his old age, not yet free from the double attraction which tore his young heart asunder, at sixteen, in the woods of Port-Royal.

The Gentlemen of the Abbey, coming and going in secret, giving as they passed their surreptitious lessons to their solitary pupil, viewed with no favourable eye his talent for making verses—a snare, no doubt, set for his feet to drag him from the strait and narrow gate ! One day the lad showed his version of the Latin hymns in the Breviary to M. de Sacy. How could he have forgotten that M. de Sacy himself had translated them in quite a different style ? The worthy Solitary glanced at Racine's verses with cutting disapproval—so hard is it for the middle-aged to understand the young —and told the young author that, clever as he was, poetry was evidently not his line—bid him, in fact, " go back to his gallipots," as the *Quarterly* reviewer bade young Keats, only Racine's gallipots were his classical studies. He had better leave verses alone ! Probably an eager, melancholy, quick-tempered boy treasured up too closely in his solitary heart the remembrance of such trifling grievances. A few years hence Racine will be very insolent to M. de Sacy. It was unpardonable, of course.

More than ninety years later—in the middle of the eighteenth century—Racine's youngest son will write his biography. He was so young when his father died that they can have had little direct communication. But Louis Racine had learned from his mother,

[1] My God, I wage a cruel war !
I find two men in me.

from his elder brother, and from the poet's friends, many details of a life which had already become a sort of pious legend, and, among other things, he has left us this account of Racine's education at Port-Royal.

His great delight was to bury himself in the Abbey woods, with some volume of *Sophocles* or *Euripides*, which he knew almost by heart. He had a marvellous memory. One day he came by chance across a Greek novel, *The Loves of Theagenes and Charicles*. He was devouring it eagerly when the Sacristan, Claude Lancelot (the great grammarian, author of the *Garden of Greek Roots*), caught him in the very act, snatched the volume from his hands, and threw it into the fire. My father found means to get another copy, which suffered the same fate. He managed to buy it again, and, determined not to run the risk of being deprived of it once more, he learned the tale by heart. He then took the book to the Sacristan and said: " You can burn it, sir, if you choose."

Evidently relations were occasionally strained between a defiant, irascible young poet and his admirable but absolute professors.

CHAPTER III

COUSIN VITART

THERE came a moment when Greek and Latin no longer sufficed for young Racine's education, when he must go to the University and study theology or law. His " Papa," Antoine Lemaistre, hoped to make of him a barrister—for, if you were not yet ripe for a hermitage, what career could be nobler than the Bar, the defence of the defenceless? So Racine went to Paris to study logic at the Collège d'Harcourt. But he could not feel drawn that way. And when, that very year, 1658, the lawyer-anchorite departed to a brighter world, the boy he had consistently protected felt free to choose a more congenial profession.

Life offered no very brilliant prospect to the lad of eighteen, but a possible opening was marked out for him. His cousin, Nicolas Vitart (his father's first cousin, which, as they say in France, is an uncle, " à la mode de Bretagne ") was now in his turn the land agent of the Duc de Luynes, and there was plenty to do in the office. The Duke's mother had married for her second husband the Duc de Chevreuse, owner of great estates in the neighbourhood of Port-Royal. In 1657 this Duc de Chevreuse had died, childless, leaving all that property to his widow, and she, in her turn, had just bestowed

it on her son, the Duc de Luynes, an eminent
Jansenist, whose young heir, the Marquis, sometimes
lived in Paris with the Vitarts, a very handsome
and engaging youth, whom we shall meet, in later
days, as the charming, absent-minded Duc de
Chevreuse, the friend of Fénelon.

A certain knowledge of law comes handy to a
land agent. Racine continued his studies at the
University, but without disdaining a stool in Cousin
Nicolas's office. Young Vitart was now a man turned
thirty, much considered and consulted by the
Ladies of the Abbey, by the Solitaries, by M. Pascal
himself. The three brothers Perrault (the doctor,
the architect, the teller of fairy-tales) frequented
his salon, and so did the admired academician,
M. Chapelain, a wretched, but eminent, poet and an
excellent man. In fact, a distinguished literary
circle assembled in the suite of rooms that M. Vitart
occupied in the mansion of his pious patron, the
Duc de Luynes. When Racine left Port-Royal
and came to board with his cousin, he made great
friends with young Madame Vitart, and his letters
are full of allusions to this charming " Aunt,"
for whom he had evidently a feeling near the
frontiers of the " Pays du Tendre." He writes
verses to her, and gives her the name of *Amaranthe* ;
they are on terms of affectionate teasing : a bright,
shallow, innocent little friendship, just the spray
tossed into the air by the irrepressible Fountain of
Youth.

At this point we come closer to Racine ; we depend
no longer on dates and anecdotes ; we possess his
early letters. Some of them are written to his
sister, Marie Racine, two years younger than himself,

who still is living at La Ferté-Milon with their grand-father, M. Pierre Sconin. She is a person of im-portance in her way. Though eighteen years old, unmarried, her letters are addressed to " Madame Marie Racine," for the Racines are noble (by the sign of the Rat and the Swan), while the poet's correspondence with his Cousin Nicolas's wife is directed to " Mademoiselle Vitart." (And when Marie Racine marries the doctor, she, too, will climb down and become just " Mademoiselle Rivière," as befits a plain bourgeoise.)

This young Racine of twenty is a handsome youth. All the portraits we possess of him are taken in a large curly wig with a great abundance of dark ringlets on the forehead and shoulders ; such was the fashion of the age, and if becoming, it is annoying to the physiognomist. How high, how broad was that smooth brow ? We cannot tell, nor the shape of the head, nor the set of the neck. The straight, long regular nose betokens sense and order. There is a pout in the charming lower lip (corrected by its upward tilt) which may mean obstinacy, and just a hint of temper. But the large full expressive eyes, the smile, are full of sweetness and charm. An open engaging countenance : one day Louis XIV will declare it one of the handsomest and most attractive faces to be seen at Court. And the bright spontaneous grace of the young man's manner accompanied this prepossessing presence, sometimes rising into a rapture of poetical enthusiasm, more often lively and satirical, full of quips and epigrams, yet sometimes fading away into a sort of dreamy woolgathering from which it was difficult to rouse him.

The first of Racine's letters to his sister was occasioned by one of these fits of inattention (caused, perhaps, by too great an absorption in his own affairs), he had forgotten an errand she had asked him to go for her.   Invited to a wedding, the young girl had wanted a muff and had written to her brother in Paris bidding him choose one and send it her at once.   But the muff had not arrived in time for the festivity.

I will not tell you [writes Racine] that I was out of town when your letter came, or that I was so plagued by business that I did not know which way to turn, for you would not believe a word of it. . . . My Aunt Vitart says that she wrote to you about the muff.   My Cousin Vitart was really the cause of my not getting it.   I was already in the street, hurrying off to buy it, when he called me back, saying that I knew nothing at all about muffs and such-like, and that I should be the cause of your getting a very bad bargain ; it would be far wiser (so he said) to let my Aunt undertake the purchase.   But her opinion was that the winter was already too far gone and that I ought to ask you to choose in preference something that you could go on wearing throughout the summer.   If you will only let her know what you would like, within the limit of two golden crowns, you shall have it without an hour's delay.

" My Aunt," of course, is Nicolas Vitart's wife. When Racine is out of town the cousins count among his most constant correspondents.   They have only one rival, a certain Abbé Le Vasseur, whom the poet had met in their rooms at the Hôtel de Luynes, a young spark in Minor Orders, a fashionable curate, already foreshadowing the eighteenth century *Abbé de Cour*.   Racine makes great play on his friend's fancied passion for a certain beautiful Mademoiselle Lucrèce, for whom the poet supplies sonnets when required ; he also writes one to celebrate the birth of the Vitarts' second baby ; and another in praise of Cardinal Mazarin—Mazarin, the persecutor of the Abbey! It was this one, I imagine, which brought down on the head of Jean Racine the vials of the Abbey's wrath. Poetry! and such poetry! Alas! the duck will take to water, the weeping willow bend its boughs, and it is very difficult to prevent the born poet from writing poetry—at any rate while he is young. Port-Royal, which had heaped favours on Racine's ungrateful head, expressed consternation, and expressed it frequently.

Every day I get letter after letter, or rather excommunication after excommunication, all on account of my miserable sonnet.

Racine is out of town, writing poetry as hard as he can, but ostensibly seeing after certain repairs to the Château de Chevreuse—that new possession of his cousin's patron ; and he complains that he has not a soul to whom he can show his verses. M. Vitart is too continually occupied. " M. Vitart est rarement capable de donner son attention à quelque chose." In despair the young poet, remembering Malherbe, has thought of reading his verses to the cook—" une vieille servante qui est chez nous "— until, just in time, he remembered that she was as arrant a Jansenist as her master, the Duke. Thus he escaped utter ruin. Still, with his Ode unread, gone in, like a checked eruption, he is out of sorts and distinctly cross. The Abbé must contrive to spend a few days at Chevreuse, were it only in order to listen to the Ode, which has been shown to no less a personage than M. Chapelain. The great man has pronounced it " fort belle et fort poétique," but suggested certain corrections. " And I have made them all (cries the poet), and am the most perplexed of mortals, not knowing now whether I ought not to correct the corrections."

This *Ode to the Nymph of the Seine* was destined to have a certain influence on Racine's future. It was written to celebrate the entry of the young Queen into Paris. There was a young King of France in those days, one year older than Racine, very nearly as handsome and as agreeable. Although he was over head and ears in love with Cardinal Mazarin's Italian niece, he was first of all a King, and had sacrificed his heart's desire, marrying instead the stupid Spanish princess in order to restore peace to Europe by signing the Treaty of the Pyrenees. And a poet of twenty-one has summoned from the vasty deeps the Nymph of the Seine to welcome the bride of a King of twenty-two. And the marvel of the affair is that the poet is Racine, and that the King is Louis XIV.

One day, when M. Vitart had less on his mind, he had (as we have learned) shown the Ode to M. Chapelain ; and the bard had observed that Racine had peopled the River Seine with Tritons. Now Tritons, it is well known, are of a constitution that requires sea-water, and are never known to swim inland, like salmon in certain seasons. The unfortunate young poet had counted on his Tritons to escort his Nymph, and was much perplexed as to what he could put in their place :

I am sure I wish them all drowned together—Nymphs and Tritons—so much trouble the plaguy things have given me !

The Ode, however, was worth the pains he spent on it. A convinced Racinian can still read it with interest and remark how the poet, in his compli-

ment to the Queen, has exactly foretold the coming
Classic Age (which that dull *mariage de convenance*
had rendered possible), the golden days which suc-
ceded the clash of war while the Seine slipped between
the most glorious shores in Europe.   But, of course,
the prophecy was accidental.   Our young man was
chiefly occupied with the hope that M. Vitart would
not forget to give the Ode to M. Colbert, and that
he, in his own good time, would hand it on to the
King. So it was ; and Louis, enchanted with his
young well-wisher's smooth and musical epithala-
mium—as clear, as liquid, and almost as colourless
as the waters of the Seine itself—sent Jean Racine
a purse with a hundred golden coins in it, and
placed him, soon afterwards, on the Civil List with
a yearly pension of six hundred livres (say, £150 of
our money) awarded him in his character of man of
letters.   And Racine began to cherish a youthful
hero-worship for this new Alexander, so like himself
in age and in looks, who, coming home crowned with
laurels, singled out among the welcoming crowd of
his adorers a young poet and gave him the means
to acquire celebrity.

Racine was heartily tired of his position as clerk
of the works for the repairs of the Castle of Chevreuse.
He dates his letters from *Babylone*.   And yet it
might appear a delightful retreat—such a picturesque
old château crowning a steep hill with a little town
nestling in the valley—quite near Port-Royal, too
—but that perhaps, at the moment, was not an
unalloyed advantage.   The Saints of the Abbey
were always insisting that our young poet should
forswear the muse and give his whole mind to
jurisprudence with a view to practising, some day,

at the Bar. Meanwhile, they allowed he might consent to accept " one of those employments which, without precisely leading to a fortune, at least procure those comforts of life which console a man for the irksomeness of depending on a patron " (I copy the phrase from Louis Racine's *Mémoires*), that is to say, he might go on being an overseer until he could maintain himself as a barrister.

Left in charge at Chevreuse, to be out of harm's way, our sonneteer spends most of his time idling about the village ; noon and night, as he boasts, he haunts the tavern where he dines and sups, yet he finds time to take a volume of Ariosto into the woods and reads poetry in the shade of the trees, a thing he always loved ; finds time, also, to write verses of his own, especially on rainy days, when he works in the Duke's bedroom, where he sleeps o'nights in the absence of the master ; and sometimes he springs on a horse and rides over to the Abbey to see his fiery Aunt and that kind grandmother, whose least indisposition melts the icy acerbity of the young malcontent into a flood of anxious tenderness. With all this (and we may reckon five or six hours a day as given to his books), he does not forget to supervise his masons, glaziers, and carpenters, " who obey my orders exactly, and ask for something to drink my health with when they have finished their piece of work. . . . And that is how I spend my time in Babylon."

If only he had spent it as innocently in Paris ! sighed Port-Royal. . . . We have no hint as yet of any moral backsliding on the part of young Racine ; but he was a slave to Poetry, and the Muse, to make matters worse, had put on the most pernicious of her masks and attracted him to the theatre, which the Saints of the Abbey considered as the very gate of Hell. Racine had somehow got acquainted with La Roque the actor, with an actress or two from the Théâtre du Marais, and even with a star from the first playhouse in Paris : the Hôtel de Bourgogne. It was rumoured that he was writing a play.

" Only (he confides to the Abbé Le Vasseur) I fear that actors in these days care for nothing save *galimatias* : high falutin' gibberish is all right if it be decked with the name of a great writer." He had written first *the* great writer, " le grand auteur." And the " grand auteur " of 1660 was Corneille— Corneille whose encumbering glory filled the throne of Fame. Corneille's defects were, naturally, especially visible to a youthful rival eager to scale the heights, push him off and take his place. A spirit of sacrilege often haunts the soul of gifted youth, ready to make a bonfire of the idols his father worshipped. The young clerk of the works at Chevreuse was willing to tackle a host of yesterday's giants : Corneille, with his Spanish emphasis and grandeur ; La Calprenède, with his old-fashioned graces and gallantry ; Madeleine de Scudéry, and all the descendants of *Astrée !* Long live simplicity and a natural elegance ! Long live a direct and immediate expression of things, sublimely felt rather than sublimely said ! Long live the new manner and the coming age ! While our young man in his retirement was meditating these revolutionary opinions, he suddenly fell dangerously ill of a fever.

CHAPTER IV

UZÈS

A STAY in a warm climate was considered necessary for the young man's complete recovery. And Port-Royal was desirous of breaking his connection with the theatres. It seemed therefore, to those pious minds, a direct intervention of Providence when Racine's maternal uncle, Father Sconin, Vicar-General of the Cathedral of Uzès in the south, Prior of Saint-Maximin, ex-General of the Order of Saint-Geneviève—evidently quite an uncle to be proud of—invited his nephew on a long visit. Racine, eager for so complete a change, set out in great haste, without even waiting to provide himself with all the papers which Church and State required from persons taking up their abode in a distant province and a new diocese.

This Father Sconin seems to have been a man of Racine's own intelligent and restless disposition, but such a character is rarer at fifty-three, which was about his age. Witty, alert and full of plans, with more than one benefice in his pocket and more than one iron on the fire, he had begun to weary of his sojourn in Languedoc, though he had built himself a fine house at Uzès, the handsomest in the town after the Bishop's palace, and enjoyed a comfortable income. One day he thought of his dead sister's gifted son—and Racine sets out on his journey in November 1661, with a view to being, possibly, made Canon of Uzès, or of exchanging that benefice for a Priory in the neighbourhood.

He had never thought of taking Orders. But his intimacy with the Abbé Le Vasseur had left him with a diminished idea of the renunciation involved in such a step. For a man who has to earn his own living there can be no easier way—none, at any rate, which leaves so much leisure for reading and writing. Besides there was time to reflect—he had made no engagement. This departure was just for a journey and a visit, which might possibly lead to a new career.

In those days it was quite a considerable undertaking : a caravan of twelve travellers rode together day after day as far as Lyons, where they stayed for two days to visit the town and its neighbourhood. In a sail of fifty hours, a boat took them down the Rhone—through some of the loveliest scenery in France ; they stopped a night at Vienne, another night at Valence, and thence, across country, by Avignon to Uzès, which is on the road to Nîmes.

The difference between the north and the south of France is surprising even in our own times. Young Racine found himself in a foreign country, an amused, excited, keen-sighted spectator.

It was at Lyons [he wrote to his distant connection, Jean de la Fontaine], that I first found out I could no longer understand what was said to me, nor make myself intelligible to others ; but here, at Uzès, it is worse by far. I swear that I need an interpreter no less than if I were a Muscovite in Paris. I am just beginning to see that this queer lingo is compact of Spanish and Italian, so (as I have a certain knowledge of those languages) sometimes I am able to make a shot at a phrase.

Uzès stands piled on a very high mountain which is but one
continual sweep of rock (this drains off the water), so that,
whatever the weather may be, one can walk dry-foot all round
the town.   The country is covered with olive-trees which bear
the finest olives in the world—to look at—but it is a fallacious
fruit, as I found out to my cost the other day.   I put one in my
mouth, with the liveliest movement of curiosity and appetite—
and, for a good four hours, I had the tongue and the palate
seared by its insupportable astringency.

The beauties of this region are not confined to those afforded
by Nature. . . .   There's not a Goody Two-Shoes among the
peasant girls but might dispute it with the prettiest Maids of
Honour at the Court.   All these women are dazzling, and know
how to set off their looks in the most natural way in the world.
Such figures as they have !

> *Color verus, corpus solidum et succi plenum.*

But there !   I'll say no more about it, which would be to
profane the pious house of a clergyman.   *Domus mea, domus
orationis.*   They said to me : " Be blind ! "   And, if I cannot
quite be blind, I may at least be mute, for I must be clerical
with the clergy, just as I was a wolf with you and all the other
wolves of your society.   *Adiousias !* as they say here.

At Uzès Racine seems at first to have been happy
enough.   He had made himself a study in a tower
standing   apart   in   the   pleasure - grounds   of   the
Bishop's palace—a tower it was called, but it was
rather a domed and columned Renaissance pavilion
(just befitting the genius of Racine), overtopped by
an immense micocoulier or nettle-tree, prodigal of
its shade.   A vaulted chamber is its principal apart-
ment, and from its balcony the young solitary could
look   towards   an   immense   amphitheatre   of   hills
across a fruitful plain, through which a river chatters
in   the   wheels   of   an   old   mill,   as   it   divides   the
fields.   In that cool place Racine studied prodigiously,
reading   Greek,   reading   Latin,   reading   theology.
Father Sconin sends to Avignon for a pile of books,

and his nephew sets to work on St. Thomas Aquinas with the sweetest docility. Not a doubt appears to have crossed his mind, either then, or at any other period of his existence. The universe was still in his eyes a machine, self-contained, exquisitely combined and balanced ; and who that sees a watch can doubt the existence of a watchmaker ? If he hesitated about taking Orders, it was never the truths of religion that he called in question, but merely his own fitness for proclaiming himself their minister.

He seems to have liked his uncle—" le seul de la famille que ait l'âme tendre et généreuse." He was a kind and friendly being, " d'un naturel fort doux " ; gentle by the hearth, but adroit and energetic as a man of business. He appeared the moving spirit of all those parts, where nothing was done without consulting him. And yet, though treated as an Oracle, how often the wily Gascons twisted him round their little finger ! His scheme was to transfer his canonicate at Uzès to his nephew, as being too good a thing to waste, although for his part he was weary of living in the south ; but, despite a hundred compliments from his colleagues, Father Sconin never obtained his desire.

At first Racine seems to have fallen in with this programme willingly enough. The beauty of the climate, the classic landscape, the grace and liveliness of the Gascons enchanted him. The Canon's new house was a fine place—" la plus régulière et même la plus agréable de tout Uzès," almost entirely completed, in great part furnished, with a garden, not yet entirely planted, which it would be amusing to lay out. The mild winter suits his health, though his fever has not quite left him when he writes to his sister in January 1662 to wish her a happy New Year. He stuffs his page with impromptu verses, an unpretending Christmas card :

> Nos oiseaux ne sont point forcés
> De se cacher ou de se taire,
> Et, leurs becs n'étant pas glacés,
> Ils chantent à leur ordinaire
> Et font l'amour en liberté
> Autant l'hiver comme l'été. . . .

> . . . Le ciel est toujours clair, tant que dure son cours,
> Et nous avons des nuits plus belles que vos jours.[1]

But, little by little, the sense of exile begins insidiously to steal over Racine (as already over his uncle, Father Sconin), and he asks himself in sharp anxiety if he can really live out his life among these amiable foreigners ?

The people of these parts, when they say *France*, mean all that lies beyond the northern bank of the Loire. And you remember that Furetière in his *History* situates the Kingdom of Gibberish, the land of *Galimatias*, in the region that extends beyond the southern shore of the same river. . . .

Not that he has any fault to find with these sonorous Gascons, save their dialect :

There is more open-mindedness among them than I expected to find. Some of them have read and admired not only M. Pascal's *Lettres Provinciales*, but M. Lancelot's *Méthodes*, and they all seem to possess M. Lemaistre's *Addresses*. At

---

[1] Our birds are not compelled to seek
    A hiding-place, head under wing ;
    The frost has never sealed their beak,
    And they continue still to sing,
    Make love, and build (in this fair clime),
    In winter as in summer time. . . .

Our skies are ever clear, through Phebe's changing rays,
And we have southern nights more lovely than your days

least, so it is with the Huguenots! . . . As for the Catholics, with a few exceptions, they are quite under the thumb of the Jesuits. Our monks here are, perhaps, the greatest fools alive, and the most ignorant. They never open a book, and I keep out of their way as well as I can. To say the truth, I have conceived a certain horror of the do-nothing life of a monk, which I cannot sufficiently dissemble. Of course I am not speaking of my uncle, Father Sconin, who is mighty little of a monk and an excellent theologian.

Young Racine admires the neat houses, the pretty daughters of the Huguenots : " Nous n'avons pas de belle catholique." It is life that interests him, not the quarrels of the Chapter—and he is beginning to bless the delays of the administration which has not yet sent after him that *démissoire*— that dismissal from the diocese of La Ferté-Milon (a sort of warrant of excorporation), without which nothing could be done in the way of ecclesiastical preferment.

But my uncle has already dressed me in black from top to toe. The fashion of this country is to wear a Spanish cloth, very fine in make, costing three-and-twenty livres the yard, and in this habit, which my uncle has had made for me, I appear one of the most prosperous citizens of Uzès.

Sometimes a passionate event breaks the tedium of his days. The young man in black has a keen eye for the dramatic. He remarks the tragic end of a love story.

I will tell you a little tale which is strange enough. A young girl of Uzès, who lived not far from us, poisoned herself yesterday. She had time to confess before she gave up the ghost. Everyone thought she must have been with child and that shame had driven her to this furious resolution. But, when her body was opened, it was clear that never yet was maid more maiden than she. Such is the point of honour in the people of this country whose passions push them to the last extremity.

The length of Racine's letters show how heavy

the time hangs on his hands, despite his studies : Latin theology, Spanish meditations, Italian histories, Greek Fathers, " and not a French book among them all." He annotates Homer and Pindar with an assiduous pen that still has plenty of leisure to write interminable screeds to Le Vasseur, to Cousin Vitart, to his " Aunt," to his sister—but that finds no hour for Port-Royal.

What can I write to my aunt the Nun ? to my great-aunt Vitart ? [he says to Le Vasseur]. It is surely enough to play the hypocrite down here, without adding a canting correspondence with my relations. For I call it playing the hypocrite to write letters full of piety and devotion recommending myself to their prayers. Not that I do not want their prayers ; but I should like them to be a free gift, and not to have to ask for them. If ever I am a Prior, I will give them as many as they want !

A fine country, a fine climate, a fine house, and fine clothes are all very well in their way, but, decidedly, they cannot bait the trap. Already in the summer of 1662 Racine writes to his Cousin Nicolas : " I think I should not always like to live in this part of the world." And in the course of July he says to Le Vasseur, " I am looking out for some dramatic theme, and think I shall soon set to work on a play."

The difficulty is to find a graceful exit from Uzès. His uncle, Father Sconin, has been very kind to the young man. But since that scheme of a Priory has mysteriously fallen through, he cannot surely suppose that his nephew is going to stay with him for ever, doing nothing.

Not for worlds would I appear ungrateful or grasping [writes Racine]. And yet he must know that I have not come so far to get nothing by it. I have shown him such an open heart and so much docility that perhaps he thinks we nay go on living together like this, friends and housemates, with no prospect for my future. I have not yet ventured to tell him that this cannot be, for I should like him to keep his good opinion of me. " J'ai peur qu'il ne me croie intéressé."

I cannot say in what way the delicate problem was solved, but it is clear that Racine did not take Orders; and though from time to time throughout his life he was inclined to bewail his lost career as a monk, he was to find another in Paris that, after all, fitted him better. In the late summer of 1663 he left Uzès on excellent terms with his uncle. It was, indeed, thanks to Father Sconin that, during the early years of his literary life, Racine found himself at last endowed with the income of the Priory of Sainte-Madeleine de l'Épinay in Anjou—an honorary clergyman enjoying the revenues of a sinecure, which he will not resign until 1673—when all Paris is acclaiming the triumphant author of *Bajazet*. Such malversations of ecclesiastical property were not uncommon in the seventeenth century, and, indeed, had their uses. Both Boileau and Racine profited by them. And it was considered very noble in the former, when, convinced at last that he had no intention of ever taking Orders, he resigned his benefices. But public opinion was already beginning to protest. Racine was compelled to abandon his priory. Its place in his budget will be taken by another sinecure. He was made treasurer of France for the town of Moulins, where he never set foot. *Autre temps, autre mœurs.* Without the Priory of Sainte-Madeleine should we have come into possession of *Britannicus* and *Bérénice*? For my part, I am more and more inclined to believe that, when genius is born without a silver spoon in its mouth, the State should put it there.

CHAPTER V

THE FOUR FRIENDS

IN 1663, when Racine returned from Uzès, Paris was full of men and women of genius. Pascal, it is true, had died the year before, under forty. But there were still various old glories encumbering the ground, quinquagenarian rubbish, such as Pierre Corneille, the Cardinal de Retz, the Marquis de La Rochefoucauld, that relic of the Fronde ; Bossuet was thirty-six ; Madame de Sévigné and Madame de la Fayette were brilliant young women in their thirties. These were not Racine's friends. He was, so to speak, on the other side.

But in his own set there were beings no less remarkable. One of his connexions at La Ferté-Milon had married Jean de la Fontaine, who was an intimate crony of Molière's. Racine soon got on familiar terms with them both, and their group attracted a brilliant young adherent, Nicolas Boileau-Despréaux.

Our poet had returned from Uzès with a sudden hunger for fame, for conversation, for pleasure. He took up his quarters as of old at the Hôtel de Luynes, but with no intention of working in Cousin Nicolas's office. He will be a writer of plays, and is already hard at work on the first of them : *La Thébaïde, ou les Frères ennemis.* To a mind as steeped in the classics as Racine's, the word expressed the Theban cycle and all the tragic history of the family of Œdipus; but the same expression is frequently used in French to denote a deep solitude, on account of those Egyptian deserts where the earliest Christian hermits built their lonely cells; and when Port-Royal heard that its pupil was writing poetry, this title of *La Thébaïde* was, at any rate at first, though a happy misconception, a balm upon the wound.

Besides the little playhouse of the Marais, where Racine's acquaintance La Roque was employed; besides the Italian Masks, who had an art of their own, there were two important theatres in Paris capable of producing a great poetical tragedy : the Hôtel de Bourgogne, which was the old Court theatre, with grand traditions and a noble style; and the new Théâtre du Palais Royal, where Molière reigned supreme. These theatres were different from ours—plain oblong halls, something in the style of the Vieux Colombier in Paris, with, in front of the stage, a pit or *parterre* where the audience had standing-room. Behind stood some twenty rows of seats, each of them raised a little higher than the one before it. On either side of the hall a double tier of gilded balconies was divided into boxes, of which the nearest to the stage contained the orchestra, chiefly fiddles. The middle of the stage was naturally reserved for the actors. At either end half a dozen straw chairs were set casually, and these were the most expensive places in the house, reserved for persons of eminence and fashion —and priced at six livres apiece (say, thirty shillings of our money), while an entrance to the pit cost only fifteen sols. The theatre was lighted by hanging candelabras, garnished with tallow candles, which on gala nights, when the King was expected, were exchanged for wax.

Of these two houses, the Hotel de Bourgogne was the more elegant. It was the Court theatre ; several of the actors, like Montfleury and Floridor, were men of noble birth and excellent education ; the first had practised at the Bar, the second had been an officer in the Royal Guards, until, stage-struck, he had thrown a good career to the winds. The profession of actor in those days was held in the gravest disrepute, at least formally, and anathematized by the Church ; yet never were actors more familiar with the great, covered with praise and favours by a public which made all the more of them here below, since it could not hope to meet them in Paradise.

Naturally, Racine, in his ambition, aspired at nothing less than the Court theatre for his play. We find him writing to his friend Le Vasseur in December 1663 :

I finished the Fifth Act yesterday. At the Hôtel de Bourgogne they have promised to accept it, but in any case it could only pass after three other plays, already received.

A long time to wait !

Meanwhile the future Duc de Beauvilliers, an eminent patron of letters (of whom I have given a portrait in my *French Ideal*), had introduced Racine at Court, and one November morning of this same year, 1663, he had made a new acquaintance there :

I met Molière at Versailles, at the King's Levée, and His Majesty paid him all sorts of compliments. I was pleased to hear him so belauded, and he, I think, was pleased that I was present.

Had the two men met before ? Probably not, though they had a mutual friend in La Fontaine. But, after eleven years spent in touring the provinces with varying fortunes, Molière had only returned to Paris in 1658, and Racine, in his turn, had been nearly two years absent. They knew all about each other and soon made friends.

" I hear you are writing a play," said the great actor-manager. " Bring it to me." And he promised to produce the *Thébaïde* without loss of time. It was a great temptation. Of course, if he took it to the Court theatre, there would be an endless wait. And Youth seldom knows how to wait. So Racine sent his tragedy to Molière.

The Palais Royal was the second theatre in Paris. Its tendencies were modern, its methods alert and brisk—none of the romantic sing-song of the Hôtel de Bourgogne. In his brief tenure Molière had already put more than one masterpiece on the stage. He was in the very hey-day of his powers. If he had not yet produced *Tartuffe*, he had written it, and had read it in private to the King and in several drawing-rooms. His star was rising to its zenith. The free and natural character of his genius delighted an audience saturated by the romantic emphasis of yesterday, and the public turned from Corneille to applaud Molière, acting in his own *École des Femmes*. He was the man of the hour, and none the less admired because his private life scandalized the clappers in the pit. (The King took it quietly enough.) For Molière, having lived openly for twenty years with Madeleine Béjart, leading lady in his company, who still adored him, had recently married her young sister—some said her young daughter—a girl of nineteen. And Racine writes to his friend Le Vasseur :

Montfleury has lodged a complaint against Molière ; he says the man has married the daughter and lain with the mother.

Son and grandson of wealthy upholsterers, who each in turn had held office at Court as Valet de Chambre du Roi, Molière had been destined to follow his father's trade, but, feeling a strong bent for books and study, he had begged his father to send him to a famous Jesuit College, where he had been brought up among the choicest sprigs of the nobility. At twenty-two he threw away all his chances in order to found a theatre, which failed, and soon lodged him in prison for debt. Thereafter came those eleven years when, with a troop of strolling players, Molière scoured the centre and the south of France, reading Menander or Plautus by the light of a farthing " dip " placed on the kitchen table of the sordid tavern where he sups, gaining priceless experience of the oddities of human character, until, having after all put something by, he is able to start afresh in Paris, as manager of the Palais Royal Theatre. In 1663, when Racine made his acquaintance, he was a year or two over forty.

The same age as La Fontaine. La Fontaine was the link that bound together men so different as Molière and Racine. The delightful fabulist was a loose liver, whom Molière could not scandalize, and yet an excellent moralist. Full of imagination and indolence, he was one of those hopeless poets, incapable of anything save poetry, who are perhaps

more profoundly poets than any of the others.
A simple-witted country bumpkin he might seem at
first sight; but "Le Bonhomme," as they called
him, "Goodman La Fontaine," was shrewd to the
point of finesse, when it was a question of observing
other people, and stupid only when he minded his
own affairs—which minding did not mend. He
lived in a state of chronic ruin, generally at someone
else's expense. He was writing his *Contes* when
Racine returned to Paris, and will not publish the
immortal fables until some five or six years
later on.

Soon a fourth poet was attracted to the coterie :
Nicolas Boileau as we call him, or Despréaux as
he was known to his contemporaries, for, being a
younger son, he had taken the title of some fief or
farm, leaving the family name, out of deference, to
his elder brother, M. Boileau. Our Boileau was
M. Boileau-Despréaux, known as Despréaux for
short ; and his brother Pierre was M. Boileau de
Puymorin, always called Puymorin by his acquaintance ; a fourth brother, the Abbé, used the
family name, for a clergyman is anyone's equal
anywhere.

Despréaux was three years older than Racine,
a lively, sparkling, charming little fellow. He had
been a student in the School of Law, when his father
died, who had been Clerk of the Court, and had
meant his son to follow in his footsteps. He left his
children each a little fortune, and Despréaux was
free to choose for his profession that of being the
most respectable of poets, unattackable in his own
private life, a born satirist, and censor of other
men's follies, yet the warmest-hearted of friends.

It was generally at his rooms that the four friends met when they did not prefer to dine or drink together in some famous tavern: the *Mouton Blanc*, the *Pomme de Pin*, or the *Croix de Lorraine*.

It was Abbé Le Vasseur who, by showing Boileau (already noted as a critic) the manuscript of Racine's *Ode to Fame*, brought the two young men together, and henceforth we can hardly think of them apart. As well try to separate Don Quixote and Sancho Panza. With Molière and La Fontaine they constituted a sort of literary club or academy, of which La Fontaine has left an enchanting account in a Preface to his adaptation of Apuleius' *Cupid and Psyche*.

Four friends who had made acquaintance on Parnassus, united in a sort of society which I would call an Academy if their number had been larger and if they had paid more attention to the Muses and less to their own delight. Their first regulation was to banish from their assembly anything approaching a formal discussion or academic conference. If some question of Art or Science should turn up in their talk, they profited by the occasion without exhausting the subject, flitting rather from one remark to another like bees who in their flight wander from flower to flower. Envy, malignity, the spirit of cabal, were allowed no entrance. They admired the works of the Ancients without refusing their praise to their own contemporaries. They spoke modestly of their own efforts, and gave each other excellent advice if any of them should be stricken by the malady of the age and write a book. Polyphile was perhaps the most subject to the complaint.

Polyphile, the General Lover, is the name which La Fontaine bestows upon himself, and we remember the lovely verses which conclude the tale of *Cupid and Psyche*.

Volupté, volupté, qui fut jadis maîtresse
  Du plus bel esprit de la Grèce
Ne me dédaigne pas ; viens t'en loger chez moi ;
  Tu n'y seras pas sans emploi :
J'aime le jeu, l'amour, les livres, la musique—
La ville et la campagne, enfin tout ; il n'est rien
  Qui ne me soit souverain bien,
Jusqu'au sombre plaisir d'un cœur mélancolique.[1]

Polyphile, then, is La Fontaine, and each of his three friends has a nickname which is a sort of label : Molière is the laugher, Gélaste ; the respectable Boileau-Despréaux is Ariste, the Excellent. And Racine ? At first we are surprised by the curious surname given to Racine : Acante, the prickly acanthus, a beautiful leaf whose thorny spikes can inflict a wound. And we remember that in later days Despréaux will declare his friend to have arrived at virtue through religion, for Nature had left him imperfect : " In his youth he was fidgety, teasing and jealous—(inquiet railleur, et jaloux) " ; and we recall a letter of Racine's to his sister Marie, in which he says that though at bottom such good friends, when they meet they spar and ruffle each other. " Le tendre Racine ! " who would have thought it ? Well, it is possible to be both irritable and tender. Racine was sensitive. One day he will confess to his son that the least criticism, though beneath contempt, " would cause him more annoyance than the pleasure of any praise could

---

[1] Pleasure, O Pleasure ! you that used to be
    The mistress of the rarest mind in Greece,
  Disdain me not, O Pleasure, stay with me,
    And I will find you various ministries.
  For Love I love, and Play, Music and books ;
  I love the town, adore the woods and brooks.
  Ay ! Everything I love ! Nor rank apart
  The sombre pleasure of a brooding heart.

compensate." And, in his young days, certainly he was quick to take offence.

Let us see what part he plays in the dialogue that interrupts La Fontaine's preface. He is the lover of Nature. It is he who drags his three cronies from the tavern-parlour in search of some remote and leafy spot :

> According to his usual habit, Acanthus proposed a walk outside the town, in some quiet place where there would be few passers-by. He was extremely fond of gardens, of flowers, and the shade of trees. These passions filled his heart with a sort of tenderness.

In the heat of their conversation he alone breaks off to remark the colours of the sunset—palest blue, the pink of dawn, orange, deep crimson ; and, as he gazes, he falls into a sort of ecstasy so that his friends have some trouble in getting him to leave the Park of Versailles where they have been walking.

> Il aimait se promener dans les jardins et converser avec les arbres et les fontaines.

He, too, knows the sombre pleasure of a brooding heart. When his friend laments the destiny of Psyche, he remarks :

> If we must shed tears, well, let us weep ! It will do us no harm. The heroes of antiquity were acquainted with wet eyes. Compassion has its charms, Ariste, which yield in nothing to the delight of laughter—indeed, I believe they bear away the palm.

He is a sensitive, quick-tempered young man, thrilled by the beauty of Nature, quick to pity, fond of his friends. No very great or deep emotion as yet has stirred his heart.

BOOK II

THE THEATRE

Τί δ'ἀισρχὸν ἀνθρώποισι τἀλλήλων κακά ;
EURIPIDES, Suppl. v. 768.

Are we not all sinners, God help us ?
J. M. SYNGE, *The Tinker's Wedding.*

ὅ, τι καλον, φίλον ἀεί.—EURIPIDES, *Bacchæ* v. 893.

A thing of beauty is a joy for ever.—KEATS.

CHAPTER I

THE BREACH WITH MOLIÈRE

I FANCY that Racine had always considered the Palais Royal Theatre in the light of a make-shift. His natural bent was all in the direction of elegance, distinction, a noble tranquillity masking a depth of feeling. These qualities, which he rated perhaps too high, Molière, it may be, esteemed too little. Racine thought that Tragedy should move in a sphere aloof from our everyday world ; he regretted the majestic tread, the modulated chant of the King's comedians at the Court playhouse. He was sure that Molière's actors played his piece too fast—almost as though it were written in prose—and walked across the stage as they might have walked across the street. And he attributed the merely modest success of *La Thébaïde* to the short-comings of its performers.

Yet *La Thébaïde* did not do so badly. It was given twelve times between the 20th of June and the 18th of July, 1664, when the dramatic season came to an end, and Molière's company moved out of town to play to the King in his different country residences. It reappeared upon the bills so soon as the theatre opened again in Paris. A young unknown writer might have thought himself fortunate. But Racine had expected greater things, and his whole nature smarted with a baulked ambition. *La Thébaïde* is not a very good play, but it is beautiful. There are passages which have already the rarest quality of Racine's verse, especially certain lines whose pure monosyllables fall heavily, drop by drop, as though wrung from a bleeding heart :

> J'ai senti son beau corps tout froid entre mes bras,

or

> Tout ce qu'ont de plus noir et la haine et l'amour,

beauties which seem to presage the cry of Hippolytus, wrongfully accused :

> Le jour n'est pas plus pur que le fond de mon cœur !

But what young, eager, ambitious heart was ever satisfied with having produced an unacknowledged beauty ? Racine determined to select for his next play a subject nearer to the times, to make concessions to the spirit of the hour. He chose the story of Alexander : *Le Grand Alexandre*, that great forerunner of Louis XIV. The youngest of poets dedicated this pæan, praising the youngest of conquerors, to the youngest of kings. There is youth everywhere in Racine's second tragedy— youth, and a showier heroism than he allows elsewhere. The play was built with an eye to the public, and while animated by a sincere and touching enthusiasm for the King, was evidently meant to startle and waylay. And yet, after all, it met with no more than the quiet, not dazzling, success which *La Thébaïde* had enjoyed in the previous year.

The new play, produced on the 4th of December, 1665, had been heralded by prophecies of triumph. In the drawing-room of Simon Arnauld, Marquis de Pomponne—a friend from Port-Royal—Racine had read it to La Rochefoucauld and Boileau, to Madame de Sévigné and to Madame de la Fayette. Great had been their enthusiasm, yet the public remained tepid when the play was put upon the stage at the Palais Royal.

Racine's chagrin was so intense that we find a trace of it remaining in the remarks of several of his contemporaries. He was always an irritable author, prone to think his play compromised, imperilled, by this or that trifling incident. And as yet he was not inured to his " dreadful trade." He appealed from Molière and the public to the King— the splendid original of the Grand Alexander. Ten days after the first night at the Palais Royal, the tragedy was played before Louis XIV in the drawing-room of the Comtesse d'Armagnac, and played by the actors of the Hôtel de Bourgogne. Between a banquet and a ball the piece was received with an enthusiasm which filled Racine's aching soul with satisfaction and delight. He himself had taught the several actors their parts. Ah ! not for nothing had the saintly Antoine Lemaistre instructed his pupil at Port-Royal in all the secrets of a moving and noble delivery ! The King was present, and his brother, and his brother's wife, *Madame*, the delicious English princess, daughter of Charles I, grand-

daughter also of Henri Quatre ; she was the real
Queen of the Court of France (where no one paid
much attention to the dull, excellent Maria-Teresa),
and all the Court had loudly applauded *Alexandre*,
noting every beauty, seizing every allusion : was
this glimpse of glory to fade without a morrow ? ·

Racine's friends encouraged him in his brooding
discontent with Molière's actors. We read, for instance, in the Anecdotes of Furetière, the *Fureteriana* :

> This fine play fell from the boards. M. Racine, in despair
> at such a desperate failure, accused his friends, who, he declared,
> had given him too good an opinion of his own work and thus
> induced him to produce it in public. The friends replied :
> " Your play is an excellent play. But you have put it into
> the hands of comic actors who play it as though it were a
> comedy ; and there is the whole secret of its fall. If the
> comedians of the Hôtel de Bourgogne were to produce your
> tragedy you would see what a success it would have ! "

This, at least, was more flattering than the opinion
of the Great Corneille, who (as we learn from
Valincour and Louis Racine) attributed this distress-
ing lack of laurels to the very modest talent of
the author. " Young man, you have no gift for the
theatre ! " so he said. This was worse than the
criticisms of M. de Sacy !

Coaxed and goaded, tempted, spurred, Racine
determined to take the law into his own hands.
On account of that performance at the Comtesse
d'Armagnac's Festival, he had already rehearsed
his play with the actors of the Hôtel de Bourgogne.
A few nights later, on the 18th of December—just
a fortnight after its first representation at the
Palais Royal—*Le Grand Alexandre* appeared on
the stage of both theatres. It was a thunderclap.
This time, at any rate, the restless Racine had

succeeded in cutting off the tail of his dog : all Paris was talking about the *Grand Alexandre*. He had not said a word beforehand to Molière. Lagrange, the Actor-secretary of the Palais Royal, records in his Register the surprise sprung upon his comrade :

> This same day, December 18th, our company was astonished to find the very piece we were acting produced on the stage of the Hôtel de Bourgogne. The thing was managed secretly in a conspiracy with M. Racine, and, as he had used us so ill, we decided to mulct him in his royalties, and so serve him out for thus rehearsing his play with other comedians.

Then for some time both the Palais Royal and the Hôtel de Bourgogne continued to give the *Grand Alexandre*,—like two nightingales singing against each other in a wood, each exciting the other to a purer triumph.

Was the acting at the Palais Royal really so poor ? The two heroines were impersonated by Armande Béjart, Molière's young wife, and by the beautiful Mademoiselle du Parc, surely at least as attractive as the plain and middle-aged, if intelligent, Mademoiselle des Œillets, and the buxom Dennebault of the rival theatre. Was Floridor in the part of Alexandre superior to La Grange ? Probably not, so far as talent goes ; but then there was that question of style : Racine preferred the Grand Manner. Whatever his taste, we should have hard work to apologize for his conduct were it not for an excuse which never fails, when the culprit is a young man (something of a Daphnis, too), with little experience of the tender passion. Racine was in love with one of those actresses of the Palais Royal on whom he had heaped mortification and annoyance. We have been told that Love sometimes begins with a little aversion. Strange, that in what was to be the great passion of Racine's amorous life, his first movement should have been to snatch himself away, to break the connexion. Perhaps unconsciously he was afraid of his own feelings. And this very movement of recoil precipitated in the young man's breast that vague, painful, quarrelsome, apprehensive emotion which made him so irascible. And he knew that it was Love. Like the shepherd of *Astrée*, like Sylvandre, he was to learn that absence is the fuel of a great passion. Once the eyes have done their work, once the blow has struck home, the fever of the wound is inflamed by solitude and renunciation.

En l'absence, l'entendement de celui qui aime agira beaucoup plus parfaitement que quand, transporté par l'objet qui se présente á ses yeux, il ne peut faire autre chose que regarder, désirer, et soupirer. C'est par les yeux que l'amour commence. . . . Mais, si jamais vous avez voulu penser profondément à quelque chose, souvenez-vous, Madame, si la sage Nature ne vous a pas appris de mettre la main sur les yeux, afin que la vue ne divertit point les forces de l'entendement.[1]

Racine could no longer look on Mademoiselle du Parc ; his own act had banished him from that which at last he knew to have been a Paradise. He was the sole Parisian who could never attend the representations at the Palais Royal, where for some time *Le Grand Alexandre* was given as regularly as at the Hôtel de Bourgogne. The rhyming gazettes,

[1] In absence, the mind of a lover acts much more perfectly than when, transported by the visible object, he can do nothing save look, long, and sigh. It is through the eyes that Love begins. But, if ever you have wished to reflect deeply on any subject, remember, Madame, how wise Nature taught you then to shade your eyes with your hand, so that vision should not dissipate the force of the understanding.—*Astrée*.

which were, in those times, the equivalent of the
dramatic *feuilletons* of to-day, trumpeted the
praise of Mademoiselle du Parc ; and our young
author discovered that he read them with a double
interest—to see what they said of himself and what
they said of her.

> La du Parc, la belle actrice,
> Avec son port d'impératrice,
> Soit en récitant, ou dansant,
> N'a rien qui ne soit ravissant.[1]

ran the jingle. Thus, though it was impossible for
Racine to see the lovely actress who played his
Queen, the circumstances of his life combined to
make it just as impossible that he should forget her.

Marquise du Parc (it was her quaint Christian
name : she was Corneille's " belle Marquise ") was
some five years older than Racine. She was the
daughter of a famous charlatan of Lyons, Giacomo
de Gorla, a native of the Grisons, who, like all the
great operating dentists of the time, employed a
band of music and a troupe of actors to distract
his patients' attention. Such were their anæsthetics :
in the midst of a burst of laughter the tooth was
drawn, while fife and drum drowned any untimely
scream. De Gorla had his headquarters at the
Lyons Fair, but radiated probably in all the country
round. His was no doubt a wild and gipsy life :
Marquise, for all her name, was not brought up
in the Faubourg Saint-Germain. Molière, in his
Impromptu, makes her complain that she shall never
be able to play the part he has set her, because it is

[1] Du Parc, the lovely actress, plays the Queen,
A perfect Empress, she, in port and mien,
Whether she dance, or whether she recite,
All that she does is done for our delight.

the part of a pretentious *précieuse* : " and never was
woman less ceremonious than I." We may imagine
her, perhaps, in her natural and passionate free-and-
easiness as a dangerously seductive creature for a
young Jansenist to encounter. Her brilliance was
a little dimmed, perhaps, when Racine first made
her acquaintance by the recent death of her husband, René Berthelot, who, some twelve years
before, had seen her at the Lyons Fair in all the
splendour of her dawning twenties. He had married
her there and then, and carried her off in his
manager's strolling company. She seems to have
been an excellent wife and mother, though perilous
to others' peace of mind, as Beauty must be—that
dissolving or healing radium of the moral world.
While the troupe was acting at Pézenas, the charms
of Marquise so turned the head of a certain poet,
Sarrasin, secretary to the Prince of Conti, that he
lost his reason. And we know the effect she produced
on the two Corneilles. She seems to have been
quite blameless in the matter, and even to have
enjoyed a certain social consideration in her native
town, for, among the godfathers and godmothers
of her several babies, we note the names of the
Archdeacon of Lyons, and of Catherine, daughter
of Nicolas de Neuville, Marshal of France and
Governor of the same city—a sign that she was
esteemed in the place which had known her childhood
and her girlhood. After the death of René Berthelot
in November 1664 she stayed on in Molière's company, for she had to earn the bread of four children
and a stepmother.

She was, as well as an actress, a wonderful dancer.
How admirable she had looked as the Spirit of

Spring, in the *Plaisirs de l'île enchantée* at Versailles, just before her husband's death ! She had worn a bright green robe embroidered in silver, and sown all over with flowers reproduced in their natural colours. In Paris, on the stage, she danced in the ballets, magically transformed into a leaping sylph, whose robes, slit up the sides, showed in her most ecstatic bounds a glimpse of slim long legs encased in satin tights. And, off the stage, she appeared a mild and gentle young widow, disconcertingly preoccupied with the memory of the late René Berthelot, attentive to the needs of her growing girls and her little son of four.

It was for her that Racine wrote *Andromaque*, which is, if not the best, at least the warmest, the most ardently pulsing of his plays, occupying, in his theatre, a place comparable to that of *Romeo and Juliet* among the tragedies of Shakespeare. Was not Andromaque also a young widow, gentle, sorrowful, and good, the sole stay of a little son about the age of Jean-Baptiste Berthelot ? There is, in Racine's conception of his heroine, a pure respect, a delicacy of feeling, an air of innocence and sorrow victorious over passion, which make the *rôle* a thing apart. Monime and Junie and Esther are good women, too, but none of them have that singular sweetness, that madonna-like charm. It was evident to Racine that Mademoiselle des Œillets, the actress of the Hôtel de Bourgogne, could never interpret Andromaque : it must be Mademoiselle du Parc, and she alone.

It was, however, a ticklish matter to negotiate, for feeling ran high between the two theatres ; more so than ever since Racine had carried off his tragedy so cavalierly to the Hôtel de Bourgogne, accusing Molière's actors of being unable to play it. Two years before Molière (thinking perhaps of Racine) had parodied a young author dissatisfied with the simplicity of his troupe.

What ! Do you call *that* dramatic diction ? You must give the thing emphasis and weight. Listen to me !

And there had followed a cruel skit of the mannerisms peculiar to the Hôtel de Bourgogne. In these conditions, how could Racine ask the friend he had offended to resign to the rival stage one of his leading ladies ? Mademoiselle du Parc was not a free agent. Actors, like servants, were engaged from Easter to Easter or from Michaelmas to Michaelmas, and she would not be at liberty to choose until the end of March 1667.

But, when that time came, although *Andromaque* was not yet ready to be rehearsed, indeed far from finished, although Mademoiselle du Parc was applauded night after night in the part she had created in the *Misanthrope*, she left the Palais Royal for the Hôtel de Bourgogne. It was at that time, I imagine, that she became the mistress of Racine, but we have no knowledge of the date of their connexion. We only know that in November she reappeared upon the stage—but it was the stage of the Hôtel de Bourgogne—playing the title part in Racine's new tragedy, *Andromaque*. The poet had taught her the words, regulating every accent, every gesture. And the result was a triumph whose echo still vibrates after three hundred years. According to the dictum of Boileau, Du Parc was not, by the gift of Nature, a great actress. But she

was beautiful, or, as the plain-spoken Boileau puts
it, a fine figure of a woman ; she was docile ; she
was in love with her young animator, and it was
enough. Her name will always be associated with
the poetry of *Andromaque* ; a halo lingers round her
still. Racine, however, had bought her love and
his triumph with the price of Molière's friendship.
The breach was never mended, though either poet
continued to admire the genius of the other.

THE BREACH WITH PORT-ROYAL

IN the summer of 1663 (for we must retrace our steps) Jean Racine had returned from the south to find his grandmother still living at Port-Royal, but such a frail old woman, so often ailing, that the young man's letters to his sister are filled with alarm and anxiety—for this, after all, was the chief affection of a life too often uprooted and transplanted, and he saw that it hung by a thread.

I cannot tell you how distressed and grieved I am. And indeed I should be the most ungrateful being in the world if I did not love a mother who has always shown herself so kind, and has cared for me more tenderly than for any of her own children. And she would have loved you just as much, if she had had the chance of letting you see her loving heart.

This letter is dated the 23rd of July, 1663 ; on the 13th of August Racine writes to his sister that the blow has fallen :

Adieu, my dear sister. My sorrow is too deep for words. Farewell again ! The death of my mother must make us dearer to each other, since soon we shall, each of us, have no one else to love us.

But from this year 1665 until 1681 we possess no other letters from Racine to any member of his family. Either the casket that contained them has been lost, or, as I am inclined to think, the breach was complete, the poet's relations having espoused, in a famous quarrel, the part of Port-Royal.

With the death of his grandmother, following on that of Antoine Lemaistre, the links were broken which had bound Racine to the home long ago accorded to his orphaned youth. Of the persons remaining at the Abbey-in-the-Fields, M. Hamon alone had touched his difficult, insensitive heart. His young Aunt's fiery admonestations, " excommunication sur excommunication," merely revolted him. He began to think Port-Royal intolerant of Art or Love or Beauty. Although in his mind a doubt never tarnished the neat mirror in which the Church reflects Infinity, he had returned from the south with a dwindling belief in the religious life. The wrangles of the Chapter, the paltry clerical intrigues, the lazy dirty monks of Languedoc, the talk of benefices and preferment—often accorded to persons not in Holy Orders—all this had weakened the respect and reverence in which he had been brought up. It is possible for a gifted imaginative youth to have been too carefully educated. When, on quitting his pastors and masters, he sets foot in the rough world, and sees it as it is, he thinks his instructors were hypocrites or liars, since they gave him no notion either of his own nature or of other men's. The cynicism of youth is often a protest. Life has not come up to a young man's expectations, and he considers that he has been deceived. He turns from his dreams of yesterday and burns the idols that he worshipped. In such a mood the harsh Acante, in his resentment, will arm himself with the biting wit, the bitter raillery, that are his weapons of self-defence.

What religious feeling he had left (and it was indestructible) appears to have transformed itself for the nonce into a passion of æsthetic sensuality. A modern novelist assures us that there is nothing more dangerous than a certain nobleness of nature in a young man leading a fast life, nothing more reckless than such a soul's contempt, disgust, for the world and men's opinions.[1] He might have been writing of Racine at seven or eight and twenty.

And, at the same time, the poet found himself in possession of a great inner force which must wreak itself somehow. Genius and Passion and Youth have taken hold of his being. The *libido sentiendi* succeeds to the *libido sciendi* ; turn by turn, he will pluck the golden apples off the Tree of Life. There is a mysterious connexion between the explosion of sensual passion and the creative instinct in art ; it is indeed doubtful if any being, wholly free from that fever in the veins, has ever attained a high intellectual development. Racine at this moment was writing his magnificent tragedy of *Andromaque*, living delightfully with the beautiful Marquise, who will soon incarnate the creature of his imagination. It was high summer with him, and he thought his love and his poetry could subdue all the powers of this world and the next—little aware of Life's secret and sly revenges.

It was in such a mood that he received the following letter from his Aunt, Sœur Agnès de Sainte-Thècle at Port-Royal :

[1] Rien de si dangereux que la noblesse dans un jeune être livré au plaisir ; le mépris d'une belle âme pour le monde, et son dégoût de la vie.—FRANÇOIS MAURIAC, *Le Jeune Homme*.

26th August (probably 1666).

Glory be to Jesus Christ and the Most Holy Sacrament !

Having learned of your intention to visit the Abbey, I had begged our Reverend Mother for leave to receive you, because several persons had told me that you were thinking seriously of the state of your soul, and I should have liked to hear it from your own lips. What joy would be mine if God should please to touch your heart ! But, during these last few days, I have heard a report which has very sorely grieved me, and I am writing to you out of the bitterness of my heart, shedding tears which I wish I could pour out in such abundance before God as they should win from Him the price of your salvation, which is, of all things in this world, that which I do desire the most. With what grief have I learned that you are plunged more deeply than before in the society of those persons who are abominable in the sight of all those who, in however feeble a degree, are truly pious ;—they are persons against whom the church-door is closed ; they are those who (unless they repent them of their evil ways) even in the hour of death must remain excluded from the communion of the faithful. Judge, my dear nephew, what that must mean to me. You know with what tenderness I have loved you ; you know that I never asked of Heaven more than that you should serve God in some honest employment. I beseech you then, my dear nephew, have pity on your soul ! Look into your own heart and see into what a pit you have flung yourself !

I trust that what I have heard may prove untrue. But if you should be so unhappy as not to have broken off communications which disgrace you in the sight of God and men, you must not attempt to come to see us here. For you know that I could not exchange a word with you, deeming you to be lost in such a deplorable error, contrary to all true Christian sentiment. Nevertheless, I shall never cease to pray God that He may have mercy upon you, and, so doing, have mercy also upon me, to whom your salvation is precious.

Sœur Agnès de Sainte-Thècle Racine.

Sœur Agnès (she was not yet Mère Agnès) was a woman still on the further verge of youth—that is to say, a little under forty. Racine had known her all his life, she was his father's sister ; they had prayed together beside the death-bed of old Madame

Racine.   He could receive these objurgations from his
Aunt without loving her less—perhaps he felt touched
by her pure sincerity.   He could not support a like
challenge from a man, from any man, not even from
one of his old masters at Port-Royal.

Some months later, in the midst of the belated
triumphs of *Alexandre*, appeared a strange sort of
promulgation from the pen of M. Nicole, the celebrated moralist of the Abbey.   No names were
mentioned, but Racine well knew who was aimed at
when the worthy man declared : "A Poet is a
Public ·Poisoner and a writer for the stage should
be considered as guilty of the murder of innumerable
souls."   Moreover, he went on to say (turning the
dagger in the wound) that a dramatic poet has lost
caste in the eyes of all respectable persons.   This
was the most unkindest cut of all.   A Public
Poisoner ?   Perhaps.   A low Bohemian ?   Never in
the world !

Acante flew to his pen.   Never was he more
completely Acante.   His opening letter has the
brilliant incisiveness of rage—it is a flash of light-
ning.

And so [he writes] the man who writes a novel or a comedy
is a Public Poisoner ?   And the man who writes the *Provincial
Letters* is a Saint !   Sir, I beg you, tell me what difference you
see between the two of them.   M. Pascal—no less than any
of us—was a writer of comedies.   What takes place, after all,
in a comedy ?   You put on the stage a sly fellow of a servant,
or a miserly old cit, or an extravagant marquis.   It is certain
that M. Pascal aimed higher.   He chose his *Dramatis Personæ*
in the convents and at the Sorbonne.   And sometimes he put
on the stage this order of monks and sometimes that, but all
of them were Jesuits.   How many parts he made them play !
Sometimes he shows us an affable Jesuit, and sometimes a bad
Jesuit, and always a ridiculous Jesuit.   Admit then, Sir, that

since your comedies and ours are so surprisingly alike, ours cannot be entirely criminal.

This was touching one of the Sacred Books of the Abbey, where Pascal took rank among the prophets. But the vindictive young man went farther still. He had his knife next in M. Antoine Lemaistre, whose death he had deplored, who had taught him Latin and Law, and that poetic diction which the pupil passed on to Mademoiselle du Parc—Lemaistre, his kind " Papa " of those first years at Port-Royal. But he cannot stay his hand.

Tell me, Sir, what were the pursuits of M. Antoine Lemaistre, when he was a man of the world, before his conversion ? He practised at the Bar, you tell me, and he wrote poetry. All that is equally profane according to your maxims. He owns in one of his letters that he retired to Port-Royal in order to expiate these crimes. And yet you permitted this guilty creature to write your books and furnish you with translations from foreign authors ! You let him labour in the cause of Grace ? Ah, you will reply, but that was afterwards. His sins had been washed white by a long and serious penance. He had spent two whole years digging up the garden, mowing the hay meadows, washing dishes, until, by dint of manual toil, he had become pure enough to serve Saint Augustine. . . . And then, you will add, clinching the matter, after all, M. Lemaistre's books were only translations. Very well. But all writers cannot hope to be as fortunate as he. Someone must compose. If the sainted Fathers of the Church had run no greater risk than M. Lemaistre, you would have had nothing to translate, at Port-Royal, except translations.

M. de Sacy, naturally, comes in for his share of the dressing.

You doubtless think it much more estimable to write a tract like M. de Sacy's *A Salve for a Burn* ? Well, mortals are not all made the same. All of us are not fit to examine these weighty matters. We cannot all of us write against the Jesuits. Happily, there is more than one path to glory !

(The young dog ! In the full flush of success, with *Andromaque* nearly finished in his writing-desk.)

All this, perhaps, Port-Royal might have overlooked. A free hand was allowed in seventeenth-century polemics. Where Racine was inexcusable was in his attack on the Abbess, Mère Angélique, that old saint who had harboured his childhood, the Teresa of Port-Royal, about whom he tells a funny story of her sheltering two wandering friars, who knocked at the Abbey gates one night, to whom, supposing them to be Jesuits, she dispensed a hunch of household bread and a cup of cider—until, finding out that they were Jansenists, she corrected her misunderstanding with the finest white loaf and the reddest wine in the pantry. Mère Angélique was in her grave five years past, and should have been the more sacred to her former pensioner. Ah, Jean Racine, the cock has now crowed thrice ! Did the verses of your pious childhood never ring in your ears ? How did they run ?

> There, hidden in a shade divine,
> Moves many an animated shrine.
> O Palaces of Innocence !
> O living Stars ! O quire of Saints !
> You a new Heaven build and grace
> In this your silent dwelling-place.

Port-Royal kept silent, wrapped in dignity, disapprobation, and offended love. And the young renegate continued to polish certain caustic pages with which he was so well pleased that he showed them one day to Boileau-Despréaux. These, he thought, would strike at the heart more directly.

" Excellent ! " [exclaimed his friend]. " They do every credit to your head—a little less, it may be, to your heart, considering all that you owe to M. Nicole and to Port-Royal."

Racine knew how to profit by a lesson ; it is indeed a salient trait in his character. He pocketed his friend's rebuff, and locked the peccant pages in a drawer of his study. So long as Racine lived no one read those last epigrams. But he had not the courage to burn them, and after his death, to his discredit, they were found and saw the light.

CHAPTER III

ANDROMAQUE

A KIND and lovely young woman, not very clever, with several children about her, such was the actress who filled with dismay and dread the pious cloisters of Port-Royal. Such was she ; and sometimes, for an hour, she was transformed into a dancing nymph who leaps and twirls and trips upon the stage before the footlights, while a thousand clapping palms proclaim her the idol of Paris ; sometimes, more dangerous still, she appears a patient schoolgirl, hanging on her author's every word, while she rehearses, hour after hour, the part he has written to suit her beauty, until she fills the personage (who is in some degree her portrait) with a life and a perfection as radiant as the golden dream of a poet before he mints it into rhyme and metre.

But it was, I think, the gentle mourning widow, the mother, that chiefly touched the heart of Racine : it was the pure magic of Andromaque, innocently striving to keep at bay a bold impassioned lover, and yet not quite to estrange him, because his protection is necessary to her little boy. Racine could not remember his mother ; he had known no home ; since the age of ten he had been at school, or staying precariously on a visit. I have little

doubt but that humble family circle increased in
his eyes the attractiveness of the beautiful Marquise.
He stood godfather at a christening where Marie-
Anne du Parc, ten years of age, was godmother.
He loved children ; when he shall have sons and
daughters of his own, we shall see what a playfellow,
what a confidant, what a spoil-child, they will find
in their father. And his eldest-born will be called,
not Jean Racine like himself, like his father and
his grandfather before him, but Jean-Baptiste. Was
it in memory of his first love's little son ?

Racine loved children. In his first masterpiece
(as in the last) the central figure is a little boy :
the frail Astyanax, who is never seen upon the
stage. Yet he is the pivot on which the whole
mechanism turns—even as on Joas in the dreadful
night of *Athalie*.

Every action in *Andromaque* is inspired by the
fate of this child :

> Un enfant malheureux, qui ne sait pas encor
> Que Pyrrhus est son maître, et qu'il est fils d'Hector.

Astyanax's mother defends him ; Pyrrhus, too, for
love of that mother ; while all the allied Greeks
combine to plot his destruction. A strange thing,
cries Pyrrhus, that the victorious nations should
conspire to bring about the death of a child.

> Qu'un peuple, tout entier, tant de fois triomphant,
> N'ait daigné conspirer que la mort d'un enfant !

Yet the babe is not thrown to the wolves ; he alone,
he and his mother, are saved from the storm (which
overtakes the humiliated passion of Orestes, the

masterful pride of Pyrrhus, the rage and fury of Hermione), they two survive, pure figures of Trust and Tenderness, of Love and Duty, against which these wild forces of the night dash themselves in vain into nothingness.

All the first act of *Andromaque* is a marvel of poetry, and also of theatrical dexterity. With a few bold strokes Racine shows us the character of his principal personages. Orestes, unbalanced, melancholy, anxious, prone to the thought of suicide, a wonderful study in neurasthenia; Hermione, cajoling in her pride, prodigal of her charms, unable to conceive that her lover may wed a mere captive, a widow, an Asiatic, suitable, perhaps, as the plaything of an hour. And Pyrrhus, the barbarian King, full of bluster and banter, breaking with his allies of the Great War when it suits his fancy, yet good humoured even in his bad faith. He sends Orestes to bid farewell to his fair cousin Hermione ere the dismissed ambassador shakes the dust of Epirus from his feet.

But, Sire [whispers the confidant of Pyrrhus], have you forgotten that old story? They say that, before the Princess was betrothed to yourself, Orestes was passionately in love with her. If the cousins meet—who knows?—old fires may break out again. They might depart together.

" —Let them! Let them! " exclaims Pyrrhus, whose heart is full of Andromaque. And he continues with a truly savage mixture of ruse and banter:

> Ah, qu'ils s'aiment, Phœnix! Je consens qu'elle parte,
> Que, charmés l'un de l'autre, ils retournent à Sparte,
> Tous nos ports sonts ouverts et pour elle et pour lui. . . .
> —Qu'elle m'épargnerait de contrainte et d'ennui!

PHŒNIX. Seigneur !
PYRRHUS.   Une autre fois je t'ouvrirai mon âme :
    Andromaque paraît ! [1]

And she rises on the scene like the full moon in a
stormy sky. And no less than Pyrrhus, we are
dazzled.

The play appeared in Paris at the Hôtel de Bourgogne in November 1667, when its fame spread like
wildfire. People were enchanted, surprised, and
shocked—startled, in fact, as the public is, by a
new sort of masterpiece. Everyone went to see
Andromaque. Young writers praised it to the skies.
Older ones complained that Pyrrhus was a savage,
and that a painting of the animal passions must
always be lacking in dignity and grandeur. To
these latter critics, the young author replied in his
first preface—(for Racine generally wrote two pre-
faces, showing himself, in the first one, fierce and
witty, as he fences with his critics ; while, in the
second, having digested their bitters, he appears
philosophic and serene)—Racine, then, in his first
preface retorts :

I admit that Pyrrhus is not sufficiently resigned to his lady's
choice, and that Céladon (the sentimental swain of *Astrée*) were
a more perfect lover. Can I help it ? Pyrrhus had not the
advantage of having read our recent romances ; moreover, he
was naturally of a violent disposition. And all heroes are not
intended to be shepherds.

By this time Racine and Mademoiselle du Parc

Ah, Phœnix, let them love ! Ay, should I hear they went,
'Witch'd with each others charms, to Sparta, . . . I consent !
Their boat shall sail unharm'd from any port o' the coast,
And take an irksome guest from her reluctant host.
PHŒNIX. Sire !
PYRRHUS.   At another time, I'll open all my heart . . .
    Andromache appears ! . . .

were living in the rue de Richelieu, not together, but (as it appears from the ingenious researches of M. Henry Lyonnet) on opposite sides of the street. Their passion was the fable of the town. All that our poet's eager heart could wish of triumph, fame, poetry, predominance, he had drunk from the cup which du Parc held out to him. . . . Were they secretly married ? Marquise du Parc's old and intimate friends, her children, her father's widow, were convinced of the fact, as it will appear from a document which I must reserve for a later chapter, and they lamented the jealousy of the unacknowledged husband. In those days when marriage was a treaty, an alliance between two families and two properties, as well as a sacrament, and when the dread of mortal sin was a very living fear, the device of a secret marriage was not uncommon. Such a tie, it was rumoured, had joined Cardinal Mazarin and the Queen-Mother ; it united, so they said, Henrietta Maria and Lord St. Albans ; one day it will bind Louis XIV to Madame de Maintenon. The example, set in high places, filtered through the ranks of society. It was the German morganatic marriage—save that no provision, no acknowledgment existed for the possible advent of children.

There are several reasons why Racine might have agreed to a secret union with the beautiful actress. She was his first love, and naturally he could not suppose that he might ever wish to dispose of his future otherwise ; in the eyes of the world he could remain a bachelor. Both he and she doubtless had their scruples, in front of that innocent circle of children, which such a wedding would appease. And he dared not hope for any open form of marriage.

How could the pupil of Port-Royal wed a dancer
who, leaping, showed her thighs upon a public stage ?
There was, moreover, another argument which
probably clinched the matter, making the jealous
Racine determined to secure his treasure.

The Chevalier de Rohan was extremely anxious
to marry Mademoiselle du Parc. It was a mad
scheme. The Rohans were already one of the
greatest families in France, and nothing in the world
is more difficult in that country, even now, than to
marry in defiance of one's kith and kin. The
difficulties diminish ; within the days of my remembrance, a man of sixty, wishing to marry, was
obliged to produce a certificate of his grandfather's
consent, or of his decease. If the Chevalier de
Rohan had persisted, the result would probably
have been a *lettre de cachet*—a sealed order, sending
him safe out of harm's way to the Bastille.

Which did not prevent the young man being
violently in love. And here again I would draw
attention to the social respect which seems to have
surrounded the beautiful Marquise. Catherine de
Neuville, daughter of a Maréchal de France, had
stood godmother to her baby ; the Chevalier de
Rohan thinks of nothing less than marriage ; the
charlatan's daughter, the dancer, must have had
a personal value. The Chevalier de Rohan was
doubtless so persuaded, during the summer of
1668, even as a dozen years earlier the luckless
Sarrasin had been when he went mad for love of the
inaccessible beauty. And we find a certain Madame
de Montmorency writing in July to Bussy-Rabutin :

The Chevalier de Rohan wishes to marry du Parc, the famous
actress. His family opposes the match.

And Bussy replies :

I admire the stars of the du Parc ! She has kindled a thousand passions in a thousand breasts, and not one of them all that was middling or mean. If the Chevalier de Rohan marries her, it will be a rare triumph for Love.

("And a rare piece of folly," he adds in a letter, to another correspondent.) A few weeks later he resumes :

The Chevalier de Rohan is really head over ears in love with the actress. He is in despair because his family forbid the bans. If the whole affair is just a means of attracting attention to himself, one may say that he has succeeded.

We enter now a reign of dark surmise. The year was not out before the actress fell seriously ill ; a mystery still surrounds the cause of that mortal sickness. Did the unhappy young woman, ashamed of bearing a child in her supposed widowhood ("C'est l'écueil des veuves !" cries Bussy-Rabutin), did she consent to frustrate the course of Nature ? And if she let an abortion be attempted, was Racine aware of it ? Was this one of those errors, those sins, those faults, which he was, long afterwards, so bitterly to repent ? Boileau tells us that she died in childbirth—a stillborn child, apparently, of whom no trace remains. And who was the father ? Racine ? Or the Chevalier de Rohan ? We know nothing.

Or rather we shall have, later on, the evidence of a most untrustworthy witness, half-demented from the cruel torture of the rack. . . . A certain Madame Voisin—a seller of lotions for the complexion, charms, receipts of all sorts, who, into the bargain, was a midwife as famous for keeping babies out of the world as for bringing them into it

—a friend of the charlatan's daughter, as she well might be ; this Madame Voisin, I repeat, will give an account of Marquise du Parc's last illness which we shall read in due time. Thence, it appears, that the midwife was never allowed to see the actress, who had often asked for her. " And it was the fault of Racine, who never left her bedside. And at the last he drew from her finger a diamond ring, and kept it." This Madame Voisin believed they were secretly married ; but I will not as yet complete her evidence.

Let us turn next to the Parish Register of the Church of Saint-Roch in Paris, printed by Paul Mesnard in his masterly introduction to Hachette's great edition of Racine. Under the rubric 1668 we read among the deaths :

13th of December. Marquise-Thérèse Gorle, widow of the late René Berthelot, Sieur du Parc, one of the actresses of the King's Company, aged thirty-five years or thereabouts, died on the 11th of the present month, Rue de Richelieu, and was buried by the Carmelite monks of Les Billettes in this town of Paris. Present at her funeral and witnesses : Rault Regnier, merchant-apothecary, and Spencer, Town-Crier.

But there were other persons present at her funeral. The sudden death of so great an actress made a considerable stir in Paris. Robinot, the rhyming gazetteer, jangles anew his rhymes in honour of the ceremony, and accompanies the lovely actress to her last home.

> Elle y fut Mercredi conduite
> Avec une nombreuse suite. . . .
> Les adorateurs de ses charmes
> Ne la suivirent pas sans larmes,
> Quelques uns d'eux incognito
> Qui, je crois, dans leur memento,

Auront de la belle inhumée
Fort longtemps l'image imprimée ;
Item, maints différents amours
Affublés de sombres atours, . . .
Item les poètes de théâtre
Dont l'un, le plus intéressé
Etait à demi-trépassé.[1]

This last mourner, "the one most concerned who was himself half-dead," of course was Jean Racine.

One day, many years later, in 1703, Racine's friend and mentor, Boileau-Despréaux, speaking to a certain Mathieu Marais, a writer of Memoirs, let fall this phrase : [2]

M. Racine was in love with the du Parc ; she was tall, a fine figure of a woman, but not a good actress. He wrote *Andromaque* for her, and taught her the part, making her rehearse it word by word like a schoolgirl. The du Parc died shortly afterwards in child-bed.

---

[1] On Wednesday last her mourners all
Accompanied the funeral. . . .
Those who ador'd her charming face
Went, all in tears, at a snail's pace ;
Others, muffled, half-disguis'd,
In remembrance keep, I wot,
The deep imprint of her they prized
And buried in a dreary spot. . . .
Likewise, many a lover sorrow'd,
All attired in sable garb,
All transfix'd by Cupid's barb. . . .
Then, the actor-people followed,
One, the most concern'd, tis said,
Look'd, himself, at least half-dead.

[2] Preserved for us by Brossette, the editor of Boileau, whose written version of the anecdote was given by Feuillet de Conches to Paul Mesnard, the editor of the great classic edition of Racine's complete works. Here it is in French :

"M. Racine était amoureux de la du Parc, qui était grande, bien faite, mais qui n'était pas bonne actrice. Il fit *Andromaque* pour elle ; il lui apprit ce rôle ; et la faisait répéter comme une écolière. . . . La du Parc mourut quelque temps après en couche."

CHAPTER IV

LES PLAIDEURS AND BRITANNICUS

THE year 1668, which ended so fatally, had
run, throughout eleven months, a merry course
enough. The last act was tragic. Spring, summer,
and autumn had been bright and sunny : it was in
these months that Racine produced his only comedy :
Les Plaideurs. The Litigants, or, as we should say,
" *Going to Law.*"

When in May 1668, with little Marie-Anne du
Parc for his " gossip," Racine had stood sponsor at
Auteuil, he signed the baptismal register of Notre
Dame de Grace, by the name of Jean Racine de
l'Éspinay : for he was still the prior of that monastery. A few weeks later he could no longer use the
title. The monks of Sainte-Madeleine de l'Éspinay
had declared that their prior ought to be as much a
monk as themselves (in which we can but think they
were right), but Racine went to law. There was a
case in Court ("which neither I nor the judges
understood," he remarked), he lost his suit, but
without too much rancour, since his uncle the
Canon found him another sinecure, which he kept
for several years.

The lawyers had amused him immensely. They
were steeped in their profession. There was at that
time in Paris an old President of one of the Courts

who, if his son wanted a new coat, used to say to him : Présente une requête !—File a petition ! The Law Courts teemed with oddities. Racine, when he left them to dine at the *Mouton Blanc*— the fashionable tavern of the age—with Boileau, Furetière, and La Fontaine, would sit down to table, primed with funny stories, which each of his companions would cap with another ; Boileau, the son and the brother of a Clerk of the Courts, was a mine of anecdotes. Racine—who had always some Greek poet open beside his writing-desk—was reading, that summer, the *Wasps* of Aristophanes : the French law-suits appeared to him just as droll as those of Athens. He wrote some verses of a modern parody of the *Wasps* and read them to his friends at their next dinner. Racine thought of giving his skit to the Italian masks, where there was, at that time, a marvellous buffoon.

The judge who jumps through the window, the dog arraigned for his crimes, the family in tears, seemed to me worthy of Scaramouche's gravity ; but the departure of the actor interrupted my design.

Still the boon companions of the *Mouton Blanc* would let the poet have no peace until he had turned his masquerade into a farce, which still keeps the boards. It was played for the first time at the Hôtel de Bourgogne in November 1668.

And oddly enough at first it had no success. The play, so nimble, alert, and gay (which seems to us moderns, like *Hamlet*, " stuffed with quotations "), the farce which has lent so many happy turns of phrase to the French language, all but fell from the boards. Paris had not yet quite outgrown the spirit of the Fronde. To make fun of the doctors, like

Molière, was permissible ; but to make fun of the lawyers and the Law was arrant blasphemy. The audience looked on dumb and disapproving. The actors did not venture on a third representation.

But Molière, who was present at the second night (although, as we know, on bad terms with the author), declared the piece an excellent comedy : " To his thinking, it was the public, not the play, that deserved to be hissed." A month later *Les Plaideurs* was given at Versailles before the King. Louis was quite of Molière's opinion, and broke into peal after peal of hearty laughter, which first of all astonished, then carried away, the Court by its infectious gaiety.

The actors, enchanted with a success for which they had not dared to hope [thus writes Louis Racine, retailing an anecdote which doubtless he had heard a hundred times from the lips of his old friend, Boileau]—the actors left Versailles late in the evening and drove as fast as they could to Paris in order to acquaint the author with this unexpected turn of the tide. And, meaning to wake him up with this good news, they called at his house. Their carriages, clattering in the small hours, startled a quiet street, which, even in broad daylight, was not accustomed to such equipages, and roused the neighbourhood. Windows were flung open ; the good people thought that the author was to be punished for having made public fun of the Judges ; they knew that a certain Master of Requests had made a great to-do about " this scandalous play " as he called it. And on the morrow all Paris thought Racine in prison, while he was rejoicing in the approbation of the King and the Court, which consecrated a comedy soon to be received with applause in Paris.

(But good Louis Racine, are you quite sure that he was rejoicing ? Those clattering coaches rattling through the still December night must have disturbed a death-bed, where your father was sitting, as if entranced, gazing with all his soul on the wan face of the woman he loved—striving to keep the wicked midwife from the door.)

The King at least meant to show his friendship. Not only did he resuscitate the *Plaideurs* (which have continued to flourish ever since), but on the last day of December he awarded Racine a pension of twelve hundred livres, on the Civil List. A year later he saved *Britannicus*, as he had saved the farce.

Racine's fourth tragedy appeared for the first time on the 13th of December, 1669. A year to the day after the funeral of Mademoiselle du Parc. How strange to think that *Britannicus* was played to an empty house ! The shopkeepers of the rue Saint-Denis, who did not mind what they paid for their seats, if they could be present on a First Night at the Court Theatre, were, for once in a way, attracted elsewhere that evening by a still more dramatic representation : On the Place de Grève a certain Huguenot marquis was to have his head cut off for high treason. Played to all but empty benches, *Britannicus* fell flat. Amid the void of the boxes Corneille was to be seen conspicuous, gloating over his rival's discomfiture. (Racine deserved it : some of the funniest lines of the *Plaideurs* are parodies and paraphrases of the heroic axioms of the *Cid*.) In the pit, a lively looking little fellow, an admirer of Racine,

did all that was humanly possible to rescue the work of a friend. His face, which might be taken for a repertory of the passions, expressed every shade of the play, one after the other, and was transformed, as quickly as the chameleon by that which it feeds upon, from verse to verse, as the actors said their say.[1]

We have recognized Boileau-Despréaux.

[1] This account of the First Night of *Britannicus* is given by a contemporary author, Boursault, in his story *Artemise et Poliante*.

What a falling off from the prodigious triumph of *Andromaque*! Racine's helpmate had failed him, she was no longer there to bear her part of the burden, to render visible and audible the most secret meaning of his mind.   For lack of an interpreter, *Britannicus* was considered cold.   And all those old relics of the Fronde, all the admirers of the heroic romances, and the party of Corneille, felt themselves justified and said : " Ah yes, this young man can do passion very well, no doubt, and love, and sentiment, and style, and that sort of thing—the baubles of his age!   But he could no more attempt the grand manner of Corneille—the Roman history, the political intrigues, the sense of right and wrong, the food for thought, that you find in Corneille— than he could equal Seneca and Sophocles."   Racine had hoped to silence once for all the tribe of these detractors when he produced *Britannicus*.   And it failed of its effect, at first.

Voltaire was one day to call *Britannicus* " a tragedy for connoisseurs."   But people do not go to the theatre to meditate, to reflect ; it is easier to touch their feelings than their mind : " Vive le mélodrame où Margot a pleuré ! "   It is seldom that a *Britannicus* —with its problem of innate evil, deep-seated, like an ineradicable cancer, in the brilliant breast of youth—it is seldom that a play showing wickedness everywhere triumphant, " Conquered good and con- quering ill " dividing a doomed civilization ; it is seldom that a masterpiece of tragedy, slowly swelling and accumulating like a wave, gathering in its advance the passions and interests and characters of a group of persons, concerned only with these interests and feelings and characters—not at all with incident, or rhetoric, or the picturesque—it is seldom, indeed, that such a play can please, at the first go-off, the shopkeepers of the rue Saint-Denis. The well-meaning Boursault, after having described the First Night of *Britannicus*, has to admit that " la pièce n'a pas eu tant de succès qu'on s'en était promis."

Racine was savage, exasperated. He laid the blame at the door of Corneille, whom he had watched gloating, lonely, in his box. And he writes bitter phrases in his preface concerning the wiles of a " certain evil-intentioned old poet, *malevoli veteris poetæ*," whom Terence had accused of going round the theatre collecting opinions against him even while the play was in course of representation. After the eighth night the tragedy came to an end, on a semi-success. But, marvel of marvels, there reigned at Versailles a King who was a man of taste—a person of no great acquirements, or learning, or originality, yet with an instinct for the beautiful, a taste, which none of his subjects could rival. The King heard of *Britannicus*, admired it, understood it even, despite his ignorance. A play the King had praised exceedingly could not be burked. And Racine could write in his second preface : " The strictures have vanished into air ; the play remains."

It is perhaps a fancy of my own, but in Nero's sudden passion for the girl he has wronged, abducted, insulted—in that love awakened by the sight of her tears—I seem to find a reminiscence of Racine's strange infatuation for the actress whom he had scorned and criticized. His mind must have been full of poor Marquise du Parc when he was writing *Britannicus* : were it only as an actress he must have missed her at every turn. And an artist transposes the truth of his own heart into his creations.

NARCISSE. Vous l'aimez ?
NÉRON.   Excité d'un désir curieux,
Cette nuit je l'ai vue arriver en ces lieux,
Triste, levant au ciel ses yeux mouillés de larmes,
Qui brillaient au travers des flambeaux et des armes ;
Belle sans ornement, dans le simple appareil
D'une beauté qu'on vient d'arracher au sommeil ;
Que veux-tu ? Je ne sais si cette négligence,
Les ombres, les flambeaux, les cris, et le silence,
Et le farouche aspect de ses fiers ravisseurs
Relevaient de ses yeux les timides douceurs ;
Quoi qu'il en soit, ravi d'une si belle vue
J'ai voulu lui parler, et ma voix s'est perdue.
Immobile, saisi d'un long étonnement
Je l'ai laissé passer dans son appartement.
J'ai passé dans le mien. C'est là que, solitaire,
De son image en vain j'ai voulu me distraire ;
Trop présente à mes yeux, je croyais lui parler,
J'aimais jusqu'à ses pleurs que je faisais couler.[1]

---

[1] NARCISSE. You love her ?
NERO. I felt a curious wish my brain excite,
And waked to watch Junie arrive to-night :
Sad, skyward lifting eyes brimfull of tears,
That glittered 'mid the torches and the spears.
Beautiful, unadorn'd, snatch'd from her sleep
In that last veil our drowsy beauties keep,
Who knows ? The tumbled robe, loose hair, wet eyes,
The torch-flare in the dark, the silence, cries,
And fierce irruption in a quiet place.
Added, perchance, an accent to her grace. . . .
Howe'er it be, charm'd by a scene so choice,
I tried to address my guest—and lost my voice.
And long I stood stone-still ; I let her pass,
Into her room, dumb-founder'd where I was !
At last I sought my couch, but could not sleep ;
I watch'd her phantom-image move and weep.
In vain I bade the unreal companion go ;
I lov'd the very tears I caus'd to flow.

It is perhaps not strange that *Britannicus* did not conquer the world at first sight. The poet may find its lines as pure as pearls. The psychologist may admire the characters of Nero, of Burrhus, that ineffectual sage, of the pure and prudent Junie, of Agrippine. But the patient votary of perfection can offer little to dazzle the passer-by. The aim of Racine, as he explains in his next preface, was not to surprise by the marvellous, or the multiplicity of adventures, but just to make something out of nothing : in fact, to create a new reality.

CHAPTER V

BÉRÉNICE

WITH every year the rivalry between Racine and Corneille became more and more exasperated : to prefer the one to the other was almost a political opinion. The relics of yesterday were all for the elder poet ; the young Court was for Racine, and the very centre of the young Court, where plays and poems were concerned, was the King's sister-in-law, Henriette d'Angleterre.

In the etiquette of France, the plain word, " Monsieur," denoted the reigning King's next-born brother, and his wife was styled " Madame " : a simplicity superior to the finest title. Henriette d'Angleterre had been barely seventeen years old when, in 1661, she had married Monsieur and entered the sphere of the Court. She rose on the horizon like a star, in sudden unexpected beauty, as new and fresh as though she had just arrived from some foreign climate. Yet she had been reared in France, in the Palace of Saint-Germain, or, more often, in the convent at Chaillot. Who could have supposed the lanky, sickly girl, sewn to her mother's apron-strings, destined to bloom into a miraculous charm ? She united the romantic beauty of the Stuarts to the wit and activity of Henri Quatre. Yet when, at nearly sixteen, the Queen-Mother of France had proposed her as a bride to the young King, Louis had been prompt in refusal : what could such an alliance add to his political situation ? Her health seemed to him undermined. And he muttered under his breath that, personally, " he had no predilection for the bones of the Holy Innocents." The meagre girl had developed into a nymph of slender grace, and if one shoulder were a thought too high, few noticed it in the general impression of bloom and radiance. Madame had ropes of flaxen hair, a complexion which—in an age of painted faces— needed no artificial heightening. And she had the most beautiful eyes of her generation—black (says Choisy), blue (say Madame de Brégès and Bussy-Rabutin), probably a changing grey or hazel. Their great charm, says Bussy, was a certain languishing glance : " on dirait qu'elle demande le cœur."

He goes on to say that this charming creature has a great enlightened mind, " un esprit vaste et éclairé." She was the King's confidant for his dreams of political supremacy, and, when he wished to negotiate an understanding with England, she was more advanced in his secrets than his Ambassador. The face of an angel, the mind of a man, seemed to promise a brilliant future to Madame, despite those Stuart whims, caprices, and love-fancies, which too often made her risk all her chances on the freak of an hour. But the physicians of the Court suspected some hidden disease at work beneath the appearance of so much beauty and so much capacity. The great Guy Patin declared himself not satisfied with the " mauvaise constitution de ses entrailles " ; already in 1664 he had written in his notebook that most English people are prone to their native malady of consumption : " Et elle est fluette, délicate, avec un penchant à la phthisie." There was something febrile in the varied activities of this young woman, traversed by fits of utter languor, when you would find her, spilt on a heap of cushions on the floor, lying prone, with her head in the lap of Madame de la Fayette.

Madame was unhappily married. Her husband's tastes were politely but vaguely described as " Italian." He was devoted to his friends, but, as Madame de la Fayette observed : " The woman was never yet born who could stir his pulses." His wife had to make for herself another sphere than the domestic hearth. There was a vacant place at Court which the Queen of France was not clever enough to occupy. Madame stepped into it, and filled it like a Fairy Queen. All the wits of the hour haunted her chamber. She was the friend of Corneille, Molière, La Fontaine, Racine. Has not Racine informed us, in his preface to *Andromaque*, that she inspired him with more than one passage in the play ?

Did Louis XIV ever regret the refusal which had made Henriette d'Angleterre his brother's wife ? Probably not. His own grandeur and the greatness of France were founded on the Peace of the Pyrenees, which necessitated his marriage with Maria-Teresa. Yet between the King and his ill-wedded sister-in-law there reigned a subtle sentimental affection. It was difficult to love merely as a cousin and a sister-in-law this too bewitching great-granddaughter of Mary, Queen of Scots. Madame de la Fayette, with her customary elegance and intelligence, has defined the situation :

She only meant the King to love her as a sister-in-law, but I fancy that he loved her differently. And she, I think, believed that she merely returned his fraternal affection ; yet, perhaps, she gave him something more. At all events, since they were both of them infinitely lovable, and both of them of an amorous disposition ; since they met day after day in a continuous round of pleasure and festivity, there were onlookers who thought they possessed, each for the other, the attraction and the charm which precede a great passion.—*Histoire de Madame Henriette d'Angleterre.*

The son of Racine (as well as Corneille's nephew, Fontenelle) assures us that, one day, Madame hinted to Corneille that a play on the impossible loves of Titus and Bérénice would interest the King. She whispered the same suggestion in the ear of Racine. Why should Louis care to hear of a love that never found its earthly close ? Well, in his youth, he had sacrificed a private passion to a regal duty, sending Marie Mancini, against his will, to Rome. *Invitus dimisit invitam.* Madame confided, no doubt, to either author that he alone could interpret so delicate a situation, but I think she meant Racine to bear away the palm ; in her heart she knew that Corneille would be grand, heroic, Roman, moral, but that Racine would track through all its mazes the deep complexities of a tortured passion (such, perhaps, as her own). From time to time she sent the Marquis de Dangeau to stimulate Racine, to urge on Corneille, bidding him never reveal to the poet he visited that he had a rival in the field. Which would show himself the better man ? It was an incomparable tournament for the curiosity of a connoisseur, of a feverish young dilettante, who sought, by incessant freaks and caprices, to give a spice to her precarious existence.

But the secret could not be kept to the bitter end. It takes some time to write a masterpiece. At last the truth leaked out, and, during the early autumn of 1670, the pens of the two poets fairly raced each other in their haste to reach the goal. Fate favoured Racine, for the Palais Royal Theatre, where Corneille was giving his play, opened late that season because the company had been requested to act the *Bourgeois Gentilhomme* before the King at Chambord. So the Hôtel de Bourgogne gained the day, producing Racine's *Bérénice* for the first time on the 21st of November, 1670.

But Madame was not there to award the prize. All through the spring of the year she had grown weaker and weaker, more and more capricious and brilliant and energetic. Sometimes she would fling herself on her cushions in a paroxysm of pain : it was a violent stitch in the side. Nevertheless, in May she had gone to England, and, in the course of three weeks' hard work at Dover, she had contrived to bring off an alliance between her brother, Charles II, and her brother-in-law, Louis XIV. She had returned home in the middle of June and had died, a fortnight later, after a sudden nine-hours-long agony, caused, said some, by poison mixed in a glass of chicory-water. But was it poison ? Others spoke of a gastric ulcer, and modern doctors breathe the word appendicitis. Anyway, the Flower of the Court had faded. " Avec elle (writes Madame de Sévigné) on a perdu toute la joie, tout l'agré-ment, tous les plaisirs de la Cour."

Not only the Court, but Letters mourned her. Bossuet deplored her death with a paternal pang. Boileau remembered that day at the Palace of

Saint-Cloud, when, tired and bright as usual, she had beckoned to him and whispered in his ear— with such a whimsical air of longing to go to bed— a line from his just-published poem :

Soupire, étend le bras, ferme l'œil, et s'endort !

Racine could not forget the tears she shed when first he read her *Andromaque*. Even the grim and gaunt Corneille, whom she had half betrayed into the hands of his young enemy, had benefits to think of.

Paris mourned her, too ; Paris, which had known her since her exiled babyhood. Everyone owned her to have been the most charming princess in all the world. Alas ! " Madame est morte ! "

When the two plays appeared in the early winter, Corneille's Roman affair fell from the stage at once, and has never recovered from that overthrow, so that in the commoner editions of the poet's works *Tite et Bérénice* does not figure at all, though the two volumes are stuffed out by sundry tragedies of Thomas Corneille's. But Racine's *Bérénice*, so close to life, so human, so moving, held the boards for thirty consecutive representations, a number, until that date, unknown in the annals of the theatre in France.

It is true there was a new actress in the part of Bérénice : a small woman with the most moving voice Paris had ever heard : " la petite merveille," Madame de Sévigné called her. She was pleasing and graceful of aspect, despite her round, naïve, and bird-like eyes, despite her brown skin ; but she would scarcely be called beautiful until one had remarked how extraordinarily expressive were those irregular features—until one had suffered the spell of her magical voice. She was a new acquaintance of Racine's when he entrusted to her the part of Bérénice. Her first appearance on the stage of the Hôtel de Bourgogne had been as Hermione in *Andromaque,* shortly after Easter in 1670. The brothers Parfait (who early in the eighteenth century wrote a *History of the Theatre in France*) have preserved for us the legend of how Racine made acquaintance with the great actress whose name will.always remain associated with his own.

" Shall we go and see the Champmeslé ? " said Boileau, one night when he and Racine were supping with their friends. " Shall we make a party and go to the theatre ? " Racine at first refused. He did not wish to see the play, so closely associated with Mademoiselle du Parc, disfigured by a faulty interpretation. However, his companions persuaded him, and they set out for the Hôtel de Bourgogne. The poet found the first two acts rather feebly impersonated—and, indeed, they require the subtlest delicacy, for Hermione's part is far more difficult than Andromaque's. But, in the final scenes of passion and rage, the young actress had risen to the occasion and filled so magnificently the *rôle* that (so we hear) " M. Racine rushed to her dressing-room, fell on his knees before her, and thanked her, with many praises, for so excellent an interpretation."

Here, at least, was part of Racine's loss redeemed : He had found an actress ! And he began teaching Mademoiselle de Champmeslé (or Chammelay, as he always writes it, in accordance with the pronunciation) just as, a year before, he had taught Mademoiselle du Parc ; and with a like result. I fancy that the feeling he had for the bird-eyed little actress could not compare with his first enchantment. Who knows ? He loved her six years ; he nearly broke his heart when she left him. Yet she seems to have been nothing more than a lovable sort of little wanton, with a dash, it is true, of genius in her composition. She was married to a husband accustomed not to reign alone, an actor in the same company. Years and years afterwards, Boileau will write one day to Racine, concerning a bottle of sour wine recently served to Champmeslé : " Poor man, who knows but it may serve him as a penance for all those bottles of good champagne he used to swill *you* know at whose expense ! "

Treating M. Champmeslé with expensive drinks, making love to his wife, Racine, at this moment of his career, gets, I fear, into very fast company. Madame de Sévigné, whose young son, the Marquis, was in the same boat, writes of him as supping with " all the Racines and all the Despréaux," as if they were the gayest of gay dogs. It is difficult for us to see them in this light, especially Boileau, consistently Jansenist and respectable from first to last. I suppose the brilliant Marquise thought that so intimate a friend of Racine's must needs be tarred with the same brush. Her indulgence seems to have been all reserved for Mademoiselle de Champmeslé ; she thought her " la plus miraculeusement bonne comédienne que j'ai jamais vue." One day, when Charles de Sévigné, who was one of the actress's numerous flames, was telling how he had shown to Ninon de l'Enclos a packet of her love-letters, the Marquise, indignant, made him get the letters back, and threw them into the fire, in order to save

" the little creature's " reputation. " La jeune merveille," " la petite Chimène," " Ma belle-fille " —the Marquise shows in every word her kindness for the actress; though, off the stage, shorn of her magic, she finds her rather dull and plain in the face. " I am not surprised my son gets tired of her."

It was her genius, doubtless, which endeared her to Racine. She was incomparable in the part of Bérénice, and showed, not merely passion, but an infinity of tender shades and fluctuations in rendering the subtlest movements of hope, love, expectation, melancholy, and regret. Your true Racinian of the inner circle sets *Bérénice* above all other plays. I did once ; but, looking at Racine's theatre through the cool grey spectacles of old age, I find that I prefer *Athalie, Phèdre, Britannicus*, and even *Andromaque*. There was a snap of truth in Corneille's objection that *Bérénice* was not a real tragedy, but an elegy, a love-poem, or (shall we say ?) a novel in verse : a psychological novel softly accompanied by the purest, the most exquisite of music.

It is Louis Racine who tells the tale, which doubtless he had often heard from the lips of Boileau. The latter, who had not an ounce of sentiment in his composition, objected that he thought the subject of Bérénice, as a matter of fact, too simple and too tender for a tragedy. Racine, who never liked the least breath of criticism, exclaimed : " It was Madame's choice, not mine ! "

" If I had been there (cried his friend), she should never have had your promise to write it, I can tell you."

This talk went on at one of those dinners at the

Mouton Blanc. Several of the accustomed coterie were present.

"And what do you think, Chapelle?" cried Racine, rounding on one of the diners, and evidently hoping for an ally against Boileau. But Chapelle merely began to hum a certain ribald song that all the streetboys sang, about Marion, who cried and stormed because she wanted to get married—

> Marion pleure, Marion crie,
> Marion veut qu'on la marie !

"And this silly stave (adds Louis Racine) made more impression on my father than all the criticisms and parodies of his enemies."

Let us admit that *Bérénice* (like *Tristan and Isolda*) is a masterpiece chiefly meant for persons under fifty. Still how beautiful it is ! "Marion pleure, Marion crie ! " If she weep and cry in this fashion, she is as eternally moving as the nightingale in May.

BÉRÉNICE.   Je n'écoute plus rien ; et, pour jamais, adieu !
> Pour jamais ! Ah Seigneur ! Songez-vous en vous-même
> Combien ce mot cruel est affreux quand on aime ?
> Dans un mois, dans un an, comment souffrirons-nous,
> Seigneur, que tant de mers me séparent de vous ?
> Que le jour recommence, et que le jour finisse,
> Sans que jamais Titus puisse voir Bérénice—
> Sans que, de tout le jour, je puisse voir Titus ? [1]

There are some of the most musical lines in Racine to be found in *Bérénice*, which, in this respect,

---

[1] Nay, not another word ! Farewell for evermore !
For ever ! Think, my Lord, think how intolerable
Is, to a lover's heart, that cruel word, Farewell !
A month hence (think, my Lord !), a year hence, can it be,
That all the waves o' the world shall roll 'twixt thee and me ?
Or that the day shall dawn, and that the day shall cease,
Yet Titus never more set eyes on Bérénice ?—
And I, the livelong day, behold my love no more ?

rivals *Phèdre*. Listen to the complaint of Bérénice's
unloved lover, the Oriental King Antiochus :

> Dans l'Orient désert quel devint mon ennui !
> Je demeurai longtemps errant dans Césarée—

words which haunt us interminably when we have
heard or read them. And yet what do they mean,
save that an unhappy man was melancholy in the
desert East and wandered for a long while in the
regions round Cesaræa. And what heartbroken
sorrow echoes in the close.

> Adieu ! Servons tous trois d'exemple à l'univers
> De l'amour la plus tendre et la plus malheureuse
> Dont il puisse garder l'histoire douloureuse.[1]

Racine, having loaded every rift with ore, felt that
he merited his triumph ; but he did not enjoy the
criticisms and the parodies which, after all, were
part of that triumph. Of course they were a
tribute, after their kind. When the Italian Masks
gave a skit on *Bérénice,* he went with the rest of Paris
to see their performance ; and laughed, and even
returned more than once, to show that " his withers
were unwrung." But there was a certain ribald
rhyme to Bérénice that distressed him greatly.
Why thus bespatter and befoul that which in itself
was noble and tender ?

And this indecent rhyme [says his son] rankled to the point
of making him quite indifferent to the crowds thronging to see
his play at the Court Theatre ; he cared neither for the tears
of the audience nor for the praises of the critics. It was in
such moments that he felt a first dim stirring of disgust with

---

[1] (*Amour*, in old French, was masculine or feminine at choice.)

> Farewell ! We three are deathless instances
> Of love, the tenderest and the most vain,
> Whose mournful story must for aye remain.

his profession as a poet, and began to think that some day he would give it all up ; for such incidents brought home to him the vanity of human wishes, and showed him the littleness of Man, whom so light a thing can humiliate.

Yet, perhaps, it will rather seem to us that the immediate effect of a mortification on a proud, eager, restless nature like Racine's was, in fact, a stimulus, urging him to " go one better " and snatch the prize withheld. Corneille and Chapelle should not complain again that he gave them a bloodless tragedy. " Le tendre Racine," as they called him, had other arrows in his quiver, and could contrive another climax than a broken heart.

CHAPTER VI

BAJAZET AND MITHRIDATE

THE Turks were all the fashion in Paris in 1670, the year of *Bérénice*. An Ottoman Embassy had visited Versailles, had been seen in the capital. The King, bitten by the mode of the moment, had asked Molière to write a play exhibiting " the customs and the costumes of the Turks," and Molière had composed the *Bourgeois Gentilhomme* with its Turkish ballet. All Paris was ready to sing *cacaracamouchen mamamouchi* with Monsieur Jourdain.

But Racine had heard another tale of the Turks, treasured these many years in a memory ever retentive of all that touched the chords of passion. An old Comte de Cézy, who had been French Ambassador to the Sublime Porte some thirty years gone by, had seen with his own eyes that unhappy prince, condemned to death by his elder brother, the Sultan Murad. M. de Cézy had noticed the young man once or twice, when he left the palace, where he lived virtually a prisoner, to take the air of an evening in the gardens of Seraglio Point, and he had thought Bajazet " un prince de bonne mine." An Embassy is always a centre for gossip of all sorts ; the Frenchman, naturally, had heard the rumour which linked the name of Bajazet with that of his still beautiful sister-in-law, the

Regent, Roxana, who reigned omnipotent in Constantinople, during the absence of her husband, for Murad, at that date, was laying siege to Bagdad. The terror and mystery of this story, told by an eyewitness, the ferocious character of the Sultana ("Hell hath no fury like a woman scorn'd"), the swift revenge of the absent conqueror; the murder of Bajazet by order of Roxana, no less than by command of the Sultan; the subsequent and speedy execution of the Empress herself—all had combined to impress the imagination of Racine. But what had touched him most was that the innocent Bajazet, solicited by his brother's wife, was himself in love with a much simpler person— a mere slave, said some; a maiden Princess of the Royal house, said others; for many persons about the Court had heard these old stories of M. de Cézy's, which seemed more interesting now that Turkey had become the plaything of the Mode, and the topic of the hour.

But a tragedy, according to the canon of the seventeenth century, should always be concerned with the Past; for the Past is heroic, a Golden Age, and all this had happened only thirty years ago. Bajazet must have left this world of woe about the time that Racine entered it. It is certain that distance lends enchantment to the view. But may not that distance lie in space as well as in time? Constantinople, in 1670, was a very long way from Paris; might not that remoteness be as perfect an isolator as the lapse of years? These questions were the subject of many musings and meditations, as our poet paced to and fro those Tuileries Gardens, where he loved to walk of a morning, ruminating the fundamental brainwork of his plays. The critics were always railing at him for breaking some rule or regulation in his love of life and human truth. So much the worse for the critics ! He decided that he would run the risk and, as he says in his second preface to *Bajazet*, substitute distance in space for distance in time—

L'éloignement des pays répare la trop grande proximité des temps, car le peuple ne met guère de différence entre ce qui est à mille ans de lui et ce qui en est à mille lieues.

A thousand leagues may serve as well as a thousand years. And *Bajazet*, when it appeared, had the scandalous attraction of being a modern political tragedy, a thing hitherto unknown.

The play was an immense success, although of course the partisans of Corneille threw up their hands in horror. " There is not a personage on the stage (said that evil-intentioned old poet to Segrais, who rather fancied himself on his Oriental tales and had composed one on the death of Bajazet), not a single one of the characters that has the sort of feelings one ought to have at Constantinople ; under their Turkish trappings they have just the same heart as beats in the centre of France ! " (ils ont tous, sous un habit turc, les sentiments qu'on a au centre de la France). And the two writers shook their heads in disapprobation of a young iconoclast whose inexplicable but evident prosperity threatened the best traditions of his art. Shades of the Buskin and the Mask ! If this sort of thing was to continue, what would be left to distinguish a tragedy from a comedy ? Madame de Sévigné, ever sensitive to the mode of the moment, was impressed by the great success of *Bajazet*. She writes to her daughter at Grignan :

Racine has just brought out a play which draws like a magnet. And it doesn't dwindle down at the finish like most of his tragedies. M. de Tallard says it is as far above Corneille's as Corneille's are above Boyer's.

This M. de Tallard evidently belonged to the party of the Court. When Madame de Sévigné has seen the play herself, she is no longer quite so enthusiastic.

Racine's play is certainly a fine thing. My daughter-in-law [the Champmeslé] seems to me the most marvellous actress that ever I set eyes on—incomparably superior to Mademoiselle des Œillets. And as for myself—who always had such a good opinion of my gift for theatricals—I am not worthy to light the candles when she appears. Seen at close quarters, she is plain in the face, and I am not surprised that my son had enough of her. But when she speaks in verse she is adorable— adorable ! Well, *Bajazet*, as I say, is a fine play, though I consider the close of it rather muddled. It is full of passion—and not such a mad sort of passion, either, as in *Bérénice* ; but, in my humble opinion, it is not a whit superior to *Andromaque*. And as for the best plays of Corneille's, *they* are as far above Racine's as his are above anyone else's.

When the play comes out as a book and she can read it at leisure, the Marquise withdraws something even of this modest appreciation.

The personage of Bajazet is glacial. Racine will never surpass *Andromaque*. He writes plays for the Champmeslé and not for the centuries to come. When the time shall come that he shall be no longer young, no longer in love—what will be left of it all, I wonder ? Long live my old friend Corneille !

But the Queen of the Cornelians keeps an undiminished admiration for Racine's interpreter. She goes to see the Champmeslé in another piece—a play of no importance.

Champmeslé is so extraordinary that in all your born days you have never seen anything like it. The piece is poor stuff and the other actors are wretched ; but when the Champmeslé comes upon the boards a murmur runs from end to end of the theatre, a spell is thrown over the house, and we shed tears at her bidding.

It is strange that, though the letters and rhyming chronicles of 1670 are as full of the praise of the Champmeslé, as of the success of *Bajazet*, not one of them tells us which part she plays. There are two heroines. Roughly speaking, the plot of *Bajazet* is identical with that of Robert Browning's *In a Balcony*. (Did he know it ?) There is an omnipotent Queen older than the hero and violently in love with him, who, dependent on her good graces, is no less passionately enamoured of a young girl, an Ottoman Princess in the one case, a Maid of Honour in the English play. The *rôle* of Roxane, in its cold and tranquil ferocity so strangely shot through with a tigerish passion, is a part for a great actress. When, in the middle of her feints and her fierceness, she suddenly breaks off and says (we almost hear the sweet, searching, throaty voice)—

> Bajazet, écoutez : je sens que je vous aime !— . . .
> Ne désespérez point une amante en furie !—

Or when she sends the man who has deceived her to his death, condemned beyond remission, in two lines full of tyranny and an implacable will :

> Sortez ! . . . Que le sérail soit désormais fermé ;
> Et que tout rentre ici dans l'ordre accoutumé—

we feel : there was a part for the Champmeslé ! And yet tradition says that Racine wrote for her the rather mawkish *rôle* of Atalide, taught it to her, put her through her paces, then made her change and impersonate Roxane, finally, however, sending her on the boards as the melancholy, sacrificed Atalide. At the last moment, depend upon it, he changed his mind again and bid her create the Sultana !

It is strange what a gift the gentle Racine possessed for delineating a monster ! They are the most living—I was just going to say the most sympathetic —personages in his plays. Hermione in her self-love and her rage is perhaps not more alive than Andromaque, but Nero, at any rate, dwarfs all the other characters in *Britannicus*. How boyish he is, how young, how pleasant almost, in the politeness of his insolence, when he says to his mother, interminably recapitulating all the crimes she has committed in view of his advancement :

> Je me souviens toujours que je vous dois l'empire—
> Et sans vous fatiguer du soin de le redire—

And what an artist—*qualis artifex*—is Nero when he re-calls the beauty of Junie in tears.

> Je me fais de sa peine une image charmante !

Terrible, terrible young man, so insidious, so ironical —and, almost, so amusing ! He is one of the most natural villains to be found in any tragedy. With Roxane and Mithridate and Phèdre, Racine completes his gallery of exasperated egoists ; but the two latter names reveal a new note in his genius. There is a deep compassion in his drawing of Phèdre —and even in his more official portrait of Mithridate, of which no trace exists in the cruel images of Néron or Roxane.

Roxane is perhaps the most dreadful, the most inhuman, of all these monsters. There is nothing to appeal to in her save amorous passion or stark revenge : a tigress would be as capable of sacrifice, detachment, or a disinterested view. Yet, because of its sincerity, there is a sort of grandeur in her fierce selfishness, and she makes us feel her force. When she bids Bajazet depart, and we know what lies on the other side the door, we tremble, when she says to him, so calmly, " We will just put Atalide out of the way, and soon you'll think no more about her. I do not ask you to take to me at once. Time works wonders."

Viens m'engager ta foi ; le temps fera le reste—

Oh, then, like Madame de Sévigné, we feel our tears fall, recognizing the cruel strength of the present as opposed to the past. The man who could write that scene has already felt the futility of passion.

Roxane and the worldly Grand Vizier, Acomat, are the two memorable figures in *Bajazet*, for no one can take much interest in the young lovers. It was Shakespeare's triumph to make Love's young dream delightful to outsiders. But there is nothing of Romeo and Juliet in Bajazet and Atalide. They remind me of those wax fruits which careful house-keepers in winter-time mingle with the genuine apples, pears and grapes in a too spacious dessert-dish. The weak point in Racine's theatre is the habit of these wax fruits. But, then, the pears are delicious !

Roxane is as real as Lady Macbeth. Acomat is living, too ; he appears an elderly Nero grown virtuous in the course of time, but keeping all his irony. Still, despite these figures, and despite the immense authority of Jules Lemaître, who had a strong predilection for *Bajazet*, if I venture to express my own opinion, it will be to place *Bajazet* distinctly in the second class of Racine's tragedies, and, in that second class, lower, a good deal lower, than *Mithridate* or *Iphigénie*.

Racine was still the young man who loved a garden and liked to fleet away the time in the " converse " of trees and fountains. On most mornings, when he was in Paris, he contrived to spend an hour or so among the parterres of the Tuileries, and here one day, during the autumn of 1672, a M. de Valincour came upon the absent-minded poet, the centre of a group of listening workmen, to whom, quite unconscious of their presence, he was reciting the tremendous close of *Mithridate*.

He had a good deal, about that time, to occupy his attention. On the 12th of January, 1673, at three-and-thirty years of age, he was received a member of the French Academy ; the next evening *Mithridate* was produced on the stage of the Hôtel de Bourgogne and enthusiastically acclaimed. *Mithridate* was the great stage success of Racine's career : " the play the King preferred," notes Dangeau. The public was never tired of praising it. There is in *Mithridate* a magnificence mixed with logic, a complexity and yet a clarity, a perfection of architecture, if I may use the word, characteristic of the Classic Age in France ; and there is also a theme of political grandeur, which alone would, in those days, hold an audience spellbound ; above all, there is the infinitely pathetic study of Mithridate himself, the old semi-barbarian tyrant, who, sole rebel of the universe, dares brook the peace of Rome.

Everyone praises the heroines of Racine ; much might be said, I think, for his portraits of elderly men : Burrhus, who knows that even in a palace life may be lived well ; Acomat, who cares for little save the stark, sheer, reality of power ; and this tremendous old rebel and warrior, Mithridate, King of Pontus, Paphlagonia and Cappadocia, Lord of the Cimmerian Bosphorus and the Chersonese. He is sixty when the play begins, and betrothed to a Greek girl who loves his son. The scene is Nymphæa, a seaport on the Crimean coast ; and the curtain rises on a scene of blank defeat. Mithridate has been left for dead on the battlefield. His two sons rally the remains of his armies, and each of them in turn confesses to the virgin-bride his own passion for her ; she discards the elder, whose treachery she suspects (and, indeed, he has already a secret treaty with the Romans), but confesses to the younger, Xipharès, who has been his father's messenger and proxy to fetch her here from Greece, that his love is shared ; they plan to fly together, when there is a cry that the fleet is in the harbour with Mithridate on board, hale and sound, escaped from the Romans, ready for his wedding.

The arrival of the terrible old king fills the stage as with the breaking of a ninth wave. Everything gives way before the accumulated force of Mithridate. Defeat has but exasperated his pride. Fly ! He means to march on Rome, conquer or die there ! But first he must marry this girl whom he loves with a jealous senile lust of possession.

Mithridate is a combative, a cunning, an Asiatic King Lear. He has no daughters, but two sons. Xipharès is his Cordelia, yet he it is who will pierce his father to the quick. For has he not stolen his one ewe lamb, deeming the old king dead and the girl in danger ?

The lynxlike glance of Mithridate has speedily detected the treachery of his elder son, and the younger one's unwitting betrayal. They must die, they and the Greek girl. Many a suspected wife or concubine has gone that way before ! He sends her a glass of poison ; but while Monime, in her Greek eloquence, reminiscent of Argos, is giving long directions to her waiting-woman and compatriot, the brusque barbarian tyrant changes his mind again : not they, but he shall quit this mortal scene. Conscious of old age and defeat, he renounces life and all the rest. Who does not remember his speech to Monime ?

> Enfin, j'ouvre les yeux, et je me fais justice.
> C'est faire à vos beautés un triste sacrifice
> Que de vous présenter, Madame, avec ma foi,
> Tout l'âge et le malheur que je traîne avec moi,
> Jusqu'ici la fortune et la victoire mêmes
> Cachaient mes cheveux blancs sous trente diadèmes.
> Mais ce temps là, n'est plus. Je règnais ; et je fuis.[1]

This is perhaps, with *Iphigénie*, the most romantic of Racine's tragedies. The power, the energy, the ruse of the old barbarian tyrant ; his utter loneliness while the Romans harry him and his children betray

---

[1] At last I judge myself, clear-eyed, and I deplore
Your beauty's sacrifice, should you, dear consort, know
All I drag after me, henceforth, of age and woe ;
So far victorious Fortune (which this battle stems)
Muffled my hoary locks 'neath thirty diadems ;
But those good days are gone ; the King's a fugitive.

him ; his intense personality, which seems to defy extinction ; and suddenly, when his vengeance is prepared, that swift abatement of desire, changed mysteriously into a deep, a bitter : *Cui bono ?* all combine to impress the reader with a sense of grandeur and compassion. The end of *Mithridate* reminds me of the end of *Wuthering Heights* (dare I write such heresy ? Yet, emotionally, it is true enough). But this romantic feeling does not prevent the tragedy from being a perfect example of classic construction. The plot is as clear as it is intricate.

This is a matter to which Racine ever gave the closest attention. His son writes in his *Memoir* that the poet, when composing a play, used to make a long scenario of every act in prose ; when every detail of construction was completed he would exclaim : " J'ai fait ma tragédie ! " counting for nothing that atmosphere and that harmony which enchant us still to-day. And he writes in the Preface to *Mithridate* :

An author cannot practise too careful an economy in that which he puts upon the stage. The most lovely scenes will run the risk of wearying the spectator if they be not strictly necessary to the action, or should they vainly interrupt it, instead of conducting it to its inevitable close.

Mithridate moves with the solemn march of Fatality from first to last.

CHAPTER VII

IPHIGÉNIE AND PHÈDRE

THE last two tragedies of Racine's theatrical career are subtly different from their fore-runners. Passion and Fate are, of course, their ostensible theme, but there is another secret intention, a mysterious esoteric meaning which transforms their accent even as we listen. Not Love, not Power, not Ambition, not Destiny supplies them with a motive, but Sin and the necessity of expiation, but Grace withheld and the inadequacy of human merit.

These Greek plays are Jansenist plays. Racine has laid to heart M. Nicole's sermon : " A poet is a public poisoner, and the man who attends a theatre an accomplice in the fancied crime he witnesses." But if the poet used the means at his disposal to inculcate a truth ? Might he not be a public healer ? *Iphigénie* and *Phèdre*, in Racine's garland, appear as olive branches offered to Port-Royal.

Phèdre does not wish to sin ; she falls without her own consent, irresistibly impelled by original sin, victim of the heredity of a monstrous race. She went blindfold where Nature bade her go. Grace was withheld. God forgot her, and she fell into the bottomless pit.

Let us turn to *Iphigénie* :

> Au sort qui m'entraînait il fallait consentir,[1]

exclaims the miserable Ériphile. Who more innocent than the Lesbian Princess when Achilles
ravished her from her devastated home ? Nature
has strange snares :

> Still, in his shady cell, where none can spy him,
> Sits Sin, to catch the souls that wander by him.

She has seen Achilles, torch in hand, fire the home
that sheltered her childhood ; she has. seen his
arms dripping with the blood of her kinsmen ;
incendiary, murderer, ravisher, he has thrown her
reluctant body, sick and swooning, into his foreign
ship—and for long she keeps her eyes closed from
the sight of her brutal conqueror. At last she steals
a glance—and lo !

> Je le vis. Son aspect n'avait rien de farouche—
> Je sentis le reproche expirer dans ma bouche—[2]

(If Freud, not Racine, had analysed the sudden
birth of passion out of terror and exhaustion, should
we not praise his ingenious psychology ?)

But though there was no purpose in her passion,
though Nature sprang it on her while God one
moment looked another way, it is not less deadly,
less sinful, less prompt to corrupt the very soul
of Ériphile, leading her through mazes of cruel
treachery to perdition ; only by her own blood
poured out on the altar in a burnt-offering can she
expiate the involuntary crime.

This Ériphile will puzzle classical students who

---

[1] Fain was I forc'd to say Yes ! to compelling Fate.

[2] I saw him ; in his face was nothing fierce or grim,
And on my lips expired the scorn I kept for him.

open Racine's *Iphigénie*. She is the French poet's
creation. I touch here on a point which inevitably
bewilders an Englishman. Most men who have
been through a public school have at least some
acquaintance with the classic poets in their original
text. Anyone in this case can but be confused by
the strange elements which Racine mixes with his
accurate translations—not only those religious inten-
tions, of which I have spoken (for the harsh Jansenism
of Port-Royal does not jar so much as one might
expect on the philosophic pessimism of the Greek
realist), but the gallant language of the Court, the
" flamme," the " flèche," the frequent ejaculations :
" Seigneur ! " " Madame ; " but a poignant modern
psychology " in which the human heart beats just
as it beats in Touraine," with, above all, new characters invented by Racine. And I, for my part,
forgive him the creation of Ériphile : she is so
interesting that Euripides might say of her as
Valentine Visconti said of her husband's bastard :
" She ought to have been mine ! " With regard to
Aricie, however, in *Phèdre*, I own that my sentiments are those of Antoine Arnauld : " Why on
earth did the man give Hippolytus a sweetheart ? "

Racine would have replied that the corrupt
audience to which his tragedies were played would
have suspected, in too complete a shunner of the
sex, the " Italian " taste then prevalent at Court.
No doubt there was a reason for all his inventions,
yet I must own that, in attempting to fit a pre-
Christian ideal to the canon of the Court, he did
somewhat deform that ideal. I know that, having
in my youth translated the *Hippolytus* of Euripides,
Phèdre for many years remained a sealed book to

me. Only after a long residence in France did I
appreciate, for instance, its extraordinary musicality
(for Racine is the nightingale of the French Parnassus), and at last find interesting that very
deformation which I have just been criticizing.
Even as the amateur of Greek wines, at first discon-
certed by the flavour of resin mixed in the cup, ends
by considering that it gives an accent to the vintage.

Racine, in his generation, was esteemed the
Sophocles of France.   Perhaps if in reading him we
took the pains we take to enter into the spirit of
Sophocles we might understand him more easily.
When we open a Greek poet we arm ourselves with
notes, consult the scholiasts, discover beauties
foreign to our native sensibilities, and so augment
the circuit of our minds.   But we pick up a play
of Racine's as lightly as the latest French novel,
expecting to be at once initiate.   Never do we
dream of consulting the useful, if sometimes pedantic,
observations of Voltaire and La Harpe ; seldom do
we refer to the exquisite appreciations of Anatole
France and Jules Lemaître.   And thus we often
fail to perceive the real originality of Racine.   One
may spend a happy hour in consulting Louis Racine's
critical Dictionary of Words and Phrases introduced
into the French language by the poet—seventy
quarto pages of them.   We all know that Racine's
vocabulary was very small.—a few hundred words,
they say.   We then perceive that the words, if
few, were fit, and, in their time, novel, as well as
choice, in their sense and combination.

Iphigénie was produced with brilliant success at
Versailles on the 18th of August, 1674, at a fête
given to celebrate the victory of Seneffe.   It was

given in the orangery in the garden, among fountains, and statues, and perfumed orange-trees, and
great Sèvres vases full of flowers.   And everywhere
dangled the banners taken by Condé the week before
from the Prince of Orange on the plains of Hainault.
The Champmeslé had never been more admirable,
and Boileau could write and seem credible—

> Jamais Iphigénie en Aulide immolée
> N'a coûté tant de pleurs á la Grèce assemblée
> Que, dans l'heureux spectacle à nos yeux étalés
> En a fait, sous son nom, verser là Champmesée.[1]

Iphigénie is certainly not one of the greatest among
Racine's tragedies.   The end, though impressive
—substituting Iphigénie's wicked rival for the white
hind offered up by Euripides in place of the
heroine—is less convincing than when, as in most
of our poet's plays, the climax is the ineluctable
conclusion of the passions to which his personages
are a prey.   (For Racine's characters are always
the prey of their own passions.)   But, if imperfect,
Iphigénie is very beautiful, exquisitely moving.
All the persons are simple, human and life-like in a
high degree—even the insidious and ungrateful
Ériphile ; and Racine (who, in this play, seems to
look at all his personages through a mist of tears)
has a movement of compassion even for her : " Was
it her fault if she sinned ? (he seems to say).   And yet
she must pay the price.   Christ has not shed a drop
of His blood for her."

Of all his tragedies *Phèdre* was to remain the
dearest to the heart of Racine—dearer even than those

---

[1] When Iphigenia in Aulis died,
The assembled Greeks, crowding the altar-side,
Wept less than we who witness'd, t'other day,
The fiction of her fate with Chammelay.

two children of his later years, *Esther* and *Athalie*. His friend, Boileau, asked him one day, when he was already on the threshold of old age, what he liked best in all his work. " I am for *Phèdre*," he replied promptly. Had not *Phèdre* re-opened to him at last the gates of Port-Royal ? And *Phèdre* expressed to the full the convictions both of the man and the artist.

The beginning of *Iphigénie* is untranslatably harmonious. When the anxious King, Agamemnon, wakes his old Squire before the dawn, the startled Arcas exclaims :

> A peine un faible jour vous éclaire et me guide,
> Vos yeux seuls et les miens sont ouverts dans l'Aulide.
> Avez vous dans les airs entendu quelque bruit ?
> Les vents nous auraient-ils exaucés cette nuit ?
> Mais tout dort, et l'armée, et les vents, et Neptune. . . .[1]

But Phèdre's desperate apostrophe to the shades of her tragical forerunners is no less musical despite the doom which condemns her to a terrible heredity.

> O haine de Vénus! O fatale colère !
> Dans quels égarements l'amour jeta ma mère. . . .

> . . . Ariane, ma sœur, de quel amour blessée
> Vous mourûtes aux bords où vous fûtes laissée.[2]

> . . . Puisque Vénus le veut, de ce sang déplorable
> Je péris la dernière et la plus misérable.[3]

---

[1] The dawn is yet too dim your groping step to guide,
Your eyes alone, and mine, are open in all Aulide.
Say, did you hear at last a rustle take the air ?
Shall the wind rise to-night in answer to our pray'r ?
No, everything's asleep, the camp, the winds, the sea. . . .

[2] O Venus' dire revenge ! Dread anger of a God !
Ah me, the devious ways that my dead mother trod !

. . . Ariadne, Sister, hear ! A cruel pang you bore,
Who died of love, alone, on that forsaken shore ?

[3] . . . Since such is Venus' will, of our unhappy line
The last, I perish, I, and the worst fate is mine !

Does an English reader catch the Virgilian music of the French ? The murmur and the wail of a lost soul ? The lucid and yet mysterious atmosphere that bathes the personages in another light than that of everyday ? One Englishman at least has felt it : Mr. Lytton Strachey. Others may follow in his track.

Phèdre is written with a sincerity, a conviction, a sort of remorse, which recall the tone of Pascal's *Pensées*. Who is Phèdre ? An ordinary human being—a woman, " ni tout-à-fait coupable, ni tout-à-fait innocente " ; no worse and no better than those who shudder at her fate and whose only chance of escaping it is the bare chance of that divine caprice, the Grace of God : a free gift, so purely gratuitous that none dare reckon on it. Who is Phèdre ? A poor heathen, ignorant of Christ, whom her own passions and the wrath of Heaven have engaged in an incestuous love. Less guilty, perhaps, than the pupil of Port-Royal, complacently parading these six years past, an adulterous intrigue with an actress, very useful to him.

Phèdre, unlike most of Racine's tragedies, bears no dedication ; in the author's mind it was consecrated to Port-Royal :

Is it the best of my tragedies ? [he writes in the Preface]. I dare not decide. But at least it is the play in which Virtue appears in the clearest light ; in which the least faults are severely punished ; in which the mere thought of crime is regarded with the same horror as crime itself, and the follies and errors of Love considered as, in reality, the follies and errors that they are.

And Racine compares his play to those antique tragedies which a Socrates ventured to approve,

and wishes that the modern theatre were framed
more firmly on their model :

> It might be a means of reconciling Tragedy with a number
> of persons famous for their piety and their doctrine, who
> have condemned it of late, and who perhaps would judge it
> less severely if the playwright sought to instruct his audience
> as well as to amuse, following, in this respect, the veritable
> intention of tragedy.

Racine is no longer so incensed with M. Nicole.
As usual, he has absorbed and assimilated the dose
he began by flinging violently in his physician's
face ; never was a man more reflective, more different
in his first and his second thoughts. For, thinking
it over, was he proud of his life during the last few
years ? Of the strange world he had moved in ?
Of the queer loose beings with whom he had come
in contact ? Of his own odd position between M. de
Champmeslé and his wife ? The best he could
say for himself would be that he was like Phèdre,
" ni tout-à-fait coupable, ni tout-à-fait innocent."

Mystery of mysteries ! When *Phèdre* was first
produced upon the stage, it was a dead failure.
There is an inscrutable fate in these things.
Usually those plays which become classic are not
admired at first. *Iphigénie* and *Mithridate* had
known triumph. *Phèdre* had no luck.

Yet the Champmeslé was no less moving and
" miraculous " in *Phèdre*, surely the most dramatic
and touching *rôle* imaginable, as our own times have
proved. The reason why *Phèdre* at first seemed
doomed to disaster had to be sought, not upon the
stage, but in the boxes of the theatre.

Racine had enemies. Sensitive and sarcastic,
with an epigram ever ready to avenge a fancied

slight, he had offended many vanities. There were those who disliked Racine because he was on the side of the young. All the lovers of old romances, heroic tragedies, emphasis, the Spanish tone ; all the partisans of Corneille ; all the relics of the Fronde—detested in him the spirit of the new Court. It is possible, too, that the queer tales which were told concerning the death of Mademoiselle du Parc had begun to affect a portion of the public. The actress's two little girls had found a harbour in the mansion of the Countess of Soissons ; they and their step-grandmother had a jealous aversion for Racine which may have spread in the coterie of Mazarin's nieces, as scandal ever spreads. One of the most charming of these Mancinis, and one of the most resolute of Racine's enemies, was the indomitable and domineering young Duchesse de Bouillon. Let us listen to what Saint-Simon says of her :

> Wherever she appeared, she gave the tone to the assembly, and seemed the dominant spirit. It was dangerous to displease her. . . . She was a personage in Paris, a sort of Queen.

By birth an Italian of no importance, a native of Rome, whose great-grandparents were wrapped in mystery, her mother's brother had been Cardinal Mazarin. When the Signora Mancini died young, the Cardinal had adopted all her children and had sent for them to France. A violent brood of young eaglets they were ! As they grew up, he married the eldest to the Duke of Vendôme, her sister Olympe to the Count of Soissons, a prince of the House of Savoy ; Marie, the third, had so very nearly snatched the Crown of France and the heart of Louis

Quatorze, that she had to be sent out of the way to Rome, where she espoused the Constable Colonna ; Hortense brought her husband (the heir of the Marèchal de la Meilleraye) the arms and style of Duc de Mazarin ; one of the brothers was turned into a French Duke, the Duc de Nevers, and the youngest girl married the Duc de Bouillon, Prince de La Tour d'Auvergne and Grand Chamberlain of France. It was the Duchess of Bouillon who had the ingenious idea of wrecking *Phèdre*.

Why ? Ah, that we can never know. Perhaps she was merely tired of hearing Aristides called the Just. She sent to Rouen for an honest Norman called Pradon, a poet of some reputation in his province, and told him to produce a tragedy on the story of Phèdre, which must be ready by a certain date. Pradon obeyed—people generally obeyed the Duchess—and the two plays were ripe at the self-same moment. On New Year's Day, 1677, Racine's *Phèdre* made its first appearance at the Hôtel de Bourgogne ; two days later, Pradon's *Phèdre et Hippolyte* trod the boards of the rival theatre.

The Duchess had engaged anonymously the entire tier of the boxes and all the good places at either theatre for the first six representations (plays were then given three times a week) ; it cost her the trifle of 15,000 livres. Racine's play was performed to empty benches, while Pradon's, of course, was riotously applauded. Valincour (in a letter published in Olivet's *Histoire de l'Académie Française*) tells us that Racine was reduced to despair, for " durant plusieurs jours M. Pradon triompha et la pièce de M. Racine fut sur le point de tomber." When one considers that the madcap caprice of one extravagant great lady nearly extinguished one of the purest masterpieces of French poetry, one understands that the generous Jules Lemaître could declare that, after nearly two hundred and fifty years, his blood boiled to think of it.

The worst of it was that the trial of this tragic fortnight had a depressing effect upon the actress. The Champmeslé had not been accustomed to play to empty houses, while all the *beau monde* trooped to the new theatre in the rue Guénegaud. She gave no support to Racine. She began to doubt of his genius, and to think he had perhaps injured her diction by insisting of that peculiar delivery which he had acquired from Antoine Lemaistre. A certain fatigue and exasperation crept into her manner. Although she made no pretensions to an exclusive fidelity, Racine had ruled her life for half a dozen years ; perhaps she was tired of him ? A sensual passion seldom lasts longer. The great actress had sucked her poet dry. (Spinoza, I believe, informs us that Love is the desire to increase our moral substance at someone else's expense.) Instinctively the Champmeslé turned towards other sources of nutrition.

There was a certain Comte de Clermont Tonnerre. The only letter which we possess addressed by La Fontaine to Mademoiselle de Champmeslé is dated 1678. There is no longer any question of Racine in it ; M. de Clermont Tonnerre has succeeded him, even as Racine had succeeded the young Marquis de Sévigné. Everything which mattered to Racine appeared to fail him at once. In vain his friends sought to comfort him by speaking of the beauty of *Phèdre*. In vain Boileau dedicated to him his finest epistle. Had they not seen Molière derided ? asks the excellent Despréaux :

> L'ignorance et l'erreur à ses naissantes pièces,
> En habits de Marquis, en habits de Comtesses,
> Venaient pour diffamer un chef d'œuvre nouveau
> Et secouaient la tête à l'endroit le plus beau.[1]

The day will come, Racine (cries the enthusiastic satirist), the day will dawn when you, the Sophocles of France, shall be given your due place upon Parnassus, and when our age will be accounted glorious because it put upon the stage—

> la douleur vertueuse
> De Phèdre, malgré soi perfide, incestueuse.

Racine would not be comforted. His first impulse was to strike back—but to strike at whom ? For, of course, at first the manœuvre of the Duchess was unsuspected, and the secret of those empty benches seemed impenetrable. And then there was the affair of the sonnet. A mysterious sonnet began to circulate and soon came to Racine's anxious ears—a really clever sonnet, for reading it some twelve score years later, we find, enumerated in its narrow room, our whole quarrel with Racine concerning *Phèdre* : the incongruity of its religious temper and the sacrilege of giving a sweetheart to the chaste follower of Artemis. Shorn of one less happy quatrain, here the sonnet is :

> Dans un fauteuil doré, Phèdre, tremblante et blême,
> Dit des vers où d'abord, personne n'entend rien ;
> Sa nourrice lui fait un sermon fort chrétien
> Contre l'affreux dessein d'attenter sur soi-même. . . .

---

[1] Ignorance, Error, damn'd the new-born play,
Dress'd as a Lord, deck'd in a Belle's array,
Quick to decry new beauties, in their rage
They shook their heads when most we praise the page

Une grosse Aricie, au teint rouge, aux crins blonds,
N'est là que pour montrer deux énormes tétons,
Que, malgré sa froideur, Hippolyte idolâtre ;
Il meurt enfin, traîné par ses coursiers ingrats ;
Et Phèdre, après avoir pris de la mort-aux-rats,
Vient, en se confessant, mourir sur le théâtre.[1]

For some reason unknown to us—probably because he was already on the scent of the Duchesse de Bouillon—Racine supposed this sonnet to be the work of that lady's brother, the Duc de Nevers. He determined on a prompt retort. Acante was not the man to take an insult lying down. In his precipitation he forgot to make sure of the true identity of the adversary with whom he meant to break a lance.

The Duc de Nevers was as fantastic a being as ever moved through a Shakespearian comedy, a recluse, a dilettante, a sort of Duke Orsino out of *Twelfth Night* : " Ce Duc de Nevers si extraordinaire qui vous glisse des mains alors que l'on y pense le moins," wrote Madame de Sévigné, who admired him immensely. She admired even his poems, which few people ever saw. " But all he writes has such a peculiar quality, as like himself as two peas ; it disgusts one with other authors." Racine, then, attributed the authorship of the sonnet to this mysterious Duke, seldom seen, seldom heard. Aided

---

[1] Pale, in a gilt armchair, limbs trembling, eyelids wide,
    Phædra murmurs her words, and no one hears a line.
    The Nurse, who seems to be an excellent Divine,
    Reads her a sermon on the sin of suicide. . . .

A blond, fat Aricie, red-fac'd, with hair like wires,
Exposes two huge breasts that fire, in Theseus' son—
The frigid votary of Dian—fond desires.
He dies, by ungrateful steeds thrown from his equipage.
And Phædra, having quaff'd a cup of rat-poison,
Crying *Peccavi* ! comes to die upon the stage.

by Boileau and a few madcap friends, he composed another sonnet on the same rhymes, ascribing to the Duc de Nevers (pale, trembling, in a gilt armchair) an incestuous passion for his own sister, the Duchess of Mazarin. Such were seventeenth-century manners.

But Nevers had had nothing to do with the sonnet, which was due to the pen of a fashionable poetess, Madame Deshoulières, chiefly remembered now for that pretty song, " Il pleut, il pleut, Bergère." And the Duke was naturally indignant at such an uncalled-for and scurrilous attack. He was not an Italian for nothing. In a moment of fury he declared that he would have Racine and Boileau assassinated, some night, on their way home from the playhouse.

They were neither of them souls impervious to fear : " l'un et l'autre des gens fort susceptibles de peur," remarks Valincourt. They protested their innocence, but no one believed them. An Italian Duke . . . bravos some dark night hiding, muffled, at some street corner . . . a sudden thrust . . . and then . . . Judgment . . . Eternity ! Here was another theme for Racine's mournful meditations.

In vain the Duc de Bourbon (Condé's son) wrote good-naturedly to the two poets : " Come to the Hôtel de Condé, where I can ensure your safety. If really you did not write the sonnet, you are innocent ; and if you did write it, come all the same, for it was an excellent piece of fooling." In vain the King promised fresh sinecures and pensions, heaping honours on Racine. Racine had received that sign, that warning, which, in the eyes of a naturally religious man, may determine a conversion. The Commendatore had supped with him ; he had seen the finger writing on the wall. Seven years

before, M. de Tréville, one of the most brilliant
young Lords about the Court, had received as
sudden a call at the death-bed of poor Madame ;
while Racine's old master, Antoine Lemaistre, after
a shock as unexpected, had cast from his feet the
dust of this world and built himself a hermitage
in the wilderness. And now the Hand behind the
veil had struck three blows : the fall of *Phèdre*,
the threat of sudden death, the inconstancy of an
adored mistress. The poet was still passionately
in love—" plein de passion," " très amoureux,"
write his contemporaries, Valincourt, Madame de
Sévigné, Boileau. Everything seemed to fail him
at once : the theatre, his incomparable mistress,
Life itself.

A sort of spiritual fear, a disgust of the world and
its works, a longing for the pure waters and green
pastures of his early life, invaded the soul of the
poet. What was Fame ? What was Life ? They
danced before you like those lovely elf-maidens,
whose faces and whose graces are enchanting, yet,
should they turn their backs, you perceive them to
be hollow, spectacles of horror. And what was
Love itself ? It had been the theme of all his
poetry : the love of the violent and brutal for the
chaste, in *Andromaque* ; the love of Nero for a pure
virgin whose torment fills him with delight, in
Britannicus ; the love of a great man for the woman
to whom he owes everything and whom he cannot
marry, in *Bérénice* ; the love of a proud old hero,
vanquished by the years, for the young girl who
adores his son, in *Mithridate* ; the diseased love of
an imperious woman for a man younger than herself
whom she murders out of jealousy, in *Bajazet* ; and

the involuntary incestuous love of Phèdre for her stepson. All Dead Sea apples, full of dust and corruption. He had tasted them too long. Strange, ominous world, was there nowhere a refuge from it and a haven ? Nowhere a Cross on which one might be nailed, like the Dying Thief, and so raised up at last into Paradise ? The prodigal son is weary of the husks and the swine. He will arise and go to his father.

Suddenly starved and deprived—not only of that bird-eyed, dark-skinn'd little woman, the Champmeslé, but of those wonderful beings, their children, created by him and her together : Bérénice, Monime, Iphigénie, Phèdre, who had knit between their parents such a complex passion—Racine felt all the forces of his nature attain a sort of watershed and flow in another direction, turning definitely away from the cherished sin, losing themselves in a state of morbid fear, anxiety, depression, perplexity ; till at last, advancing from the background of his unconscious life, a new love arose, a new life began, —till one night in the darkness of his chamber, the poet embraced a crucifix.

In a paroxysm of sincere remorse, of that loving faith which longs to have something to renounce, and yet, perhaps, moved no less by the pettish anger of a disappointed child, Racine determined to fling the world and the flesh to the Devil and seek his salvation through the narrow gate. A voice out of the Past sounded in his soul, and, counting the world well lost, he announced his determination to lead a new life, as a monk, in a Carthusian monastery.

BOOK III

THE PRODIGAL'S RETURN

Wer immer strebend sich bemüht,
Den können wir erlösen.
Faust, 2nd Part. *Chorus of Angels.*

CHAPTER I

MARRIAGE AND A NEW START IN LIFE

RACINE'S spiritual director, while approving, perhaps exacting a complete separation from the theatre, dissuaded his penitent from attempting to scale the dizzy heights of sanctity in some remote chartreuse. A Christian marriage would suffice to mend his ways.

When a man of eight-and-thirty, famous, handsome, charming in manner and disposition, informs an anxious family that he intends to turn over a new leaf, and wishes to settle, it is seldom long before he finds himself in presence of a suitable young lady. In Racine's case her name was Catherine de Romanet. She was twenty-five years of age, pious and well-connected; her father had been in the Civil Service; her maternal grandfather a prosperous Parisian notary; but the girl was an orphan and lived under the roof of her guardian, a cousin of the Nicolas Vitarts; this guardian's wife was related to the Coulanges, and distantly connected with Madame de Sévigné. The young lady was not a great heiress, but had a little fortune of her own. She was well brought up, sensible and religious.

And Racine accepted the bride that his family and his spiritual adviser proposed to him with a grateful heart.

They were married on the 1st of June, 1677, exactly six months after the fiasco of *Phèdre.* The great Condé and his son came to the wedding, with Colbert, Lamoignon, and other names of note, among which it is pleasant to read those of François Le Vasseur, Prior of Ouchy—that frivolous little Abbé, the friend of Racine's salad days, now sage and solid in his white friar's frock—of Nicolas Vitart, Seigneur de Passy, and of Nicolas Boileau, Seigneur des Préaux : these two last were Racine's " best men." A few weeks later (having left a due interval for the honeymoon) the *Mercure Galant* informs all and sundry that—

M. Racine has married Mademoiselle de Romanet. The lady is possessed of a fortune as well as of wit and birth, and M. Racine well deserves to find these advantages united in the shape of an amiable young lady.

The *Mercure Galant* does not pronounce the word beauty ; none of her contemporaries mention the looks of Racine's wife ; they were probably in no wise remarkable. " Ni l'amour, ni l'intérêt n'eurent aucune part à ce choix." According to her son, Louis Racine : " Neither love nor money influenced my father's choice. Reason alone prompted so serious a decision."

The modest dowry of his wife, his scanty savings, and the pensions and offices which he held from the King, enabled the poet to set up house without counting on the labours of his pen—henceforth he will ask nothing from the theatre. He was not poor. He was not rich. Supposing the livre to count as a little under four shillings of our present English currency, they made up between them about £1,600 a year, shall we say? Catherine de Romanet brought her husband an income of 3,600 livres, and a small estate valued at 22,000 livres ; Racine had about a thousand livres a year of his own ; a Royal pension of £1,500, a sinecure as Treasurer of France for the town of Moulins, which brought him in 2,400.

Besides these sums, the inventory made for his wedding shows him in possession of a library (valued at 1,500 livres) and some fine furniture : a best bed of gold and silver brocade, richly fringed and lined with saffron-coloured satin ; another bed upholstered in green silk damask, with chairs, armchairs and curtains to match, several pictures, a tall mirror, a clock with a pendulum, and several sets of tapestry, Flemish and Italian. For the first time in his life our poet now enjoyed a real home of his own. He had no leisure to feel time hang heavy on his hands, for almost at once there opened out before him the prospect of a new career, that " other chance " which most of us, at some moment, must have wished that Life might hold out for us. The *Mercure Galant* announces it in October of the same year, 1677 :

The theatre is threatened with a great loss. It is rumoured on all sides that one of our most illustrious dramatic authors quits the stage in order to dedicate himself entirely to the pursuit of history. He is capable of writing the history of this reign : it would be impossible to find a finer subject or a more enlightened guide.

Every one was not so pleased with Racine's appointment (conjointly with his inseparable Boileau-Despréaux) as *historiographe du Roi*. On the 15th of October of the same year we find Madame de Sévigné writing to her cousin, Bussy-Rabutin, who would, she thought, as a soldier and a man of great

birth, have fitted the position more appropriately
than " ces deux bourgeois." " I should like to see
what they will make of it ! " she cries. " The King
gives them two thousand crowns a year a-piece,
and require them to write his history. He will
supply the necessary material." About a fortnight
later she returns to the subject ; the King had then
returned to Versailles from the armies in the North.

Four days ago he said to Racine and Despréaux:
"I am vexed that you did not witness my last campaign.
That would have shown you what war really is. And the
journey was not so long as to prove fatiguing."

" Sire [replied Racine] we are two quiet cits, who live in town
and have no country clothes. We ordered them; but your
Majesty had taken the cities he was laying siege to, before the
tailor could finish our coats."

" The remark was well received," concludes the
Marquise ; she was somewhat pacified by Racine's
pretty repartee, but on the 14th of March (1678)
all her indignation against the two bourgeois flames
up afresh.

What do you say to the fall of Ghent? It was a precious
long time, my cousin, since that town had seen a King of
France! Ours is indeed an admirable monarch! He deserves
a better historian than two poets! We know what *poet*
means! He has no need of poets! Neither fiction nor fable
are necessary to place him above all others! All that he
needs is a manner of writing direct and pure and clear, such
as flows from the pen of a man of quality who is also a man
of war. And I know such, my cousin !

Strange transformation brought about in a few
months' time. Our Racine, the amorous, restless,
jealous man about town, dramatic poet, lover of a
theatrical star, finds himself changed into a comfortable bourgeois, a husband, and a historian ! He
seems to have been quite happy. His wife was
warm-hearted, kind and simple, quite devoid of

social ambition, and yet not without a certain
elegance by her own fireside. She was devoid of the
faintest tincture of literary taste, and took no
interest at all in the matter. She was deeply
religious, and there she shared his thoughts.

One must admit [writes Louis Racine] that Religion was the
only force .that could fuse into a perfect union two characters
so entirely different. My father's vivacity took the least trifle
with an excessive sensibility, while my mother's tranquil temper
never even seemed to notice the ups and downs of daily life.
Often in later years, when domestic anxieties (such as the illness of one of his children) would agitate my father, he would
exclaim : " Why did I run the risk of such misfortunes ? Why,
oh why did my friends prevent me from turning monk ?
A monk leads a quiet life ! " . . . Yet his companion, by the
sweetness of her disposition, her dutiful behaviour as wife and
mother, her admirable piety, knew how to captivate him entirely,
and stood him in stead of all those societies he had renounced
on quitting the theatre.

Thus Religion united what in the eyes of the world must
ever have seemed but ill-matched partners. My father had no
passion in his heart so lively as the love of poetry. My mother's
indifference to the Muse was such that, in the course of a life
spent in the society of poets, she never learned the structure
of a verse. She never read, and never went to see, one of her
husband's tragedies, and if she knew their titles it was only
from hearing them spoken of in the course of conversation. But
a man, though none so impassioned for the movements of the
mind, may yet perfer, in a wife, an excellent mistress of his
house and mother of his children, rather than a companion
enchanted by the same delights. My mother, though she read
nothing save sermons and pious tracts, had none the less a solid
judgment of her own, and was on all occasions a sensible adviser.

Boileau, extending his affection and esteem for
Racine to his wife, had a very genuine liking for the
lady, for he appreciated good sense and fidelity.
When his friend was at Court, or with the armies,
Madame Racine and her little brood were welcome
guests at his cottage at Auteuil on any sunny afternoon, or he would look in on them in Paris to

exchange with them his news of the absent husband and father. But Boileau found more incomprehensible than Catherine Racine's indifference to poetry, her indifference to money. Boileau was imbued with that comfortable French and bourgeois form of avarice which does not exclude a habitual disinterestedness and a not too infrequent freak of generosity. When Boileau resigned a benefice, or gave a present—and he was capable of doing either very handsomely—he knew the value of his act. Catherine de Romanet, good housekeeper as she was, and careful mother, was deaf to the clink of coin— the only deafness Boileau never suffered from. One day, when Racine was on duty at Versailles, he had arranged to call for his wife and children at Auteuil on his return, and, pushing the gate of Boileau's garden, he arrived towards evening, excited and happy.

" Congratulate me ! " he cried. " The King has just given me a purse of a thousand livres ! " Boileau appreciated the boon ; but good Madame Catherine was full of some obstinacy of one of the children's, who would not learn his lesson as he ought.

" These two days passed I have not been able to get him to his book ! " she cried.

" Well, well ! " said Racine. " We will talk of all that by and by. Let us rejoice to-day in the King's liberality ! "

But my mother [continues Louis Racine] could not take any interest in the unexpected boon, and went on lamenting that there was no getting the child to hear reason, and that his father must take him to task on his return to Paris, until Boileau, who had been pacing to and fro in his astonishment, lost all control of his temper and broke out :

" What insensibility, to be sure ! How can one pay no attention to a purse with a thousand livres in it ! "

CHAPTER II

PORT-ROYAL REVISITED

RACINE'S marriage, honourable, prosperous and happy, was a satisfaction to his family, and perhaps to no one more than to his aunt, Mère Agnès de Sainte-Thècle Racine, the Prioress of the Abbey. It is probable that she had had a hand in it, for her nephew wrote, many years later, to Madame de Maintenon :

> She it was who taught me to know God in my childhood, and she, also, was God's instrument in withdrawing me from those erring paths in which, for fifteen years, I had wandered.

During the greater part of those fifteen years our poet had been an outlaw from Port-Royal, nor was it a light task to secure a welcome for the prodigal on his return. Nothing was easier than to obtain the full and free forgiveness of the gentle Nicole ; but Antoine Arnauld, even more sensitive and fiery than was Racine himself, could not pardon those poor jokes that Racine had fired off at the expense of Mère Angélique the Abbess, Arnauld's sister.

All the clan of the Racines and the Vitarts at the Abbey began to prepare a reconciliation. A certain Abbé du Pin, whose mother was a Vitart, accompanied the poet to the house of M. Nicole ; but the good man could do nothing with that obstinate

Jansenist, Antoine Arnauld, who refused to receive the stray lamb back into the fold, deeming him still a wolf in sheep's clothing. The Abbey then resorted to Boileau as an intermediary, and could not have found a better ; for he was equally devoted to Arnauld and to Racine, and a man whose Jansenist proclivities were above suspicion ; for some reason, too, Boileau's poetry never was anathematized by the Solitaries—perhaps because, despite its music and its wit, it was essentially unimpassioned and unpoetical. Boileau asked nothing better than to make peace between the theologian he revered and the peccant poet who was his closest friend ; he set to work at once.

After prudent and patient negotiations, he at last succeeded in persuading the heady and passionate old doctor in divinity to admit Racine's conversion, and the next time that he visited the Faubourg-Saint-Jacques, where Arnauld was living more or less in hiding, Boileau put in his pocket a copy of *Phèdre*, bent on reading aloud that passage in the preface where the author expresses a hope that his play may reconcile with the Tragic Muse " a number of persons famous for their piety and their doctrine." When he reached the quiet convent where two great ladies, the Duchesse de Longueville and Madame de Saint-Loup, had taken up their abode —in one or other of whose parlours the great Antoine Arnauld held his secret receptions—he found several eminent brothers in the persecuted faith already present. They were all theologians, more or less, and excellent debaters, so Boileau began at once on the subject of Racine's play and the interest of a tragedy, explaining the vanity of human merit

deprived of saving Grace. The visitors began to
argue the point, some for, some against Racine's
pretensions, but the objectors were still in the
majority, when suddenly old Arnauld broke forth :

" If really things are as he says, Racine is right
and his tragedy is innocent ! " (And thenceforth,
as we know, Arnauld was *Phèdre's* most ardent
admirer, though he marvelled that the poet should
have given Hippolytus a sweetheart.)

Thereupon Boileau took his leave, enchanted
with his success, and returned a few days later
accompanied by the pale and trembling prodigal.
The sensitive Racine could scarcely support the
ordeal. Again Boileau sought the tranquil apart-
ment of Madame de Saint-Loup, again they were
admitted, and again they found the room full of
surreptitious visitors, for the two poets were not
expected. Boileau went forwards. Racine advanced in his wake a few steps, and then, as he saw
his old master rise to receive him, he sank on his
knees in a paroxysm of shame and contrition.
Arnauld stooped as if to raise the poet, and then, in
his turn, overcome by his feelings, knelt down beside
him upon the floor, where, each of them flinging his
arms about the other's neck, they embraced, repentant and forgiving. After that day, Racine was a
welcome visitor not only at the Abbey, but also in
that pious Faubourg-Saint-Jacques, which, in the
corrupt and brilliant Paris of Louis Quatorze, appears as a sort of catacombs where converted and
persecuted Christians met to pray. Three great
convents : Port-Royal of Paris, the Carmelites,
and the Visitandines, harboured many great ladies
growing old, weary at last of the world and its vani-

ties, of politics and passion ; there, in retirement, they still kept their court, and deeming themselves aloof from all sublunary affairs, still were persons of importance whose influence spread afar. " Le quartier fournit une très bonne compagnie," wrote Madame de Sévigné's cousin—Madame de Coulanges, " on n'a qu'à l'habiter pour être une personne audessus des autres," and the Marquise herself half-dreaded, half-desired, to be caught one day by the sacred bird-lime, the " glu," of the Faubourg-Saint-Jacques, which never loosed its hold on those with whom it had come in contact, and which in fact will catch her son. Two of its repentant goddesses, its Magdalenes " de bonne compagnie" —the Duchesse de Longueville and Madame de Saint-Loup—were heart and soul at the disposal of Port-Royal. It was in their drawing-rooms that Antoine Arnauld, a wanderer on the face of the earth, made his appointments when he ventured to visit Paris, sure that no search-party, or sudden perquisition of the police, could ever reach him in those pious quarters ; for the Faubourg-Saint-Jacques was a perfect honeycomb of innocent conspirators in coif and veil, the private rivalries of the great religious houses being forgotten in their common distrust of, and resistance to, the tyrannic pre-tensions of the Crown.

But the King did not like the Faubourg-Saint-Jacques, which he considered, not without reason, as a wasp's nest of sectarians and malcontents ; and he had been informed of Antoine Arnauld's visit to the convent-lodging of Madame de Saint-Loup. Seething the kid in its mother's milk, one day he sent to that address an Arnauld, his Minister, the

Marquis de Pomponne, the great Arnauld's nephew, with a prompt and peremptory message.

His Majesty disliked too great an intimacy between a number of persons of one way of thinking, such as was frequent in the Faubourg-Saint-Jacques. He desired that Monsieur Arnauld should live like other people. The King especially desired that no peculiar union, sect, or coterie should excite remark.

Thenceforth the days of Arnauld were not to be long in the land—at least, not in the land of France.

One Wednesday (it was the 17th of May, 1679), at Port-Royal-des-Champs, Racine was saying his prayers, kneeling before the altar in the chapel, when, looking up, he saw the Archbishop of Paris enter " like a flash " and walk across the church. It was barely nine o'clock in the morning. This M. de Harlay, the Archbishop, was, like Racine himself, one of M. Hamon's old pupils, but he was no friend to Port-Royal. In his swift traject across the nave, Racine saw him stoop an instant to read an epitaph, muttering, " Odd, very odd! " He then hurriedly retraced his steps and left the building. In his brief apparition the Archbishop had noticed not only a singular monument, but Racine on his knees, and desired to say a few words to his illustrious friend, his colleague at the French Academy.

Like M. de Pomponne, M. de Harlay had been sent on a mission which was a warning. A man naturally gallant of mien, and infinitely courteous, he had some difficulty in getting his message out. " He was so gentle, so cordial, so polite (wrote the Abbess on the morrow of this visit), that one felt persuaded that, though under constraint, the Archbishop may be forced to *act* unkindly, he could never bring himself to *say* a harsh word." Yet Port-Royal had no more redoubtable enemy than this amiable cleric.

See him walking about the grounds, bearing his part in an eloquent and gracious conversation with the Lady Abbess, Mère Angélique de Saint-Jean, with M. Racine, with M. de Sacy! In the course of the talk he let it be understood that the King had been much vexed by some recent small success of the Jansenists before the Papal Tribunal at Rome. Port-Royal would have to pay for it! Another turn or two, and M. de Harlay, no less urbane, contrived to enunciate the King's command : that the Abbey must at once dismiss all its pupils, all its pensioners, and receive no fresh novices until the natural process of time should have brought the number of the nuns down to fifty. Finally, and just as he was going to leave, the Royal delegate turned back, still smiling, to say to M. de Sacy :

" I was about to forget to tell you ! It seems that you, sir, and all the other Solitaries of Port-Royal must quit the Abbey—at once ! at once ! " And he was gone.

So much for the Abbey-in-the-Fields. In Paris, Antoine Arnauld had received more than one private warning : it were well that he should quit France while yet he could ; the world is a wider prison than the Bastille. One day, very sore at heart, he took his departure for the Low Countries. Though still hale and hearty, the great Arnauld was sixty-eight years old. Fifteen years thence he will die in exile —and what an exile ! a perpetual hiding ! For the arm of the King of France reached far. During the years that the old philosopher went to earth, so to speak, in a quiet street of Brussels, he dared not take his walks abroad. There was a little garden to his house, with a wall on either side conterminous with other garden plots. When Arnauld wanted an airing, his maidservant hung out the sheets to dry on a line stretched in front of either wall; washing day was walking day; and the violent old man paced up and down his white cloister, unperceived, like a polar bear left stranded on too narrow an icefloe. Then he remembered Port-Royal. He will see no more (save with the mind's eye) the Abbey-in-the-Fields, the huts of the Solitaries, his own innumerable and ardent family, or the quiet parlour of Madame de Saint-Loup, and the eager colloquies of his co-religionaries in the Faubourg-Saint-Jacques. Antoine Arnauld died in banishment. But, once dead, and buried secretly, " for fear of wolves "—(did the Jansenists fear that the King would scatter their prophet's ashes to the winds ?)—a pious conspirator was found to take charge of the great heart of the outlaw and carry it home to the Abbey-in-the-Fields. There it was privily buried before the altar, Racine, alone of those without the walls, being present at the secret and anathematized sepulture.

During those years of solitude and peril Racine had proved a true friend to the exile. Letters, messages, passed between them; the poet was always ready to act at his master's command. He was a faithful agent. Despite his admiration for the King, notwithstanding a naturally timid and gentle disposition, he showed himself full of courage as the champion at Court of the persecuted saints.

He rather likes to be pointed out as a Jansenist [wrote Spanheim, the Duke of Brandenburg's agent, in his Memoirs, quoted by Paul Mesnard in his Introduction to Racine]. He seems to court the suggestion, although Jansenism is quite out of fashion in France ; perhaps he thinks such intrepidity makes him appear the more a gentleman and a man of the world. In fact, M. de Racine almost flaunts his Jansenism, which, however, has been remarked upon, not a little to his discredit. He is the Oracle of Jansenist doctrine, and states his decisions with a grave and decent modesty that carries weight.

The risks were great. In covered language, for the post was not safe, Madame de Sévigné (a Jansenist at heart) informs her distant daughter of the peril of Port-Royal, in October 1678 :

The Jesuits are now more powerful than ever. They have re-opened that old quarrel [with P. R.] about the Five Propositions. One has been obliged to lower one's flag and disavow one's principles, and say Aye, aye ! to whatever they wish. For the Lettres de Cachet [sealed orders securing imprisonment] with which one is threatened are powerful arguments for the doctrines of the Jesuits. . . . God will judge between us in the Valley of Jehoshaphat. Meanwhile, let us live with the living, say I !

Racine, the timid, the tender-hearted Racine, was almost the only courtier not to lower his flag— stouter in that than the bright, vivacious Marquise, or many another. Port-Royal had few friends at Court, and was to have fewer still. Towards the end of November 1679, Simon Arnauld, Marquis de Pomponne, brother of Mère Angélique de Saint-Jean, nephew of Antoine Arnauld, and hitherto, despite all this, a man of mark at Versailles, a Secretary of State, was suddenly dismissed, disgraced. No excuse, no reason was vouchsafed. Pomponne was a Jansenist, and the King disliked their coterie.

CHAPTER III

POETS ON A BATTLEFIELD

WE have seen our poet suddenly wrenched from a career in which he had attained a glorious mastery ; then, by an act of voluntary discipline, accepting a task for which he had no natural aptitude and in which he will never achieve greatness. And we could weep for the apparent perversity of such a choice, were we not convinced, with Goethe, that the only way to sublimate a poem is to sublimate the poet. If nothing remains to-day of Racine's *Histoire du règne de Louis-le-Grand*, yet may it be that a ten-year-long spell of discipline and self-sacrifice alone enabled him to climb those pure heights where, one day, he will pluck for us that blue gentian, *Esther*, and the dazzling edelweiss of *Athalie*.

The post of *historiographe du Roi* was not a sine-cure, like the Priory of l'Éspinay, like the Treasury of Moulins : blessed iniquities which enabled one of the great poets of the world to come to maturity. The King's historian had to work hard for his living and to lose no time about it. " When the King wanted anything done he would not listen to reason : he must obtain it at once, without objection or rejoinder. He had been too long accustomed to have his own way to possess the patience that listens to an argument." So wrote a woman who loved him well and knew him shrewdly, the plain, perspicacious second wife of " Monsieur," the Princess Palatine.

In March 1678 the King invaded the Low Countries. Racine and Boileau accompanied the armies. It
was a new life, so remote from the studious tenor of a
poet's days, that Racine must indeed have felt himself
born again. The two bourgeois rhymers and their
inexperience are at first just food for laughter to the
merry Madame de Sévigné (who had wanted their post
for her cousin Bussy-Rabutin). She writes to him :

The two historian-poets have followed the Court to the
front, more wonderstruck more thunderstruck, than you, my
dear Cousin, can imagine ! Sometimes on horseback and sometimes on foot, with mud up to their ears, sleeping in the open,
as befits two poets, under the beams of Endymion's fair mistress,
they gaze with all their eyes and try to observe what is going
on around them. . . . I fancy they have rather the look of
two Simon Softlys, our poor poets ! The other day they said
to the King that they marvelled no longer at the courage of
fighting-men, for they thought it reasonable to wish to be killed
at once and thus quit of an intolerable existence.

Boileau on a battlefield was indeed a poet out of
place. Deaf, asthmatic, hunched up all on one
side of his charger in a visible tremor, his figure
inspired the King with a feeling between mirth and
scandal (" The two poets have succeeded to the
King's jesters," writes Madame de Sévigné), so that
after the first campaign Boileau remained in his
cottage at Auteuil. Meanwhile, Racine, on the
front, sends him the material necessary and soon
adapts himself to circumstances, giving news of
himself to his friend in letters which still are excellent
reading, full of the liveliest interest in trench and
fortification, of pity for the soldiers' hardships, of
quick admiration for the brave, of devotion to the
King and all his works. And Racine the historian
and military correspondent tries to forget the
existence of Racine the poet.

When Racine and Boileau left Paris in the spring of 1678, in the capacity of war correspondents to Louis XIV, it was the first time that two historians had been asked to follow an army—though of course a soldier had often turned historian—and the Court was full of funny stories concerning the two poets turned Knights-at-arms. Many were the practical jokes played upon their inexperience. The bluff, bright, Boileau, the dreamy and delicate Racine were the easiest persons to hoax in all Versailles. A certain M. de Cavoye sent them all over Paris looking for a farrier who would warrant his horseshoes to last at least six months—and this was but one of many a fool's errand. The King himself was diverted by Racine's astonishment when first the bombs fell round them at the siege of Namur. " You were the braver, I think ? " he said, in later days, to Boileau. But Boileau never tried it a second time ; while Racine, though no hotspur by temperament, accustomed his high-strung nerves to the life of trench and tent, got used to them, and followed the King in many a campaign.

In camp as at Court he made friends : never had a man more devoted or truer ones. On the front, his best comrade was that M. de Cavoye, whose name has just dropped from my pen. He was one of those persons to be found in every brilliant society, who, without anything to boast of in the way of birth, wealth, or talent, are generally recognized as the umpire of elegance, the dictator of fashion. M. de Cavoye's real name was Oger ; although he cut so brave a show he was but a modest gentleman whose nobility was not much more imposing than that of our poet. Nevertheless he was a man to reckon with at Versailles. He was one of the handsomest men in France, brave as a lion and dressed to perfection. His good looks, in their time, turned many a woman's head, but none so effectually as that of a certain Breton Maid-of-Honour of the Queen's. " Elle était laide, sage, naïve, aimée et très bonne créature," says Saint-Simon, who tells the tale. When on one occasion the King sent Cavoye to the Bastille for having served as second in a duel, Mademoiselle de Coetlogon had a fit of hysterics, raved, scolded the King, and threatened even to scratch him. She sulked all the time that Cavoye was in prison ; refused to wait upon His Majesty at supper ; the glances she gave him were daggers drawn, and she grew lean, yellow, plainer than ever, suffering continually from the vapours. When Cavoye came out of jail, the King said to him (in the language of the times) : " Really, Cavoye, you must marry that girl ! I will make it up to you in other ways." Somewhat reluctantly, Cavoye submitted—and was the happiest husband at Court, bathed in an atmosphere of comfort and perpetual adoration. In Paris, the Cavoyes had their house quite close to the Racines. The husbands were close friends ; the two wives followed suit. I fancy they were plants of the same slipping, the two good ladies.

Boileau's health was not strong. He was deaf, and if this is sometimes an advantage on a battlefield, it is an affection that is not improved by sleeping out of doors, like Endymion. He was asthmatic, and somewhat hypochondriacal, as befits an old bachelor. When the armies laid siege to Mons in 1691, to Namur again in 1692, and to Le Quesnoy in 1693, Boileau remained at Auteuil, while Racine followed the armies and sent his colleague a full, true and particular account of his experiences on the " front." But these letters suffice to show that Racine had nothing of the historian's grasp of events, or even of Froissart's graphic and living view of the world about him. When he wrenched himself from his dream, it was to tell the truth as simply as he could—generally a truth of no particular importance.

That first campaign of 1678 came soon to a triumphant conclusion : on the 10th of August the Peace of Nimwegen was signed between the King of France and the Prince of Orange, which was the first step to putting an end again to that ever-renascent European war. But Orange was savage at a treaty so disadvantageous to his country. The King's messengers raced from Nimwegen to Mons, where the Maréchal de Luxembourg, commanding the French army, was laying siege to the city ; but Orange was in no such hurry to let his party know that the war had come to an end. And so it happened that while the French camp, full of flags and wine, was banqueting to celebrate the good news, the Dutch fell upon them in a treacherous surprise. Luxembourg managed to turn this alarm into a victory for France, and returned to Paris as the conquering hero, while Court and capital echoed to a little song, sprung from nowhere, which had caught the public ear.

> Luxembourg dînait en paix
>   Avec sa phalange ;
> Il trouva, dit-on, mauvais,
>   Et le cas fort étrange,
> Qu'il eût, pour son entremets,
>   Une orange—un Orange !

CHAPTER IV

THE GREAT POISON CASE

THIS Maréchal de Luxembourg was a friend of our poet's. He was one of the King's greatest generals, a lion on the field of battle, and not only brave, but full of resource, audacity and range of view. Once back in Paris, he became the laziest of mortals, too often sunk in frivolous pleasure, but, even then, witty and engaging to a notable degree, and of so charming a conversation that one forgot to remark his queer ugly face, or his double hump— a little one before, a very large and pointed one behind. The Marshal's pen was almost as brilliant as his sword, but people said that, for his pamphlets, he often had recourse to the talent of Racine.

About fifteen months after his triumphant entry into Paris, the Maréchal de Luxembourg was paying his court to the King at Saint-Germain; it was a Wednesday, the 24th of January, 1680. The King received him with his customary amiability. But while the Marshal was still at Court, though no longer in the sovereign's presence, he was informed that there were sealed orders out against him; he was condemned to the Bastille. Aghast, and perhaps surprised, M. de Luxembourg hurried back to the King's chamber and besought his protection. In vain; Louis, unmoved, begged him to go quietly, and

of his own accord, to give himself up to justice.
" If there is really nothing against you (said the
King), no harm can befall you. I believe there are
good judges in this sort of cases, and I make it a
rule not to interfere."

Finding no help in princes—and remembering ,
that the Jesuits were supposed to be far more
powerful—the Marshal drove up the steep hill
where Father La Chaise had his house and gardens,
and stayed with him an hour, with no better result,
so that, towards the end of the afternoon, he
followed the King's advice, went to the Bastille and
became a prisoner.

A few days later, Madame de Sévigné, writing to
her daughter, expatiates on all the circumstances of
Luxembourg's arrest.

> They put him in one of the rooms in the tower—those horrible
> rooms with grated windows out of which one scarce can see
> the sky. All visits were forbidden. My Dear, what food for
> thought is the fate of this poor man, whose brilliant fortunes
> you remember, and the honour he had of commanding the
> King's armies. Think what he must have felt when he heard
> the doors shut to, and the great bolts slide ! If he slept, as he
> may have done from sheer exhaustion, think of his waking !
> Not a creature believes that there is a trace of *poison*, really,
> in his affair.

The Great Poison Case was an immense mystifica-
tion which spread, like an unholy vapour, round a
crime that ramped and ramified, sank underground,
and sprang up again like certain tropical trees. Four
hundred and forty-two persons were accused (and
for the greater part, I believe, wrongfully accused)
of all the sins and follies of Byzantium : mysterious
and magical poisons, alchemy, witchcraft, astrology,
fortune-telling, the calling-up of spirits, sorcery,

conspiracy to murder.   Many of the principal persons
at Court were involved in the affair : Racine's old
enemy, the Duchesse de Bouillon ; her sister the
Comtesse de Soissons the King's old playmate,
who for years had been his confidant and Egeria ;
the Duke of Vendôme, Madame de Polignac—
scores on scores of great names.   No one felt safe.
Certain great ladies (Madame de Tingry, Madame
d'Alluye, Madame de Dreux) were called out from
a card-party, where they were playing with their
friends, and carried off to the Bastille under sealed
orders ;   the first was accused of poisoning her
children, the second of poisoning her father, the
third of poisoning her husband.   In vain their
families protested of their health and happiness,
and beseeched the King to send the ladies home :
Madame de Dreux was kept for a whole year in a
miserable cell, more than half-dark, lighted only by
a hole under the ceiling.   The scare, the contagious
panic, was so great that any horror seemed believ-
able.   One day the King was shown a small note
discovered among the papers of the principal culprit,
Madame Voisin.   It consisted of one line in the
handwriting of the Duchesse de Foix : " Plus je
frotte, moins ils poussent."   The more I rub, the
less they grow !   What could it mean ?   The Duchess
was immediately sent for and questioned.   The
poor woman blushed, and admitted that she had,
indeed, bought of Madame Voisin a lotion supposed
to give to the flattest chest the noble proportions
of a statue.   To return to the Maréchal de Luxembourg, he was accused of a pact with the Devil,
to bring about his son's marriage with the daughter
of Louvois, the Minister of War.   There was more

folly than guilt in most of the counts. Madame de Polignac, for instance, was accused of ordering a philtre which should procure her the love of the King ; charms, pacts, and prophecies were more frequent than downright crime. Yet this we must say : not one of the accused seems to have been completely spotless and without reproach. That sort of mud can only stick to a robe already soiled. No one, for instance, thought of accusing Arnauld, or even Boileau, of dealings with Madame Voisin.

Racine was accused of having poisoned Mademoiselle du Parc.

This Madame Voisin had been a friend of the dead actress. They had known each other some fourteen years—long before Marquise du Parc had any connection with Racine. Madame Voisin was a person of some importance in her way, no miserable sorceress living with a lean black cat in some wretched garret, but a sort of Parisian celebrity : a Beauty Specialist, as our modern slang would put it, and a Public Entertainer. She was a fashionable clairvoyante, and was often asked to amuse with her white magic the guests at some fête or party. Many of the humbler culprits of the Great Poison Case began after this fashion : their queer trade put them in possession of many secrets ; they became the confidantes of discontented women of the world before they thought of being their accomplices, sold a wash for the complexion, an eyelash-cream, or a bust-producer long before advising a love-philtre, and provided many an amorous charm before suggesting a dose of arsenic to remove a tiresome husband.

" La Voisin " was also an experienced midwife

—one of those who knew how to keep a baby out of the world as well as to bring one into it, while apt to supply an heir to order where Nature showed herself remiss. She was quite at the head of her profession. When her husband, a jeweller, failed in his trade, she turned to account (as she said in her evidence) " the science which Heaven had imparted to her," and added to all these accomplishments a more secret art : the Black Mass, where the naked body of the supplicant formed the altar, while the chalice was filled with the blood of an infant. In one way or another she made a good income, representing well over two thousand a year of our currency. She dressed expensively, lived in the grand style, kept open house. And alas ! during some three years Racine had been on terms of acquaintance with this dreadful woman—the three years, half-forgotten in 1679—in which he had known and loved Marquise du Parc.

Madame Voisin was arrested on the 12th of March, 1679. Following close on the trial of the Marquise de Brinvilliers, the accusation of secret-poisoning, on so large a scale, made an intense impression on the public, a still more tragic one on the Court, from which were drawn so great a proportion of the four hundred and forty-two persons incriminated. Madame Voisin's revelations slurred with suspicion such great names that a special court—a *Chambre Ardente*, or Star Chamber—was instituted in the following April for the secret examination of witnesses. Despite all that was done to keep things dark, enough leaked out to fill Paris with horror, revolt, suspicion and dismay.

On the 21st of November, under torture, Madame

Voisin accused Racine of having poisoned Marquise du Parc. I quote her cross-examination, still preserved in the Bibliothèque de l'Arsenal, and printed by M. Frantz Funck Brentano in his *Drame du Poison* :

Question. Who introduced the prisoner, Voisin, to Mademoiselle du Parc, the actress ?

Answer. She had known her for fourteen years and they were intimate friends (" très bonnes amies ensemble "), so that during those years she had known all Du Parc's private affairs. Some good while ago deponent had meant to inform the Court that Du Parc must have been poisoned (devait avoir été empoisonnée). Suspicion fell on Jean Racine (l'on a soupçonné Jean Racine). It made a great stir at the time. The prisoner also said that what confirmed her in her opinion was that the said Racine had always done everything in his power to keep her, Voisin, away from the said Du Parc who was her familiar friend ; so that she had not seen the actress one single time during the course of her last illness, though Du Parc was always asking for her. And though she, Voisin, often called at the house to inquire after Du Parc, never once was she let in, and it was all by order of the said Racine. Deponent knew it, through Du Parc's stepmother, Mademoiselle de Gorle, and also through the daughters of the said Du Parc, who are living under the roof of the Comtesse de Soissons ; they told her that Racine was the cause of all their misfortune.

Question. Had she ever been approached with a proposal to remove the Du Parc by means of poison ?

Answer. She would like to have seen them come ! They would have had a warm welcome !

Question. Does she know whether the woman, De la Grange, was approached with any such proposal.

Answer. She knows nothing about it.

Question. Does the prisoner know a lame comedian ?

Answer. Aye, to be sure ; 'tis Bejart the younger, of Molière's company. But the prisoner only met him twice.

Question. Had Béjart any ill-will against the said Du Parc ?

Answer. No ; and what the prisoner said anent Racine, she knew it first of all through Mademoiselle de Gorle.

Question. Let the prisoner attempt to recall as exactly as possible just what Mademoiselle de Gorle said to her.

Answer. Deponent heard from the said De Gorle that Racine had secretly married Du Parc. He was jealous of everyone who approached her, and especially of herself, Voisin, against whom he harboured an uneasy, suspicious feeling. Deponent said that Racine ended by getting rid of Du Parc, because of his excessive jealousy. During her last illness Racine never stirred from her bedside, and he drew from the dying woman's finger a valuable diamond ring and kept it, with other trinkets and valuable effects of the said Du Parc, who had everything most handsome about her. And he would not let her speak to Voisin's waiting-woman, Manon, who was a midwife, though Du Parc had asked for Manon, and had even written to Manon, as well as to the witness, Voisin, asking them to come to Paris.

Question. Did the said De Gorle ever inform the prisoner what kind of poison was used, and in what way it was administered ?

Answer. No.

And there the evidence, so far as Racine is concerned, comes to an end.

A young Jansenist, who thinks himself a gay young spark, yet who retains much of his early education, is head over ears in love with a beautiful actress, a dancer, in no sort of way a vile woman, but free-spoken, loud of laughter, " la moins façonnière des femmes," brought up among all the riff-raff of a fair, and acquainted with some very queer fish. One of these, the beauty-specialist and midwife, fills him with unsurmountable suspicions ; and he does all he can to keep her at bay, especially when he discovers that his mistress, or secretly married wife, is pregnant. Can we not see him seated by her bedside, drawing from her finger the ring, which, doubtless, he had given her, that was, perhaps, their wedding ring, while the stepmother and the wicked midwife lurk in the doorway ?

That question about Béjart, who was Molière's brother-in-law, seems to indicate in the judge's mind a doubt whether the death of Mademoiselle du Parc may not have been a vengeance for her desertion of the Palais Royal Theatre. But this seems to have been a false scent. If there was a crime, it was probably abortion. And her sad end may have occurred in the course of Nature. Boileau tells us that she died in childbirth. The editor of Boileau's works, Brossette, declares that in 1703 he heard from the lips of Mathieu Marais these words, which Marais had had from Boileau:

M. Racine was in love with Du Parc, who was a fine woman, tall, and well made, but not a good actress. He wrote *Andromaque* for her. He taught her her part, line upon line, as one teaches a schoolgirl. . . . Du Parc died, a little later, in child-bed.

How terrible that in 1679 these old passions, these old sins perhaps, should start to life again, when Racine was no longer a poet and a lover, but a married man rising forty years of age, with a post at Court, and a couple of babies in the nursery!

The *Chambre Ardente* continued its arrests and its imprisonments until the middle of July 1682, with frequent applications of torture; but nothing further came to light concerning the crime of Racine. We find only one reference among all the trash and litter of that trial. On the 11th of January, 1680, the great Minister, Louvois, writing to a member of the Star Chamber, Bazin de Bezon, affirms the King's intention to pursue the inquiry to the bitter end; and he concludes his long letter with these words:

His Majesty wishes to learn day by day all that may come to light concerning, for instance, Madame de Vivonne. Herewith I send you an order for the arrest of Madame Larcher. An order for the arrest of the Sieur Racine shall be sent you as soon as you shall ask for it.

Bazin de Bezon never asked for it! If he was a member of the Star Chamber, he was also a member of the French Academy, where Racine was his colleague. Our poet was easily able to prove his innocence to the King, who, ignorant as he was, and with no great mental power, had, in the discrimination of character, a penetrating insight which was akin to his rare taste in literature and art. Louis Quatorze was a *sourcier*, a well-finder. Something within him quivered when he found himself in presence of genius, beauty, deep sincerity, noble and genuine gifts of any sort, so that he was able to surround himself with a galaxy of great individuals. Rarely mistaken in his estimate of a man, he never doubted Racine.

Of all the four hundred and forty-two persons incriminated by the Star Chamber, he came off, perhaps, the easiest. The Comtesse de Soissons escaped to the Low Countries. Madame de Montespan fell from her high estate, at once guilty, sullied, profane, and ridiculous; Luxembourg was at the Bastille; Madame Voisin herself was burned alive, chained to the stake on the Place de Grève. Meanwhile in Paris the tide of opinion had turned: not the culprits, but the judges were hated and condemned.

The general tone to-day [writes Madame de Sévigné] is to affirm the innocence of the accused and the horrible wickedness of calumny. Perhaps to-morrow people will say just the opposite. One never can tell with these sort of general sentiments.

The Duchesse de Bouillon found herself quite a popular heroine. She had walked into the Star Chamber with, on one side of her, the old husband she was supposed to have tried to murder, and, on the other, the handsome young nephew, who was considered the cause of her crime. And, resolutely, she " cheeked " the magistrates—there is no other word for it. She exclaimed, for instance :

" Really, I never could have believed that such clever men could ask such stupid questions ! "

She walked in like a little Queen [writes Madame de Sévigné], laughing a little in her careless way ; and, when she walked out, she was welcomed by her family and friends with a sort of adoration, so beautiful she looked, so artless and natural, so well bred, so deliciously serene.

Like Madame de Sévigné, and copying her phrase, I am inclined to think that, where the judges painted black, there was as a rule a shade of grey : much lamentable folly, degrading superstition, envy, hatred and malice. Perhaps some rare cases of murder. The Princess Palatine believed that Madame de Montespan had really poisoned the unfortunate Fontanges. Yet, in re-reading the evidence of this vile and odious trial, what chiefly strikes the mind is the savage character of the repression, worthy of the Dark Ages. Other times ! you may say. But many persons in those days were just as shocked as we are now. Madame de Sévigné writes to her daughter in a mood of indignant irony :

The Voisin was burned alive, by a slow fire, on the Place de Grève. They sat her firmly down on the piled-up logs and fastened her to the stake with iron clamps ; then they heaped straw all round her and set it alight. She swore a good deal, and, once or twice, she tried to push back the straw ; but, as the flames grew stronger, we lost sight of her, and, at the present moment, her ashes are in the air. . . .

My son, the other day, said to a magistrate, that he thought it a strange thing to burn a human being alive at a slow fire. The Judge replied :

" Ah, well. There are certain palliatives which come into play when it's a question of the fair sex."

" Do you strangle them ? " said my son.

" No, sir, no ! But the executioners throw a log or two at their heads ; sometimes the varlets go so far as to tear their heads right off with their iron hooks."

You see, my Dear, things are not so terrible as they seem ! What do you think of this little story ? It made me gnash my teeth !

CHAPTER V

THE DEATH OF CORNEILLE

THE King was deeply affected by the revelations made to the Star Chamber. All his conduct at this time appears inspired by a horror of disorder. " La peur du diable," writes Saint-Simon ; " la crainte de l'enfer," confirms the Princess Palatine. His own conduct had been flagrantly immoral : he saw the necessity for reforming it, convinced at last that our pleasant vices make a scourge which our own bare backs shall be the first to feel. In fact, though a man of a very different trend of nature, he went through much the same phase of feeling as that which some four years before had determined the conversion of Racine ; it may be that such a similarity increased his sympathy for our poet.

The King had suffered sorely from the suspicion cast on so many of his intimates. The Countess of Soissons, to whom for years he had paid a daily visit, whom he had made Mistress of the Household to his young Queen, in whose society he had acquired (says Saint-Simon) " that air of politeness and gallantry which he knew so well how to combine with the severer aspect of majesty " ; Luxembourg, his victorious general ; countless others. Worst of all, the principal culprit, after Voisin, was his mistress, Madame de Montespan. In the amorous life of Louis Quatorze there had been many incidents, some accidents, one great event : his passion for Madame de Montespan, whose beauty ("une beauté surprenante," says Madame de Sévigné), whose wit, whose infallible amusingness, so precious to a man ever dogged by the *tedium vitæ*, had transported the King with a veritable enthusiasm of love, so that he had carried her off from an indignant and equally enamoured husband. For years their double adultery had been the scandal of the Court—a more serious affair than the seducing of one of Madame's Maids of Honour, a La Vallière or a Fontanges. In the course of time Madame de Montespan had borne her Royal lover eight children, of whom, if four were dead, four had been legitimated, and took rank among the princes and princesses of France.

The King knew what was due to his children's mother. He checked the course of the Star Chamber inquiry ; Madame de Montespan returned to the Court, and queened it, not officially in disgrace, until her own son informed her of the King's wish to see her no more. She left Versailles " en furie et en larmes," to retire to the Convent of Saint-Joseph, when her place was taken by her children's governess, the pious Madame de Maintenon. Her place was taken, that is to say, in so far as regards the sympathy, the mutual confidence, which had reigned between her and the King—Madame de Maintenon was not a Royal mistress. After the death of the Queen, in 1683, she became the King's wife by a secret marriage.

In the quiet sober Court, over which Madame de Maintenon presided in this transformed Versailles —where her influence, never officially recognized, permeated the very atmosphere—Racine found a favoured place. The King had always loved the poet ; he praised his quick repartees, admired his talent for reading aloud, his easily fired eloquence, and even his expressive face, which Louis considered one of the handsomest at Court. And now, in this new mood, the King (a rake reformed) was touched by Racine's conversion, his firm repentance for youthful disorders less flagrant than Louis' own. He counted Racine among his intimates.

Sometimes [writes Saint-Simon], when the King had no business with his Ministers—of a Friday afternoon, for instance, especially if it were in winter and the weather too wild for him to go out-of-doors, His Majesty would send for Racine, and bid him read aloud to him in Madame de Maintenon's room.

On one occasion, when the King was ill, Racine slept in a closet off the Royal chamber, and would often charm the watches of the night by reading to the invalid.

No one had a mind more solidly informed than Racine's [again I quote Saint-Simon] or more agreeably cultivated. There was nothing of the poet in his manner or behaviour— everything of the gentleman, the man of the world, the modest man, and, in the course of time, of the good Christian. He counted as many friends among the greatest of the Court as in the rank of men of letters.

Now let us listen to Spanheim's less friendly and yet practically identical estimate :

For a man sprung from nothing, M. de Racine has easily acquired the manners of a courtier. His friends, the actors, had given him in his youth a sort of spurious courtliness, which he has since amended with excellent effect. He is presentable in any circle, and even at the bedside of the King, where he has sometimes the honour of reading aloud to His Majesty, for which art he has a peculiar gift. If he were a preacher or an actor, he would surpass all others in that line. The Duchesse de Bourgogne is charmed to have him at her table and consults him on various matters in which he is considered competent. There you may see him in all his glory—*C'est là qu'il triomphe.*

While Racine, in early middle age, seemed placed upon the pinnacle of Fortune, the oracle of ravishing princesses, the comforter of a King, Corneille, grim, dour, quixotic old Corneille, cut a far more unfashionable figure. He had survived his genius by some ten years, during which, in the words of his nephew, Fontenelle, " he did not think much of the theatre, and, finally, did not think at all."

In those days, plays of a very different character from Corneille's triumphed on the stage ; they were full of tender feeling and gentle, endearing sentiments. If they did not reach the sublime beauties of the elder tragedian, neither did they fall into his offensive defects. They were lofty in tone, though not of quite the supreme elevation ; they were full of love, and written in a most agreeable style with a purity which never falters ; bespangled, too, with the most charming flashes of wit, with touches of nature, wonderfully ingenuous ; what is more, they were written by a young author. No wonder these plays pleased the ladies ; and their word was law in the theatres. They were enchanted. Save for a few women who have the minds of men, Corneille, thenceforward, was only old Corneille.—FONTENELLE, *Vie de Corneille.*

In these bitter words did Corneille's nephew consecrate the triumph of Racine.

Old Corneille, so romantic in the plays of his old age, stuffing his tragedies with extravagant situations, passions torn to tatters, and quixotic heroes—old Corneille seemed as out of fashion as Amadis of Gaul—and the connoisseurs of Versailles spoke of his ancient merit with an indulgent smile—until the first days of October 1684, when, suddenly, the full splendour of his genius burst upon a world that had long forgotten it. What had happened? Merely, Corneille had died. He was no longer old Corneille, the senile and the silly. He was the great Corneille, a glory for all time.

Racine was prepared for the revelation. In this instance, at all events, his renunciation proved ' useful ; for, since he no longer looked on himself as a poet, Corneille was no longer a rival. Perhaps the truest test of a sincere conversion is the new power it gives a man to love those whom he has cordially detested, and to understand those whom he has set at naught. Racine saw at last that Corneille and he were part of the same movement, were associates, not adversaries. Henceforth he can admire his great contemporary with an unbiassed mind. He can teach his little children to learn by heart, not his own poetry, but Corneille's. There was a line in *Cinna* which he loved to repeat to them :

Et, monté sur le faîte, il aspire à descendre.[1]

" We all say ' aspires to rise,' my father would say to us (writes Louis Racine), but Corneille understood the heart of an ambitious man." Racine, no less than he, had risen to the pinnacle of Fame, and had seen nothing but a giddy void all round him. He, too, had aspired to descend.

" Do not suppose (he said to his children on another occasion) that it is my talent which attracts the attention of the great. The poems of Corneille are a hundred times finer than mine, and who ever paid any attention to him ? "

It was with something of a pang that Racine recalled how malevolent, how ironical, such notice as

[1] Stands on the pinnacle, aspiring to descend.

he had taken of old Corneille had been. He wished at last to render a supreme tribute to the dead master. When the armchair which Corneille had occupied at the French Academy was offered to his younger brother—himself an estimable poet and writer of plays—Racine, receiving Thomas Corneille, was able to liberate his soul in praise of the dead poet's genius. Racine's speech was delivered with a generous effusion of the heart which must have surprised the listening Academicians, who certainly had not forgotten the rapier-thrusts, the fine fencing, which used to occupy the two tragedians in their frequent encounters. Only five years earlier, what a dagger would have gleamed among the flowers of that funeral wreath! Evidently Racine had experienced a change of heart. And then, after all, it *was* a funeral-wreath ; and poets dearly love their rivals—dead.

" Corneille fait des vers cent fois plus beaux que les miens." With a simple and a single heart Racine could now make this admission which, during nearly twenty years, had seemed impossible, absurd, almost dishonouring. In the *Discours de Réception* he could compare the dead poet with Æschylus, with Sophocles, with Euripides (and, indeed, if we take Corneille only at his best, the praise is not exaggerated) ; at last he could assure an audience hanging on his lips that Corneille had immensely out-distanced those futile rivals his contemporaries " who vainly attempted, by a frivolous criticism, to underrate a merit which they could not hope to equal."

That Thursday, 2nd of January, 1685, the French Academy had to receive two new members :

Thomas Corneille and a M. Bergeret. But having strung such a sounding chord upon his lyre, our poet could not condescend to applaud a Monsieur Bergeret. He began a dithyramb in praise of the King, who was present. In Racine's eyes Louis was still the " Grand Alexandre," the paragon of princes, brave, wise, triumphant, generous, and now at last, in addition to all the rest, full of virtue and regularity. " I could have praised you more for your speech, M. Racine (said the King), if you had praised me less."

But in Racine's eulogy there was an innocent ingenuous quality which distinguished it from flattery, while, in the nostrils of Royal persons, even flattery, as a rule, has a pleasant flavour. " The King likes to be admired by everybody—and anybody," remarks, rather grimly, the Princess Palatine, who loved, and understood, her illustrious brother-in-law. The King liked praise.

Nothing seemed to exceed the merit of his triumphant royalty. And when the ladies of the Court, passing through the Royal chamber, incommodiously situated in a long string of magnificent saloons, made a sweeping curtsey to His Majesty's empty bed, as though it had been indeed an altar, the King saw nothing to cavil at in their reverence. He found it natural that the Duc de la Feuillade should keep a perpetual light in front of the Royal portrait. Doubtless, that Thursday at the French Academy, in his heart the King murmured, as he so often said :

Racine a bien de l'esprit,

and appreciated our poet all the more.

CHAPTER VI

RACINE AND BOILEAU

IN the spring of 1687 Nicolas Boileau-Despréaux caught a heavy cold and lost his voice. Never was an attack of aphonia so long or so loudly bewailed, at least in writing. Boileau was in despair. For several years he had been a sufferer from asthma ; an increasing deafness troubled him greatly ; but the loss of voice, rendering a witty satirist incapable of conversation, appeared to him the unkindest cut of all. Week after week dragged its slow length along while Boileau perforce kept silent : " the most miserable of mortals, a deaf mute," and, as he wrote to Racine, " a man who no longer takes rank among the living."

To us of a later day who are aware that, six months later, Boileau will talk as brilliantly as before, the pain and inconvenience of his disorder are chiefly important as having given rise to a really enchanting exchange of letters between the invalid and his friend, Racine. Boileau is at Auteuil, in his cottage, nursing his cold ; a little later we shall find him at Bourbon taking the waters, with all their accompaniments of purging, bleeding, cupping, starving, sweating, and so forth. Racine is at Versailles, or at Marly with the Court ; or else at home with his family in Paris ; and sometimes on the front of

battle with the King. Wherever we find him, he
has no dearer pleasure and no more pressing duty
than to write to his depressed and doleful friend ;
and his letters are most engaging, full of a feminine
tact and tenderness, imparting all the news, cheering
the sufferer, providing material for the history, with
which he enjoins his correspondent to amuse the
silence of his solitude. Boileau is grateful. On the
19th of May he writes :

> I need your virtue, and especially your Christian virtue, in
> order to console my sad case. For I was not brought up like
> you in the Holy of Holies. A mere Quietist virtue would help
> me mighty little in this quandary. No, I must have Grace,
> and efficacious Grace into the bargain.

Racine is far too wise to sit down and write a
sermon. A grain or two of hope in a drachm of
patience is his prescription. He is quite sure the
errant voice will return. He has just been putting
the case to a very learned physician—one no less
than the great Denis Dodart, a botanist, a doctor,
a member of the Academy of Science, and a notable
Jansenist to boot. Dodart, from the heights of his
knowledge and experience, recommends an apricot-
syrup, to be taken neat, in drops, or, if that be
considered too strong a dose, diluted in a little tepid
water. There is a deal of virtue in an apricot.
But after all the syrup is only half of his prescription
—the rest is silence, complete silence, not to fatigue
the vocal chords even in the most moderate degree.
And, in further addition, " to keep the mind
continually cheerful."

Of all the doctors we shall meet with in this
correspondence, Dodart is certainly the most sensible.
To drink warm, keep silence, amuse the mind, is

even to-day a good prescription for aphonia. The letter which contains this excellent advice is despatched by Racine from the front. Having paid his respects to his friend's inflamed larynx, he strives to distract his attention from his woes by a brilliant description of M. Vauban's wonderful new fortifications, and concludes his communication with a list of all the persons of importance who have inquired after the health of M. Despréaux, " avec des expressions fortes, vigoureuses, et qu'on voit bien qu'elles partent du cœur." Such a letter must have been worth at least a pint of apricot-syrup to the lonely, moped invalid.

Racine needed all his tact, all his kindly penetration, to hit just the right nail on the head in writing to his nervous correspondent. To take his illness too seriously was to plunge him in abject depression ; it was still worse to take it lightly. Boileau is comforted, perhaps, to hear of other persons who, having lost their voice, have got it back again ; but it must be plainly understood that their case was not quite so serious or so interesting as his own ; he is not sure but their complaint was an infringement of patent. " Si je suis original en quelque chose c'est en infirmités ; mes maladies ne ressemblent jamais à celles des autres. . . ." Meanwhile the year slips away ; a month after midsummer the truant voice is still as absent as ever. Racine has hard work to keep his friend's spirits from a complete collapse. One of his letters brought a solid piece of comfort to the sufferer, for Boileau was consoled to hear that his sore throat had formed the principal subject of conversation at the Royal dinner-table one evening at Versailles.

M. de Louvois said these very words : " He was grieved to hear it had lasted so long a while." Both Monsieur and Madame expressed their sympathy ; in fact, though I am sure I hope you will soon regain your voice, I doubt if ever you will have enough of it to return all the thanks you owe for kind inquiries.

Disgusted with the Paris doctors, the dumb poet decided to try the springs of Bourbon, which, in those days, were thought a panacea for all human ills. Certainly the treatment ought to have some effect : Boileau is bled and purged to such an extent that he can scarcely stand upright, and faints more than once in four-and-twenty hours. But still no voice ! At last an extreme measure is proposed : he shall not only drink of, but bathe in, the healing waters—not a complete immersion, evidently ; that would be too great a risk, but a " demi-bain," apparently a sort of sitting-bath. The suggestion of this drastic treatment strikes horror into Court and camp.

It was Dr. Fagon, the great Fagon, Physician-in-Ordinary to the late Queen, who had ventured to recommend the *demi-bain*. But doctors disagree. The local authorities are dead against it, and state the case of several patients, " qui ont perdu la voix pour s'être baignés." Persons have even been known to expire on contact with the unaccustomed liquid. Yet Fagon, at Versailles, maintains his view, supported by a certain Dr. Amyot, while the local luminaries, Bourdier and Baudière, shake their heads in gravest disapproval : " What a thing it is (cries Boileau) to see one's poor body the sport of a most conjectural science—' une science très-conjecturelle ' (he had the phrase two centuries before Renan). The one says black, the other

white ; and Bourdier, with Baudière, persists that
it is a case of life and death.   I may very possibly
die of the experiment."

Imagine the effect of this melancholy communication on our tender-hearted poet ! He is with the
King at Marly when he gets the letter.   His alarm,
his commiseration have soon infected all the Court
—or at least all that intimate and holiday-making
fraction of the Court which is at Marly—Marly, the
week-end cottage of the greatest monarch in Europe.
Nothing is talked of save M. Despréaux and his
parlous plight, and the danger of a sitz-bath.

" For my part," cried Madame la Princesse de Conti (who
was seated at table next to the King), " for my part I would
rather remain mute for thirty years than risk my life to regain
the power of speech."

You cannot imagine [continues Racine] what an agreeable
life we lead in this house of Marly.   The Court is quite on
another footing to that of Versailles.   No one is present who
has not been especially invited ; one sees nothing but smiling
faces, honoured at having been asked.   The King is free and
caressing in his manners.   At Versailles he is given up to the
business of the State ; at Marly he has time for hospitality
and pleasure.   More than once I have had the honour of being
invited to a private talk, and I leave these interviews, as always
on such occasions, enchanted with His Majesty, impatient with
myself.   Most strange it is, but I am never so dull as when I
chiefly wish to be agreeable.

A frequent subject of these Royal parleyings was
the health of the absent historiographer.   Should
he stake his all upon a throw of the dice : take the
sitz-bath, find his voice, or lose his life ?   The
King, with his usual sound sense, opined that it was
not necessary to risk so much.

He said, in these identical terms :
" Tell M. Despréaux to resume his ordinary way of life.   His
voice will come back when he leasts expects it."

Before Racine's letter could arrive at Bourbon, the Court is startled by the news that, reduced to despair, Boileau has taken the sitz-bath. He stayed in it an hour. It did him no manner of harm. Indeed he felt wonderfully sprightly in consequence : " the legs lighter, the chest relieved, the mind more cheerful." The bath had done everything—except restore the voice. And now the forlorn hope has failed, what use is there in staying on at Bourbon ? How sad to re-traverse all the stages, all the inns, of the long journey to Paris, as dumb, as deaf, as helpless as he was when he set out on his travels ! " Count me no longer among living things ! " Yet who knows ? The revulsion occasioned by that extravagant bath may have worked some salutary movement in the system which may yet operate after a lapse of time? And, in fact, a few weeks later, Boileau's voice did come back. Though growing steadily deafer, the poet was no longer mute ; he could still cut a brilliant figure in a soliloquy, if not in conversation.

Health occupies a great space in this corre- spondence, for Racine also is delicate and subject to sore throats. We hear a great deal of the virtues of the herb erysimum, apparently a sort of cress, sovereign for the larynx. And then there is that English doctor—the red-faced and plentifully- pimpled Dr. " Chmith "—who cures all sorts of fevers by his new drug, quinquina. (Here is another introducer of the Jesuit's bark than Madame de Sévigné's English doctor, M. Talbot.) Still, the two friends have other than sanitary subjects of conversation. They recount with pleasure the tribu- lations endured by the company of the old Palais

Royal, turned out of their handsome theatre in the rue Guénégaud, and unable to find another anywhere, for Paris has grown so pious that no one cares to let to the actors. " They say they will have to build themsleves a theatre quite on the edge of the town, out by the common sewer—which will prove a handy receptacle for the plays of M. Pradon," writes Acanthus, evidently scotched, not killed.

As the years run on, the health of Boileau grows regularly worse, and he becomes more and more the hermit of Auteuil, deprived by deafness of all intercourse save the most familiar. Pen in hand, he sits in his study or his garden, while Racine scours the plain in search of material for the history. He visits the battlefield. In 1691 we find him present at the attack on Mons.

I saw the whole affair quite plain—from a good way off, it is true ; but I had a pair of excellent field-glasses, which I could scarce hold to my eyes because my heart beat so quick to see so many brave men in mortal peril. . . . A truce was called that we might each of us bury our dead.

In 1692, at Namur, Vauban pilots Racine through the new redoubts and trenches, and the poet writes to Boileau :

Our trench is something prodigious, embracing several hills and valleys with an infinity of twists and turns—almost as many, I should think, of these by-ways as there are streets in Paris. While all these miles of earth were being delved, the people of the Court, who are here in camp with the King, found the time hang monstrous heavy on their hands, yet they saw the good of it when, as soon as we attacked, the enemy, aware of the strength of our position, beat the drums for a parley.

This stirring life of his never blinds the gentle Racine to the peculiar trials of his friend in a

sequestered suburb. He is grieved to think of
Boileau all alone, " dans une fort grande solitude
à Auteuil."

" Is it possible that you can live so much alone
and not write poetry ? I hope I shall find the
Satire des Femmes quite finished on my return."
Racine has had to cut off his right hand, to pluck
out his right eye, in order to enter the kingdom of
heaven ; it is a rare grace in the self-maimed to see
that others may be just as holy while enjoying the
use of all their members. Racine is continually
urging his friend to further flights.

I have instilled into the breast of Madame de Maintenon a
great desire to see how you mean to celebrate her new institution
at Saint-Cyr. She was deeply touched that you had even
thought of such a thing. And she spoke of you in the kindest
way in the world. Believe that I share her impatience and long
to see your verses. . . . If you send them to me, I will read
them aloud to Madame de Maintenon, and they shall not suffer
in the process.

About this time, 1687, Racine began to see a great
deal of Madame de Maintenon ; one day she made
him a communication which sorely distressed his
delicate mind. He took up his pen and wrote to
Boileau :

Madame de Maintenon tells me this morning that the King
has settled the affair of our stipend as Royal historiographers :
I am to have four thousand francs a year, and you will have
two thousand. Of course this is exclusive of our several pensions
on the Civil List. I thanked Madame de Maintenon warmly,
both for you and for me. I have just been to thank the King.
He seemed grieved and reluctant to cut down our salary, but I
told him we were perfectly content. And I insisted even more
on your grateful feelings than on mine, and said you would
write to His Majesty in this vein, for you would never venture
to cost him the trouble of raising his voice in a conversation.
In fact I said, word for word :

" Sire, his mind has never been clearer, never has he had more zeal for your Majesty, nor a greater wish to labour for your glory."

And so, you see, things are arranged exactly as you wished. But I cannot get rid of the oppressive thought that I enjoy an advantage obtained at your expense, although I am quite aware you vastly prefer that I should be the better treated. Your heart is full of friendship. And of course there is the fatigue and the cost of those journeys of which I am very glad you should be quit. . . . I stay on here at Versailles until the affair is quite concluded, but hope to see you soon, and am entirely yours.

One more extract from this delightful correspondence will give the measure of Racine's feeling for his friend.

The more I watch diminish the number of my intimates, the more my heart warms to the few that remain about me. And, to speak frankly, it seems to me that there is only you. Farewell! If I dwell too long upon this thought it will melt me into tears.

Excellent Racine!

BOOK IV

THE POET OF THE BIBLE

ἀλλ, εἰ δοκεῖ σοι, στεῖχε· τοῦτο δ'ἰσθ', ὅτι
ἄνους μὲν ἔρχῃ, τοῖς φίλοις δ'ὀρθῶς φίλη.

SOPHOCLES: *Antigone*, **v.** 98.

CHAPTER I

ESTHER AT SAINT-CYR

TOWARDS the fiftieth year of Louis Quatorze, in all the new perfection and grandeur of Versailles, a change began to steal over the spirit of the Court. The tediousness of system and routine has sometimes the result of driving inward an ideal; it encourages a mystical religion. The King himself took on an unexpected likeness to his melancholy father; a new note began to sound in the great classic literature of his reign—plaintive, romantic as a chime of haunting bells; even as the King reproved and persecuted the hermits of Port-Royal, their dream of solitude began to invade the precincts of his presence-chamber, and in those dazzling galleries of mirrors a new desire awoke, for something remote, aloof, interior. Persons occupied all day with great affairs met in a new conception of religion, secretly, as though it were a catacomb. Fénelon and his flock, Madame Guyon inundated by the internal " torrent," Racine in his contrition, and even the uncrowned Queen of France herself—Madame de Maintenon—counted among these Solitaries in disguise. In the pages they have left us, and especially in their spiritual letters, there breathes a peculiar melancholy charm, still as the fall of autumn leaves on windless afternoons, pure and vast as the view from balustraded terraces commanding a great expanse of country, for in them all there reigns a like spirit of renunciation or, as Fénelon would say, " un *Amen* continuel au fond du cœur."

When we read to-day the name of Madame de Maintenon, a lappet of her black mantilla swings across the page and hides from us the fact that even in her fiftieth year she was a very charming woman, admirably framed to attract a high-minded, intellectual man—still grace itself in her bearing and movements, tall, slender, with, under her trailing coifs and veils, an abundance of hair faintly powdered, which still retained in its ashy softness a hint of warm chestnut-brown. In addition to all this (as the ladies of Saint-Cyr consigned in their notebooks) she had " eyes of fire, the sweetest sound of voice, and the natural, expressive gesture of the most lovely of hands."

No less than Fénelon, Racine will feel the charm, the spiritual grace of the gifted lady. To him, too, she will seem a sister-soul, full of sympathy and inspiration. Was she not the King's Egeria ? More than that : Had she not saved the Lord's Anointed from the bottomless pit ? One after the other Fénelon and Racine will confide in her ; and she will abandon either in the hour of need, even as, on his death-bed, she will desert the King. And yet she will leave behind her, in these forsaken hearts, no sting of anger or rancour, so firmly will the sufferers feel that, if she play them false, the fault lies only in her feminine fragility, her timid and fantastic scruples. She had no vile intent to betray; hers is the dereliction of a Peter, not the treachery of an Iscariot.

Eleven years had elapsed since Racine's renunciation of the theatre, when, one day in 1688, he received a letter from this enigmatic lady. They were friends. Already, the year before, Boileau had written to Racine:

You do well to cultivate Madame de Maintenon. Never was any person so worthy as she of the post she occupies; hers is perhaps the only virtue on which I never have remarked a speck. The esteem she has for you is a proof of her fine taste.

There was nothing, therefore, unusual in the fact of her writing to Racine, but this letter contained a request more serious than a desire that he should read aloud to the King, or give herself his opinion on that School for Noble and Impoverished Young Ladies which she had recently founded at Saint-Cyr in the neighbourhood of Versailles. She now wanted our poet to write for her, not a play, but a sort of poem on a pious subject, interspersed with songs for a chorus, and with sufficient dramatic interest to disguise the absence of a love story. M. Racine's reputation could not be affected by a trifle of this sort, destined to be buried in the depths of a ladies' school.

The receipt of this letter threw Racine into a state of violent agitation. His first impulse was to refuse, but, before sitting down to write, he showed the disturbing missive to his faithful mentor, Boileau.

The satirist, who only liked fine ladies in their proper place, was little less indignant than he had been with poor Madame when she had requested his friend to compose the tragedy of *Bérénice*. Racine had renounced the theatre. Was he to go back on so immense a sacrifice, without pleasure or profit, in order to amuse a pack of schoolgirls ? But on reflection Boileau remembered that Madame de Maintenon's favour was important to the King's historiographers. Had Racine thought of a subject ? What : Esther ? An admirable subject ! In the twinkling of an eye Boileau took in the subtle resemblance between the Jewish Queen of a wicked heathen Court, which she redeemed, and the position at Versailles of Madame de Maintenon. After all, the effort would be slight ; a convent is not a playhouse ; and what could be more meritorious than to instruct these young ladies in the Apocryphal Scriptures ?

Racine decided to accept. The lady was grateful. And the poet, setting to work on the plan which she had suggested, discovered that he was realizing a project that had haunted his brain for years (as he tells us in the Preface to *Esther*), " which was to combine, as in the antique tragedies of Greece, the action of a Play with the chant of a Chorus."

So *Esther* came into being, and, as it grew in beauty, the original idea of a mere amusement for the young ladies of Saint-Cyr developed into something new, surprising. In her chamber at Versailles Madame de Maintenon was often confronted with the difficulty of her task, which was, as she herself declared, " to amuse the Inamusable." How

often would she willingly have left her royal charge
to visit the new buildings at Saint-Cyr, inspect the
school, confer with the mistresses, instruct the
adoring girls.   In the playgrounds of the convent
she renewed her youth.   Saint-Cyr was her passion.
And now she had the brilliant idea of connecting
her two duties.   The King should attend the play !
He liked Racine.   The project would interest him.
The sight of those fresh young faces, the sound of
those sweet young voices reciting the pious harmony
of Racine's incomparable verse, would refresh the
King's jaded fancy as a glass of new milk the palate
for which spices and wine have lost their relish.
And there was another reason which perhaps no
single person among those privy to the production
of the play ever directly formulated, a thing left
unexpressed yet in all their minds : *Esther* was a
sensitive tentacle extended, a feeler timidly stretched,
to test the state of opinion as to a public declara-
tion of the King's secret marriage.   For Esther was
obviously Madame de Maintenon.

In the boredom of Versailles Louis XIV was
greatly interested in the scheme.   He sent to
Saint-Cyr the cast-off splendours in which, as a
young Prince, he had loved to dance a ballet before
the Court—brilliant, embroidered, diamond-bespat-
tered garments out of which Esther and Haman
and Ahasuerus might fashion their turbans and
caftans and Oriental robes.   He listened while
Racine recited some passage which he had finished
the night before.   The play was indeed the thing !
It soon became a frequent topic of conversation at
Versailles.

It is odd to find a school for girls occupying so

central a place in a splendid Court, but so it was
in France when the same bevy of damsels that
confessed their sins to Fénelon and raved of Madame
Guyon's interior orisons rehearsed *Esther* with
Racine. Madame de Maintenon had opened the
school in 1686. The King named the candidates.
And the pupils were two hundred and fifty young
ladies of poor but noble parentage, who were housed
in a palace built by Mansart, surrounded by a park
of sixty acres, educated with the last refinement,
and chiefly dedicated to the religious life. One may
say, therefore, that Saint-Cyr was a normal school,
a college for preceptors. Pedagogy was at once the
sport and the science of the hour. The improve-
ment of a Chosen Few, destined to hand on the
torch, excited as ardent and as curious an interest
at Versailles towards 1688 as our own age brings to
bear on the amelioration of horses. Kings had a
School then instead of a Stud.

Racine was not only the poet of the play, but the
stage-manager of the representation. There were
daily rehearsals at Saint-Cyr. The excited young
things, fresh from their provinces, were soon converted into accomplished actresses, their rough
country speech polished into an imitation of our
poet's rare and beautiful diction. They knew him
well by reputation, for they had already played
Andromaque with such fervour and with so fresh a
passion that Madame de Maintenon had declared,
smiling, they should never act the piece again.
And now they hung upon the lips of an author no
less happy than themselves, almost as great a
child. Fifty years later, when Louis Racine shall
visit Saint-Cyr, several old ladies (who had been

fifteen years old in 1688) said to him " with a sort of enthusiasm " :

" Vous êtes le fils d'un homme qui avait un grand génie et une grande simplicité."

Racine was happy with his doll's-house of a convent-theatre, where, constantly accompanied by Boileau, he spent a part of most of his days. And Madame de Maintenon was happy—but no child, she ! I think of her as an aspen rooted in a rock : such a wavering in the wind of the delicate leaves and branches ; such fickle fancies and swift withdrawals ; and yet, deep below this fugitive and volatile grace, a staunch groundwork where Order, Principle and Regularity hold her, half against her will, for ever and evermore a prisoner.

" In her (said Fénelon) eternal wisdom spoke through the lips of the Graces."

It is said that there exists in the forests of Paraguay a small flower so pale of aspect and so faint of fragrance that none remarks it. Yet if any by chance should bruise, in treading on it, that frail imperceptible blossom, he is thenceforth impregnate with a perfume so delicious that he can no longer live without it, and turns back on his path, like a man demented, to discover the mysterious plant. Such a charm, such a magic was Esther's. And yet she was a virtuous woman of fifty.

She kept the King's affection for two-and-thirty years, being a little his elder. He who had loved so many women never wished for any other after he fell in with her. Racine, in *Esther*, gives us an inkling of her secret.

Je ne trouve qu'en vous je ne sais quelle grâce
Me charme qui toujours et jamais ne me lasse. . . .
. . . Tout respire en Esther l'innocence et la paix !
Du chagrin le plus noir, elle écarte les ombres
Et fait des jours sereins de mes jours les plus sombres.[1]

And again :

Oui, vos moindres discours ont des grâces secrètes ;
Une noble pudeur à tout ce que vous faîtes
Donne un prix que n'ont point ni la pourpre ni l'or.[2]

With what a beating heart, under the demure magnificence of her robes, must the Lady, the hostess (and, so to speak, a hostess on her trial) have watched her guests when Esther tells how the Persian tyrant, finding he could have her at no cheaper price, at last consented to set on her meek head a crown !

Dieu tient le cœur des rois entre ses mains puissantes ;
Il fait que tout prospère aux âmes innocentes
Tandis qu'en ses projets l'orgueilleux est trompé.
De mes faibles attraits le Roi parut frappé.
Il m'observa longtemps dans un sombre silence,
Et le ciel, qui pour moi fit pencher la balance ;
Dans a temps-là, sans doute, agissait sur son cœur.
Enfin, avec des yeux où règnait la douceur,
" Soyez Reine ! " fit-il.[3]

---

[1] I feel in you a charm, I find in you a grace
That wins upon the heart nor ends in weariness. . . .
. . . Esther exhales an air of tranquil innocence !
She comes, and lo ! our blackest trouble melts away !
She smiles ; a ray of light transforms the darkest day.

[2] Caught in your lightest word, a secret grace shines through ;
A noble modesty confers on all you do
A worth beyond the price of purple or of gold.

[3] God holds the heart of kings in His Almighty hands ;
That mild and guileless souls shall prosper, He commands,
While the proud man beholds his project come to harm.
And so the King was struck with my poor feeble charm.
He, in a sombre silence, watch'd me, long and late ;
Then, in my scale, the hand of Heaven cast a weight,
And in that hour, no doubt, God touch'd the tyrant's soul.
At last, with eyes in which a novel sweetness stole :
—" Reign ! Be a Queen ! " he said.

But Louis Quatorze was harder-hearted. Though he espoused his saint, he never proclaimed her a queen.

On the second story of the convent at Saint-Cyr, in the great hall which divided the dormitories, Madame de Maintenon had improvised a charming theatre; the hall itself was divided into two parts, of which the smaller formed the stage, the long bedroom behind it being turned into a green room, lighted by a profusion of wax candles, where a large wood fire blazed comfortably. Here, in the brief December afternoons, Racine and Boileau would instruct their eager little flock; one alone of the actress-apprentices was more than fifteen years of age.

The larger half of the vestibule was reserved for the audience, of which the pupils and mistresses of Saint-Cyr would form an important part. A stand of seats which ran round three sides of the hall gave ample sitting room. In the middle, several rows of large square stools and chairs were reserved for the guests, with two or three armchairs for Royalty.

One Wednesday afternoon, the 26th of January, 1689, the play was performed before Louis XIV, who was accompanied by the Dauphin, by four or five Dukes (La Rochefoucauld, Beauvilliers, Chevreuse, Noailles), and by the great Louvois; and people whispered, in the Court circle, that if Esther represented Madame de Maintenon, the iniquitous Haman was a portrait of Louvois—" but not too much like," murmured Madame de La Fayette. " Racine did not wish to emphasize the resemblance." Several Bishops, among them Bossuet,

were also present and several ladies of the Court.
The King was enchanted ; the girls played their
parts delightfully. There was, however, a little
hitch in the green room. Racine was very nervous
that night. At one moment the child who played
the part of Esther's confidant forgot her words.
There was the halt of an instant till Boileau, who
was doing prompter, came to the rescue. On the
other side the stage the little interval had scarcely
been noticed. But Racine, in the wings, was in a
fever. When the child came off he marched up to
her, glowering with solemn eyes, and in a voice
which she had never heard otherwise than sweetly
modulated, but which suddenly had turned harsh
and eager, he said :

" Mademoiselle, qu'avez vous fait ? Voilà une
pièce perdue ! "

Ah, Racine, you have no longer in front of you a
professional actress, a case-hardened Champmeslé,
but a timid schoolgirl of fifteen—" la petite
chanoinesse," as they called her ! She broke into
tears—loud, wailing, childish sobs. Racine immediately relented. Of all the young improvised
comedians at Saint-Cyr she was the nearest to his
heart, for she was an Arnauld, a scion of Port-
Royal, a great-niece of his old master, Antoine
Lemaistre. He whipped out his handkerchief and,
half in tears himself, attempted to dry the pretty
eyes that he had drenched. " Hush ! hush ! " he
murmured ; " they will hear you in the hall ! "
And when the child, consoled, had stepped back on
to the stage (where the King remarked her red
eyes and whispered, smiling, to his neighbour : " La
petite chanoinesse a pleuré ! ") Racine stole out to

the chapel and, kneeling before the altar, strove
to calm that fever of his unregenerate heart. This
angelic fairy-tale, written for a convent school, had
revived all his old passion for the theatre, had
turned him again into a dramatic artist—a vain,
sensitive, inconsiderate, cruel man capable of making
a good child cry her eyes out !

Esther at Saint-Cyr was a triumph. But a little
girl had wept, Racine had prayed in renewed
remorse, Madame de Maintenon herself had felt
some qualms as she noticed the arrogance of the
Blues, the elder girls, those who sang in the chorus
and played in the piece : they would no longer sing
in church lest they should strain their voices ! One
person, however, was absolutely satisfied, and that
was the King. *Esther* became his hobby. Not a
beauty was lost upon him : the pure and exquisite
quality of the verse, the subtle likeness between
the heroine and his secret wife, the fresh youth of
the carefully-trained and nobly-born young girls on
the stage, and the quaint theatre filled with nuns
and schoolgirls. Between the end of January and
the beginning of Lent the girls of Saint-Cyr had
time for little else than the repeated rehearsals of
the performances of *Esther*. When Madame de
Maintenon timidly suggested, in the interests of
discipline, that perhaps one might have too much
of a good thing, the King protested. He liked the
poetry, he liked the pretty girls, the simple atmosphere of youth and innocence ; he was not yet
weary of taking his friends over to Saint-Cyr to
see Racine's new play. The King and Queen of
England (James II and his wife), the Duke of
Orleans, Monseigneur, Monsieur, Madame and Made-

moiselle, a whole galaxy of Jesuits (twelve or fourteen at a time, says Madame de La Fayette), the celebrated Madame de Sévigné were all invited. The piece, performed on the 26th and 29th of January, the 3rd, 5th, 15th and 19th of February, was then, perforce, brought to a close because the Court went into mourning for the young Queen of Spain, the King's own niece, the daughter of Monsieur by his first wife, Henriette d'Angleterre.

Madame de Sévigné was present at the last representation of all. She had been longing to see the play. Her letters to her daughter ring a dozen changes on the theme of *Esther*. " Racine has surpassed himself ! He loves God as he used to love his mistresses, and is as ardent for sacred things as he used to be for profane ones." So she writes on the mere report of M. de Pomponne, whom Racine (ever mindful of a Jansenist) had begged the King to invite. When at last she has seen the play with her own eyes, the vivacious lady can find no words to express her admiration :

We were in the second row, just behind the Duchesses. Field-Marshal de Bellefond came and sat beside me. We both of us listened so earnestly that our attention was remarked in high quarters ; and every now and then I whispered a quiet word of praise, placed at the right moment, such as, perhaps, all the ladies present could not have fetched from under their lace head-dresses.

I cannot tell you what an exquisite spectacle it was ! A thing so difficult to put upon the stage, and which never can be reproduced in the same conditions : it is a harmony of the music, the poetry, the chorus, the performers, so perfect, so complete that one can wish for nothing better. The young girls who represent such great personages fill their *rôles* to a perfection ! It is simple, touching, innocent, sublime ! I was enchanted ! And so was the Marshal, who got up from his

place and went to pay his respects to the King. He said how
charmed he was with the representation, and that, next to him,
was a lady who was worthy of the invitation which she had
received to see *Esther*.

The King then came our way, and, turning round, addressed
himself to me.

" Madame, I am told you are pleased with the play ? "

And I, without losing my head, replied at once :

" Sire, I am more than pleased ! I find no words to express
my feelings ! "

The King then said :

" Racine is a man of great parts."

" Great indeed ! " said I. " But, Sire, these young ladies
are also most extraordinary. They enter into the subject as
naturally as if they had done nothing else all their days ! "

" True ! " said the King. " Very true ! "

And then His Majesty withdrew, leaving me the object of a
general envy.

M. le Prince and Mme. la Princesse also came and said a few
words, and Madame de Maintenon also, just for the twinkling
of an eye, for she retired with the King.

And that was the end of *Esther* for the time
being. But in the following winter, when the dark
afternoons returned and again were hard to while
away, the ladies of Saint-Cyr resumed their representations, which the King attended with an undiminished pleasure. By this time *Esther* was in
print. Not only Saint-Cyr, not only Versailles,
but Paris and all France applauded the poet of
the Bible.

Like Milton's *Comus*, with which it is interesting
to compare it, *Esther* is a lyrical drama, written for
music, intended to be sung. The beauty of either
poem is that mysterious thing called *tone*, that tone
which in Racine, as in Milton, is often superior to
the words, or even to the ideas expressed. The
tone of *Esther* is that of a mystical ravishment.
Few French persons, of any sensibility to poetry,

could read or recite without a peculiar emotion
that prayer of Esther's to the God of Israel which
begins : " O mon souverain roi ! " and ends with
the supplication :

> Accompagne mes pas
> Devant ce fier lion qui ne te connaît pas !

Love for and confidence in the Eternal is the
theme of *Esther*. Hitherto carnal love—a love passionately sexual—had been the subject of all Racine's
tragedies : the love of the violent and the brutal
for the chaste in *Andromaque*, and, in *Britannicus*,
the love of Nero for a pure virgin whose torment
fills him with delight ; the remorseful tenderness of
a great man for the woman to whom he owes everything, and whom he must not marry, in *Bérénice* ;
the love of a proud old hero, vanquished by the
years, for the young girl who loves his son, in
Mithridate ; the diseased love of an imperious woman
for a man younger than herself, whom she ruins out
of jealousy, in *Bajazet* ; in *Iphigénie* the rape of
Ériphile, with her sudden passion for her ravisher
because he has the blood of her kinsmen on his arms ;
and the involuntary incestuous love of Phèdre for
her stepson. . . . In *Esther* there is no love. It is
not Ahasuerus but the God of Israel whom Esther
adores and invokes.

Esther is still capable of communicating to the
reader something of Racine's religious exaltation.
Like those old engraven mirrors which show us
dimly, behind the frosted fancies chased upon the
glass, something of our own resemblance, so each
of us may catch our secret there. The Court of
Louis Quatorze saw the image of the Court with
Madame de Maintenon and Louvois. Port-Royal

remarked in Mardochée a likeness to the great
Arnauld, and whispered in passionate prayer the
song of the Young Israelite :

> Dieu d'Israël, dissipe enfin cette ombre !
> Des larmes de tes saints quand seras-tu touché ? [1]

So, in our own age, the pure poetry of *Esther* reflects
the soul of a religious reader, and yet reveals—in
that slow mystical dance of the final chorus—
Racine's own intimate thanksgiving for a soul at
last redeemed from death.

> Que le Seigneur est bon ! Que son joug est aimable !
> Heureux qui dès l'enfance en connait la douceur !
> Les biens les plus charmants n'ont rien de comparable
> Aux torrents de plaisirs qu'il rèpand dans un cœur !
> Il s'apaise, Il pardonne.
> Du cœur ingrat qui l'abandonne
> Il attend le retour. . . .

> . . . Pour l'enfant qu'elle a mis au jour
> Une mère a moins de tendresse.
> Ah, qui peut avec lui partager notre amour !

Listen ! The wonderful, mystical dance before
the Ark is woven out of quite ordinary words,[2]

---

[1] How long, O Lord, till Thou dispell the gloom ?
When wilt Thou wipe the sad eyes of Thy saints ?

[2] How lovely is the Lord ! His yoke how light to bear !
Thrice happy they who chose in youth the better part !
The world's enchanting boon hath naught that can compare
With those enraptur'd floods which inundate a heart !
Before the Soul repents,
Forgiving, He relents ;
And if the ungrateful heart forsake the upward track,
He waits till it turn back. . . .

. . . A mother's tender cares for her young babe are naught
To all His love prepares for them He miss'd and sought !
Ah bring, ah bring in offering
A love no mortal shares !

simple, undistinguished. The poem is stripped of all adornment. Nothing is very precisely stated save the mercy of the divine, eternal Lover of the Soul. But what a tone, what a sentiment are exhaled from these quiet phrases! Sweet, invisible violets that we trample in the dark have no such perfume!

CHAPTER II

ATHALIE

THE name of Milton again rises to our lips when we open *Athalie*. Who else, save they two, could animate a sphere composed only of innocence, of awe, of a sublime compassion, where the vain cruelty of human pride is vanquished and annihilated by the Will of God ? In this atmosphere all colour is absorbed into a trembling intensity of light.

The visible hero of *Athalie* is a child of seven years, Joas, or as we say Joash, the orphan prince of Israel, the only scion of the House of David, saved from the massacre of all his kin, and hidden, by his uncle the High Priest Joad (or Joiada), in the inner sanctuary of Solomon's Temple. There he was reared in secret, under the name of Eliakim, to carry on that sacred branch of David which one day was to flower in the Messiah. And the contrast of the frail and threatened life of so young a child with the august impersonal destiny which he must fulfil is the first mystery of *Athalie*.

In a poet's eye, a thing, a person, is always, in addition to itself, another thing, another person. " Alles Vergängliche ist nur ein Gleichnis." And these symbols have echoes and strange reverberations ; this mysterious child, Joas, has more than one shimmering reflection. Doubtless in the eyes of *Athalie's* first audience, and partly no doubt in the intention of the poet, Joas symbolized the eventual heir to the French Crown, the little Duc de Bourgogne, the pupil of Fénelon and Beauvilliers —a violent, sensitive little lad of eight years old— on whom centred the hopes of such as dared to hope for France—for was he not the scholar of the Saints, trained to inaugurate a nobler earth ? Listening to Racine's play, the devout glanced at the Royal child and murmured :

> Te duce, si qua manent, sceleris vestigia nostri,
> Inrita perpetua, solvent formidine terras. . . .
> . . . Magnus ab integro sæclorum nascitur ordo.

A little child, *parvulus puer*, might yet lead his people to salvation.

But, I think, less in the poet's intention than in his deepest memory, his almost unconscious being, there was yet another interpretation of this little child reared in the sanctuary : a dim, remorseful remembrance of Racine himself, a lonely boy, reared in secret at Port-Royal. Else why should Joad, the Priest, in his prophetic trance foretell so bitterly the backsliding of the child he has cherished ? foresee so cruelly that Joas—the lamb saved from the slaughter, the brand snatched from the burning— shall prove an ingrate in after years, a criminal, rending the hand that fed his helpless youth ?

> Comment en un plomb vil l'or pur s'est il changé ?

Is there in any literature a scene more tremendous than that which shows us Joad, in the hour of fulfil- ment, suddenly transported by the spirit of prophecy and foretelling, as he quivers in the sacred rapture, not triumph, but only horror, ruin, desolation ? He beholds the Temple of Solomon destroyed, the sacred tribes dispersed, and Joas imbued with the blood of those that saved him ; and it would be too painful (since it destroys our interest in the hidden child) were Joas indeed the hero of the tragedy. . . . But he is only the visible hero.   The real protagonist of *Athalie* is the Eternal God of Israel.

We can imagine the impression produced on the first public—on Beauvilliers, on the little Duke dissolved in tears, on the listening King (who supposed that they were to hear some amiable parable like *Esther*)—we can imagine their terror, their surprise, perhaps their displeasure, when the High Priest, shaken by the authentic oracle, can only cry : Weep! Weep! Jerusalem! Woe! Woe ! . . . Flames, ashes, captivity, destruction fill his eyes—until, rapt to a higher Heaven still and seeing farther afield, the Visionary bursts forth at last in a solemn chant of joy :

> Quelle Jérusalem nouvelle
> Sort du fond du désert, brillante de clartés !
> Et porte sur le front une marque immortelle ?
> Peuples de la terre, chantez !
> Jérusalem renaît plus charmante et plus belle !
> D'où lui viennent de tous côtés
> Ces enfants qu'en son sein elle n'a point portés ? . . .
> Lève, Jérusalem, lève ta tête altière !
> . . . Cieux, ripandez votre rosée
> Et que la terre enfante son Sauveur.[1]

---

[1]   Behold a new Jerusalem
Rise from the distant desert sands, and shine !
See, on her brow she bears the immortal sign !
   Come, let us sing with them
That sing,—the assembled nations of the earth :
   " Jerusalem is born again
More bright, more lovely in her second birth ! "
. . . But who are these that come, that troop, that pour ?
These bands of children that she never bore ? . . .
Lift high, Jerusalem, thy brows empearl'd !
. . . And, Heaven, shed thy dews in rain,
While Earth brings forth the Saviour of the world !

The particular is abolished, the city of David is destroyed, the veil of the Temple is rent in twain. But the reign of the universal has begun. Not a mere tribe is saved for ever, though it were the tribe of Judah; not a people alone, though it were the people of Israel; but all humanity, through the sacrifice of Christ, with, instead of the altar of Abraham, the Catholic Church as wide as the world itself!

Such was the theme of Racine. All things have worked together to righteousness. The crime of Joas is effaced, for God has no need of human merit; the unjust, like the just, can prove His instrument. After the chorus has debated the terror of the immediate future and the infinite hope that dawns in the dimmest distance, the scene croons itself to sleep with a lullaby as simple as the cradle-song of a child :

> D'un cœur qui t'aime,
> Mon Dieu, qui peut troubler la paix ?
> Il cherche en tout ta volonté suprême,
>   Et ne se cherche jamais.
> Sur la terre, dans le ciel même,
> Est-il d'autre bonheur que la tranquille paix
>   D'un cœur qui t'aime ? [1]

This sense of the *Deus abscons*, ever mysteriously working, " shaping our ends, rough-hew them how we will "; the pæan of thanksgiving telling how the doomed nation shall yet be saved from the pit ;

[1] The heart that loves Thee, Lord,
Need never fear the peril of its peace.
In everything Thy will he seeks and sees,
    And nothing seeks for self.
On earth, in Heaven itself,
Is there another bliss than that unruffled peace
    Of hearts that love the Lord ?

the prophetic vision of a new Heaven and Earth lift *Athalie* above the rank of a tragedy.

The only English poem with which we can compare *Athalie* is *Paradise Lost*, although here Milton's majesty has melted into grace. The two poems have similar qualities of musical beauty and religious grandeur. They are classical poems and, we may add, poems of national importance, for England would rather be shorn of a colony than shorn of *Paradise Lost*, and Tonquin itself is less essential to the grandeur of France than *Athalie*.

But *Athalie* is, at the same time, a play—a very interesting, historical and political play, with a rightful heir cherished in concealment, a wicked Queen, Jezabel's dreadful daughter, tarnished with all the crimes which Racine had observed at Court, and yet keeping a strange, horrible fascination, an almost sentimental charm, in her darkened eyes and painted smile. Athalie is a masterly portrait of a wicked princess, corrupt and cruel, and yet with a certain grandeur in her crime, a sort of Comtesse de Soissons or Madame de Montespan. She tries first to seduce and then to destroy the Hope of Israel, but, hoisted by her own petard, she, not he, falls a victim to her own iniquity.

Having a Prophet for one of his personages, Racine was able, in *Athalie*, to inculcate a few home truths. Joad, in his instructions to the child-King, also warns the ageing Louis Quatorze of the dangers inherent in absolute power; the deadly peril of flatterers disguising every fact; the insidious persuasion that a sovereign is superior to the Law, and even to moral right and wrong; that the common people are necessarily condemned to a life of tears

and hard labour, so that it would be folly to attempt
to ameliorate their condition ; that, on the whole,
they prefer being governed by an iron hand ; that,
if the King did not oppress the lower class, they
would oppress him and so endanger the safety of
the State. Kings never learn and seldom love the
truth, for it is the interest of their ministers to
keep them in ignorance.

Hélas ! ils ont des rois égaré le plus sage !

No monarch will find by his throne a counsellor
to repeat the golden rule.

Entre le pauvre et vous, vous prendrez Dieu pour juge.

Versailles had not often echoed to such accents.
It is perhaps not astonishing that Versailles did not
relish them.

Neither the magnificence nor the enthusiasm
which had been lavished on *Esther* were accorded
to *Athalie*. The wind had veered. Madame de
Maintenon had heard on all hands that her school
at Saint-Cyr would degenerate into a hotbed for
vice and folly if she allowed her pupils to act in
private theatricals before the Court.

As a matter of fact, two of these young ladies
had made brilliant marriages, and another had
sorely compromised her reputation. Madame de
La Fayette wrote in her *Mémoires sur la Cour de
France* : " It really is not reasonable to suppose
that three hundred young girls can be kept in the
neighbourhood of the young lords of the Court
without one or other of them sometimes leaping
over the wall." A pamphlet published in Holland
had dared to print that Saint-Cyr was " little better

than a Seraglio which an aged Sultana was preparing
for a new Ahasuerus."

Infinitely susceptible to opinion, Madame de
Maintenon had decided not to renew the experiment. As she herself wrote in her *Lettres Edifiantes*
to her pupils at Saint-Cyr, " L'approbation des
honnêtes gens était mon idole ; une belle réputation
était ma folie ; il n'y a rien que je n'eusse été
capable de faire et de souffrir pour cela." So there
should be no more stage plays at Saint-Cyr : no
diamond-bespangled caftans and turbans, no Kings
and Queens and Dukes and Duchesses grouped in
applauding audience.

Athalie was played once, in the classroom of the
" Blues " at Saint-Cyr, before the King, almost
unattended save by the King of England, the
Dauphin, the little Duc de Bourgogne, and four or
five grandees in waiting ; but it was played without
any scenery, by the girls in their school uniform,
enlivened only by a few knots of ribbon, a few
strings of beads. If Fénelon and Boileau declared
Athalie the most perfect of modern masterpieces—
" equal to Sophocles " (and what could they say
more ?)—there was no general enthusiasm ; the
piece appeared more terrible than beautiful, cold,
and the fate of a mere child a motive insufficient
to sustain a tragedy. A few rare spirits—I have
quoted two, the great Condé and Madame de Maintenon may be added to their number—continued
to exalt *Athalie* ; the King from time to time would
send a couple of coaches to Saint-Cyr to fetch a
dozen young ladies to Versailles, where they would
act the play, without the chorus, in Madame de
Maintenon's room. Boileau was present, by acci-

dent, on one of these occasions, and wrote at once
to his friend that " the King was ravished, enchanted ! " Still there was no disguising the fact
that if *Athalie* was not precisely a failure, like *Phèdre*,
it was, at best, a *succès d'estime*.

And Racine, the too sensitive Racine, was almost
as much cast down, almost as embittered and
unhappy as after the fiasco of *Phèdre*. He lan-
guished ; he looked ill ; his friends could not
persuade him that he had written a masterpiece.
His conversion had left him very human. He had
let his feet be caught in the snare. He had tasted
again of the honey of poetry and praise : " *paullulum
mellis—et ecce moriar.*" How happy he had been
in combining those movements of the chorus which
had left the scene never for an instant empty from
the first word to the last—a thing hitherto unknown
in any modern play ! Ravished into an ecstasy, he
had shown the Unseen Hand framing to its own
design the incoherent and contrary events of our
mortal life ! How much he had delighted in the
(doubtless sinful) pleasure of verse : number and
harmony, measure and rhythm, the sweet mystical
malady of visions ! Henceforth he would write
nothing save hymns and canticles.

We possess several hymns written by Racine at
this period, and especially four spiritual songs or
canticles which the King asked him to compose for
Saint-Cyr. In a letter to Boileau, dated from
Fontainebleau the 3rd of October, 1694, we find
Racine hard at work polishing his stanzas, asking
his friend's advice, suggesting different versions.
" Je vous conjure de me donner votre sentiment
sur tout ceci. J'ai dit franchement que j'attendais

votre critique avant que de donner mes vers au musicien—et je l'ai dit à Madame de Maintenon." The musician was a certain Moreau, of whom, I think, nothing remains, yet well known in his day; he had composed the music for *Esther* and for *Athalie.* He cannot have been long about his business, for, on comparing Dangeau's Journal with Racine's letter, we find that on that same evening of the 3rd of October, the King, who was in bed with the gout, sent for Racine and Moreau and the singers to his chamber, and listened to a rehearsal of the canticles.

Moreau's music was probably nothing very striking, but the poems have their music in themselves: a melancholy music, a morbid grace, which, combined with the most winning naïveté and an evident sincerity, recall, to an English ear, the religious poems of Cowper—sad verses, especially when we remember that they are the last we shall hear from Racine, full of

> La pénitence tardive
> Des inconsolables morts.[1]

One of them offers us so true an image of Racine in a mood of depression that I will quote a couple of stanzas here.

> Mon Dieu, quelle guerre cruelle!
>   Je trouve deux hommes en moi:
>   L'un veut que, plein d'amour pour toi,
> Mon cœur te soit tougours fidèle;
> L'autre, à tes volontés rebelle,
>   Me révolte contre ta loi.

---

[1] The tardy penitence
Of dead men ever unconsoled.

> . . . Hélas ! en guerre avec moi-même,
> Où pourrai-je trouver la paix ?
> Je veux, et n'accomplis jamais,
> Je veux, mais (ô misère extrême)
> Je ne fais pas le bien que j'aime
> Et je fais le mal que je hais.[1]

Perhaps it is as well for Racine's final sanity that another war than that interior battle distracted his attention during those anxious years. The European war which, without ever subsiding into an honest peace, had died down for some while flamed up again fiercely in 1692 when William of Orange vowed that he would make an end of France. Racine followed the King from Court to camp, from camp to Court, during the whole of the ensuing campaign, and doubtless the constant alarms and shocks, the continual hardships of a battlefield, so little consonant with his gentle nature, appeared to him as at once a relief to his remorse and a Heaven-sent expiation for the crime of having made immortal verse.

> [1] My God, how fierce a fight is here !
> I find two men alive in me.
> The one, devoted, Lord, to Thee,
> Would arm my heart to persevere ;
> But there's another voice within
> Whispers revolt and bids me sin.
>
> . . . Myself is with myself at war !
> How shall I stem the long asaults ?
> My virtuous wishes end in faults ;
> My will is weak, too faint by far ;
> The good I love I never do,
> And hated evil still pursue.

CHAPTER III

A HISTORIAN AT COURT

SPANHEIM, that wise collector of old coins, who was the Elector of Brandenburg's Envoy to France, gives us a portrait of Racine at Court.

M. de Racine has risen from the theatre to Versailles, where he has become an able courtier. He is one of the devout. The merit of his dramatic works can scarce compare with the art he has shown in acquiring the manners and tone of a sphere where now he plays all sorts of personages. Complimentary enough and acquiescent when he is one among the many, in an intimate circle and a private conversation he can blame and exclaim with the best. He has a hand in all sorts of combinations and contrivances, especially if they aim at a pious end, for he manages to keep in with all the leaders in that line. . . . He is a good Greek scholar and a good Latinist, too ; as for the French that falls from his pen, it is of the very purest, sometimes lofty in tone, sometimes moderate and measured, but always of a fresh novelty of diction. I do not know if M. de Racine will acquire as great a reputation in History as in Poetry, but I fancy that he will scarcely prove an exact historian. He is most eager to be thought of use ; but though he have the desire to serve and the best will in the world to write his history, I doubt if he possess the ability. 'Tis about as much as he can do at present to keep his head above water at Court.

These notes of Spanheim, which I have used more than once (they were first published by M. P. Mesnard in his Introduction to Hachette's great edition of Racine), are interesting and, on the

whole, perspicacious, despite an accent of acrimony.
I fancy the German was right about the history.
Perhaps we did not lose immensely by that fire at
Saint-Cloud, which (burning to the ground Valincour's house there during the night of the 13th of
January, 1726) destroyed every vestige of the
Histoire du règne de Louis XIV. When he saw the
flames raging, Valincour, who was Racine's successor
as *Historiographe du Roi*, promised a purse with
twenty gold pieces to the rescuer of the manuscript.
A poor fellow dashed into the fire, and emerged,
blackened and burned, triumphantly displaying—a
bundle of old Gazettes ! Then the roof fell in, and
we shall never know what Racine and Boileau had
made of their glorious task.

In what degree was Racine a historian ? A few
pages of studies for the history—mere notes—are
all that remain, except his *Abrégé de l'Histoire de
Port-Royal.* He wrote this short history of the
Abbey with the intention of enlightening the new
Archbishop of Paris, Noailles, who had succeeded
the unfriendly M. de Harlay. The Cardinal de
Noailles was a high-minded man, a friend of Madame
de Maintenon's, of Beauvilliers'. Port-Royal raised
its head, began to hope, and entrusted to Racine
the sacred duty of removing the possible prejudices
of a prelate. But, in the course of events, we often
see the most iniquitous actions accomplished by the
best of men. Had Racine, as he stooped over his
page, entered into a visionary trance, like Joad, he
would have seen, under the reign of Noailles, the
Abbey dismantled and destroyed, stone wrenched
from stone and cast upon the fields, while the
reluctant nuns were torn from their home by

soldiers, and carried off by force, some this way and some that. " Comme des créatures publiques qu'on arrache à un mauvais lieu," says Saint-Simon.

The Short History of Port-Royal was Racine's latest work, and it remains unfinished. Its plain and exquisite simplicity of its prose has something of the charm which Flaubert found in that bare wall of the Parthenon—more admirable, he thought, than even the frieze of the Metopes. It is flawless, but without an ornament. Here is a subject in which Racine is at home, where he writes with liberty and grace. I choose for an example a passage from the opening of the second part, where our historian records the unjust persecution of the saint he most revered by the King he most admired, Louis XIV :

Hitherto we have seen calumny do its best to destroy the Abbey of Port-Royal ; but now we shall watch the storm, which has been so long gathering, blast the roof to ruins ; we shall behold the passion of the Jesuits armed not only with the authority of a Minister, but with the consent of the Throne. I doubt not that posterity, observing, on the one hand, all that the King has done to further the Catholic religion, and, on the other, M. Arnauld's labours in the cause of the Church, together with the rare virtue of Port-Royal—I doubt not, I say, but posterity will wonder how so holy a house could be overwhelmed by order of a King so full of piety and justice ; and our children shall marvel that M. Arnauld should have been forced to finish his days in a foreign country. Yet it is not the first time that God has let His Saints be condemned as malefactors by the most virtuous of princes, and we must admit that never was a prejudice apparently better founded than the King's prepossession against Port-Royal.

And here is another passage from the first part, in which, with equal impartiality, Racine attempts

to explain the cruel animosity of the Jesuits against
the Jansenists.

It is difficult to understand how a company so venerable in
its institution and composed of members so pious as the Society
of Jesus could advance and spread such strange allegations
against Port-Royal. Had the spirit of true religion suddenly
expired in their breasts ? Certainly not ! That same spirit of
religion breathes in their very calumnies. The Jesuits, at least
most of them, are convinced that their Society can only be
assailed by heretics ; as a rule they have read nothing save
the writings of their own Fathers, the arguments of their
adversaries being printed in books which are on their black list.
It follows that, in order to know whether a thing be true or false,
a Jesuit can only consult a Jesuit. They confine themselves,
as a rule, to copying one another, and we may see them any
day advance, as incontestable and certain facts, things which
have been disproved these thirty years gone by. How should
they know it ? The greater part of them entered the Company
when they were but striplings and exchanged their school-
benches for the postulant's ward. When they were at College,
they heard their masters abominate Port-Royal, and now they
repeat the lesson to their pupils.

And there is another thing. It is an inherent vice in most
communities to think that one can do no harm in defending
the honour of one's corps, until, at last, that honour becomes
a sort of idol to which everything else must be immolated :
Justice, Reason, Truth—yes, everything ! One can only say of
the Jesuits that this general defect is more common among
them than in any other body. Some of their casuists,. indeed,
have gone so far as to say that calumny, or even murder, are
permissible if employed in defence of the Society of Jesus.

Racine had several esteemed acquaintances among
the Jesuits : the Père Rapin, the Père Bouhours, the
Père La Chaise, notable men, great scholars ; and
no doubt sometimes, in the sacred precincts of the
Abbey, he had missed their more liberal atmosphere,
had suffered from that sectarian spirit (inherent in
Port-Royal as much as in the Society of Jesus)
which holds that one can do no wrong in defending

the honour of one's corps. But, if Racine sometimes esteemed and occasionally liked the enemy,
he never let there be any doubt as to which was
the side he fought on. At Court he was the agent
of the Abbey. Had a farmer a tax that he wanted
remitted—was the great Arnauld, or Du Guet, or
any illustrious Jansenist exile in need of an intercessor—did the Abbess require a diplomatic friend
to negotiate with the Archbishop the nomination
of a new spiritual Director—one and all they applied
to Racine, who accounted no pains too great, no
steps too wearisome, no strain on his own favour
too imprudent, if the result might prove an advantage to Port-Royal. " À un aussi bon ami que
vous, si généreux et si effectif," begins old Antoine
Arnauld, and the letter is, of course, to recommend
a protégé. Racine must have been a busy man in
those seventeen-nineties !

Yet sometimes, communing with his own heart,
he deplored the unwariness of the Abbey. Knowing
the Court as intimately as the cloister, he could
estimate the injury that the Saints had done to
their own cause by their partisanship of the Cardinal
de Retz and their familiarity with the long-extin-
guished, superannuated, and yet still dangerous
firebrands of the Fronde. All those old beauties,
weary of the Court, who sheltered their chagrin and
their infirmities at the Abbey-in-the-Fields, gave it
the air of being a nest of malcontents, the natural
resort of those in disgrace at Versailles. And the
Jansenists themselves, by setting themselves apart
as a city within the City, an empire within the
Empire, had insulted the King in that which he
held most dear and sacred—the conception of his

own universal supremacy; so that he looked on an Augustinian as little better than a Republican disguised, and held the Abbey to be a hiding-place for rebels as well as heretics.

Racine knew all he risked by making himself the indefatigable advocate of Mère Agnès, of Antoine Arnauld, of the very farmers and field labourers on the estate of Port-Royal; but he had a debt to pay, a dereliction to expiate and a faith to affirm. He did not flinch. One day he said to a friend of his (a M. Vuillard, or Willard, whose letters I shall often have to quote): " I don't care if I fall into disgrace, nor should I mind if I came tumbling head over heels one of these days, so long as thereby Port-Royal might flourish as of old." " And these were his very words," adds the worthy Vuillard, rather horrified at that realistic expression, " faire la culbute."

But Racine was still a favourite with the King. After *Athalie*, to show his royal appreciation, Louis made the poet a present of a handsome office at Court, the place of Gentleman-in-Ordinary to the Chamber, with ultimate reversion to young Jean-Baptiste Racine. There was a good salary attached to the post, which, had it been bought as a commission, would have cost the purchaser at least fifty thousand livres; it might therefore be considered a noble gift and a provision for the future of Racine's elder son. But, like everything in France in those last years of the seventeenth century, it was heavily taxed. Before the new beneficiary could enter into possession, he would have to pay down some five thousand livres, which as a matter of fact our poet did not possess; for all his income was derived either from pensions or from landed estate, his conscience forbidding him to touch the money he might so easily have had from the Paris theatres. The only way he could think of was to save the sum out of his yearly revenue, which would be considerably increased by the new stipend. He therefore begged Madame de Maintenon to ask either for some abatement of the amount, or at least for some extension of the time in which the payment must be completed, a grace which had been granted him once already when he had received that sinecure at Moulins. It was a grave mistake. Times were altered. Racine had solicited too many favours for Port-Royal to be able properly to ask a kindness for himself. In his situation at Court, as a man esteemed for his genius and his character, yet rather dreaded on account of his indiscriminate befriending of Jansenists, he would have been far wiser to have borrowed the money from the Jews. Boileau, who was a practical man, should have told him so.

It was, I imagine, while talking with Madame de Maintenon about this tax that Racine let himself go into an enthusiastic protest against the over-taxed condition of the poor and the possible means of alleviating it. They were discussing the sad results of glory, the miserable poverty of the king-dom, when—says Louis Racine—

My father said that a general impoverishment was the natural consequence of great wars, but that those in high places might, in some degree, mitigate the general distress if they themselves were sufficiently enlightened. And as he spoke his face shone, he breathed his very soul into his words (as was his wont when a subject really touched his heart), so that he entered into that fine frenzy, that enthusiasm of which I have already spoken which inspired him with so agreeable an eloquence. He enchanted Madame de Maintenon, who said that, since on the spur of the moment he could improvise such pertinent remarks, he ought to think the matter seriously over and give her the result in writing. He might rest assured the paper would never go out of her own hands.

Worse luck, he accepted her suggestion, not out of a courtier's complaisance, but because he really hoped to be useful. He gave Madame de Maintenon an eloquent and solidly reasoned memorandum. She was reading it in her room one day when the King came in, took it out of her hands, glanced through it, and hastily asked to be told the name of the author. She answered that that was a secret, and the writer had her word for it. But her resistance was vain, and the King expressed his will in terms so precise that she was obliged to say it was Racine. The King, while admitting his zeal, took amiss that a man of letters should meddle with politics, and said, rather testily :

" Because he writes fine poetry, does he think, forsooth, he knows everything ? Because he's a great poet, does he fancy he's fit to be a Minister of State ? "

Had the King imagined the effect these words would have on Racine, he would never have uttered them, but how could he dream with what a force and weight they would fall on too sensitive a heart ?

Thus Louis Racine, who repeats the family tradition, heard many a time no doubt from his mother, his brother, and from his beloved old friend Nicolas Boileau. The memorandum itself, like the history, has utterly vanished. (It was perhaps in those archives of Valincour's that perished in the flames.) There have been found modern critics to doubt its very existence; not, however, those who knew Racine the best, neither Sainte-Beuve nor Jules Lemaître. To their arguments I might add this : the heads of such a memorandum to the King in favour of the poor are to be found scattered across the pages of *Athalie*. Racine had slipped so easily into the place of advocate for the oppressed that, in pleading the cause of the poor, he would seem to himself but to exercise a natural function.

I believe therefore in the existence of such a memorandum confided to Madame de Maintenon by our poet (the friend of Vauban, of Fénelon, of Beauvilliers, of all those who desired a reform of the government), and surprised in Madame de Maintenon's hands by the King. The King was vexed ; Racine had a hint of the cold shoulder shown him at Versailles. Saint-Simon has an absurd story—the very same that Louis Racine far more plausibly relates of deaf old Boileau—that Racine offended the proud monarch by maundering on in an absent-minded manner about Scarron's over-rated comedies while speaking in the presence of Madame de Maintenon—Scarron having been the lady's first husband. At any rate, for some reason Racine fell out of favour at Versailles.

Imagine him in his study in Paris, racking his brains to discover what could have been his " crime " —for he could not believe, says his son, that the memorandum was sufficient to cast him so completely overboard—and feeling very sore at heart because of the evident dereliction of his dear Egeria, whom he no longer saw nor heard from.

For my part I believe that neither Scarron nor the memorandum was the real cause of Racine's semi-disgrace. His Jansenist sympathies explain it all. In those years of the 'nineties the Jesuits were supreme at Versailles. If we turn to the Letters of the Princess Palatine we find a score of instances of their authority. You had but to say (she tells us) that a man was a Huguenot or a Jansenist for the King immediately to lose all interest in him. On one occasion the sturdy old German lady was shocked because, His Majesty having been assured that a certain person could not really be a Jansenist since he was well known for an Atheist, the King was said to have replied : " So much the better. That is of no importance."

The same accusation of Jansenism would perfectly account for Madame de Maintenon's falling-off. The poor woman, conscious of her Huguenot parentage and upbringing, aware that she had been converted at last almost by force, was ever afraid lest a taint of original sin still might cling to her haunted soul. Agrippa d'Aubigne's granddaughter—how could she escape her doom ? If one of her friends should run off the moral rails—as was the case with Ninon de l'Enclos—she or he could count on the faithful friendship of the charming prude. But at the least hint of heresy she turned restive, mistrustful of her own resistance to contagion. Racine, accused of Jansenism, will fare no worse than Fénelon accused of Quietism. She will give them a wide berth, for fear of endangering her soul's health. And yet, in her heart of hearts, she will esteem them still.

And now let us return to Louis Racine's narrative :

My father's friends used to banter him and tease him because of his ill-founded anxieties, which grew deeper and deeper as time went on, owing to his regret at seeing no more of Madame de Maintenon, to whom he was deeply attached.

And here again I must interrupt the commemorative son, for I should like to quote from a despairing letter which our melancholy Racine sent the lady. It is dated from Marly, the 4th of March, 1698. The very fact of its being dated from Marly (the most intimate recess, the cosiest corner of the

Court) shows that, although Racine might, as I have said, have felt the subtle chill of a cold shoulder, there was nothing open or official in his disgrace.

The letter begins as a mere business letter concerning that tax on his new charge which Racine found it so difficult, so impossible even, to pay. But writing to so dear a friend, he soon lapses into a confidential strain, unburdening his heavy heart :

> Ah, when I wrote that chorus in *Esther*,
>
> " Rois, chassez la calomnie ! "

little did I think that I myself one day should be its victim! I know that, in the King's mind, a Jansenist is a man rebellious alike to Church and State. Did you ever notice in me any tincture of that heresy ? Did you ever know a man more devoted to the King than I, who spend all my days thinking about him, writing an account of His Majesty's great and noble actions in the hope of inspiring in others the same sentiments of admiration and of love ? As for myself, I may truly say that the great world has ever sought after me rather than I have sought after it. At least I can say that, in whatever society I may have found myself, Heaven has lent me the grace never to blush for the King or for the Gospel . . . Well, I think I can trace the origin of this suspicion of heresy. I have an Aunt who is the Superior of Port-Royal, to whom I am infinitely indebted. She it was who taught me to know God in the days of my childhood ; and it was she again who, as God's instrument, drew me from those paths of error in which I had wandered fifteen years. . . . I heard, nearly two years ago, that she had been accused of rebellion and disobedience. Could I, unless I had been the meanest wretch that breathes, refuse her my aid in her necessity ? . . . I seek my consolation in my studies. But think, Madame, what a shadow is flung across that work by the fact that the very King with whose virtues I am perpetually occupied regards me as an object fit for his displeasure rather than for his kindness !

Madame de Maintenon, although in her timid fugacity she dared no longer receive our poet at Court, desired none the less to fall in with him by accident, so as to have the opportunity of a little friendly encouragement. One day, while walking in the Park of Versailles, she crossed Racine, and, glancing at him, drew aside into a less frequented avenue, where he was not slow in joining her ; and as soon as he had greeted her, touched, doubtless, by his ravaged face—she began to reassure him as to his reinstatement in favour.

Of what are you afraid ? I am the cause of your misfortune and consider myself in honour bound to repair my inadvertence. The cloud will soon drift by ! I can promise you a speedy return of finer weather.

But I will not translate a conversation which Louis Racine cannot possibly have overheard (he was six years old at the time) but whose results were obvious, and doubtless the subject of a pious household legend which he must have listened to, many a time. In consideration of which I pass him again my pen, after skipping an imaginary dialogue.

While the two friends were talking, a sound of wheels was heard on the gravel behind them.

"The King!" cried Madame de Maintenon. "It is the King! He is driving this way. . . . Quick! Get out of sight!"

Racine beat a speedy retreat and concealed himself behind a clump of trees.

Like Adam and Eve in Paradise, he hid himself in the garden. Supreme humiliation ! " Il se sauva dans un bosquet." I think our poet should have stood his ground. But he was not the man of a prompt, immediate reaction, and he had to consider the reputation of a lady. What a leper the sad over-sensitive soul must have felt himself—not fit to be recognized, a man in disgrace, that a woman must not be seen with ! " Il se sauva dans un bosquet." He doubtless felt fit to hide there on all-fours.

Racine was very ill at this moment. The King's displeasure did not kill him, as his contemporaries and some of his biographers believed. But a chronic disease of the liver, which had already begun to poison his existence, made him brood more bitterly on his disgrace. In such a condition of health, this encounter, after all, was almost a death-sentence. And I cannot forgive Madame de Maintenon her silly fit of the flurries. It is with satisfaction that I repeat Saint-Simon's appreciation of her personality :

She had no coherency in her character, unless she was forced to it. Her natural taste was to hover and change. Her fancies flamed up, and died down as rapidly. . . . Her constitutional instability often made her seem twice as perfidious as she really was.

Poor woman ! I think that she was weary of Racine's attachment and, at the same time, deeply touched by it, and sorry for the harm she had done him by encouraging him too freely. Above all, she was anxious to grace her own position and to save her own soul.

CHAPTER IV

THE FATHER OF A FAMILY

Racine was the kindest father of a family that ever lived. Le meilleur père de famille qui ait jamais été.

SO said Valincour, in his *Discours de Réception* at the French Academy. And Valincour knew Racine well, and all his household. Louis Racine, in his *Memoirs,* tells us how his father loved to play with his children, as delighted as themselves with their pious games, carrying the cross in a procession. Best of all, we have Racine's Letters to his Son. Compare them with Lord Chesterfield's and admire the wide gamut of paternity ! These, and his correspondence with his sister, show us our hero in another light. The Poet, the Prodigal Son, the Penitent have all disappeared, giving place to a mild and generous being, very simple, full of a child-like piety ; a near relation, one would say, of the Vicar of Wakefield.

Family feeling was strong in our poet. We have seen him deeply attached to his grandmother, to his aunt ; but when his children were born, he felt the full power of the love that lurks in the blood. That younger sister of whom he had seen so little in their orphaned childhood, with whom he used to spar sometimes in their eager youth, grew also very dear to him when she likewise married and had a child. Mademoiselle Rivière (she had lost the noble rank of Madame on marrying the doctor), cuts an important figure in Racine's correspondence. She was a devoted aunt, and frequently requested to find wet-nurses for the poet's ever increasing family. The babies were generally sent to La Ferté-Milon, where they were put out to nurse, and many of Racine's letters are occupied with different details concerning their health and convenience.

What chiefly interests us in this correspondence is the light it throws on Racine's disposition, revealing an unsuspected side of the great man whom we find, in these unstudied pages, to be constantly charitable, full of pity for the poor, always ready to reach out a helping hand. The Racines, the Sconins and the Vitarts represented the prosperous portions of one of those immense provincial families which ramify far and wide and occupy a good many rungs of the social ladder. The poet, who had left La Ferté Milon at the age of ten, knew little of these unnumbered cousins, but they were kith and kin—all these Des Fossés, La Hayes, Moufflards, Dassys—though it might well happen that he had never set eyes on them ; and his sister has but to breathe a word of their distress for his heart and his purse to open wide. Here are a few extracts from Racine's letters to Mademoiselle Rivière, written between 1685 and 1697. They bear the sign of a sweet, a tender, a generous temper.

16 *Aug.*, 1685.

Give four or five gold pieces to that poor Mademoiselle des Fossés, who, you say, is old and unhappy with her husband. Was it her daughter who was married at Neuilly some two years ago who is now a widow ? Let me know, for if she be in need of assistance I will try to help her, and will send whatever you think necessary in the way of money. . . . Keep what you have of mine to come to the aid of any of our poor relations who may require it in these hard times. And if you know of other poor persons suffering much distress, although they be not of our family, I beg you do not refuse them! I count on you for this, and I shall never reproach my sister with having given away too much.

Times get harder and harder, so that a few years later he writes :

My mind misgives me that those forty francs a month which I send to poor Cousin Des Fossés are not enough. Give her whatever you think she ought to have.

Yet this is at the moment when Racine is sorely put to it to find money for the tax on his new post at Court, and he tells his sister that he is obliged to practise a severe economy in his household expenses. . . . Well, let us resume the list of his poor pensioners :

You wrote to me about a son of Madame d'Acy, or Dassy. Tell me what age the lad is and whether he ought not to be apprenticed to some trade or craft. An honest craft, it seems to me, is the happiest means of livelihood for people of that sort, far better than teaching them to read and write, which, at best, would make of the youth some wretched bailiff, or perhaps a regular ne'er-do-well. I will gladly bear the expense of his apprenticeship if he be already old enough to profit by it. Let me hear what we can do for him.

Life is so difficult in these hard times that I beg you to use my money freely in helping the poor.

And again in 1688 :

Cousin Fourrure can count on her hundred crowns as surely as though she had them already in her money-box. . . . I am glad to learn the marriage of the daughter of our cousins the Moufflards. Give her a hundred francs from me for a wedding present. I wish I could do more, but we are such a large family! I like to help such of our kin as need a helping hand, and my own affairs at present are much embarrassed.

I heartily approve the alms you propose to give our poor cousin De la Haye. Although he has led but a dissolute life, and there is, I fear, not much to be made of him, still we cannot abandon him in that depth of poverty to which the poor wretch has sunk ; and I will give more than you propose if you think it wise.

I think it must have been this same cousin De la Haye who was one day to rekindle in Racine's gentle breast a spark revived from the nervous and irascible Acante.

Jan. 10th, 1697.

Cousin Henry has been here, to Paris, dressed like a beggar, and called me Cousin before my wife and all our household ! You know that never in my life have I disowned a relation ; you know that I try to help my kinsmen to the best of my ability ; but I own I do find it hard that a man who has brought himself down to the condition of a tatterdemalion by sheer debauchery and drunkenness should come and bespatter me here with his beggary. I spoke to him as he deserved. I told him you would never have let him want if he were worth his salt—but whatever you give him he spends at once at the tavern. All the same, I did not let the poor wretch go away empty-handed, and gave him for his journey home. Prithee help him in secret, and never let him guess that I have a hand in it. If we could manage to haul him out of the mire I would make a sacrifice.

Pray continue the monthly dole to poor Marguerite, my old nurse. If you think poor Cousin Des Fossés needs a little more than what I allow her, pray increase her pension.

And so on, and so on. What between the money he distributed to the poor, and the money he would not receive because it came from the theatre, it is not surprising that Jean Racine, with all his girls and boys at home, was never a rich man.

The prettiest of all our poet's letters are those addressed to his elder son, Jean-Baptiste, or more properly *Racine.* The seventeenth century still preserved a great respect for the first-born : from his

babyhood the heir of the name and arms is *Racine*.
When, many years later, at the tail end of a long
family, a second son is born (little Louis, who was
to become his father's biographer), he was given
the style of Lionval from some farm on the parental
properties : M. de Lionval, he was intended to be,
leaving to his elder brother the undisputed usage of
the name Racine.   But centuries change, and sometimes progress ; the eighteenth century, already in
the offing, will make short work of this ridiculous
custom, and Louis Racine will lay aside the name
of Lionval with his primers and his pegtops when
he comes to grow out of childhood.

Meantime he was Lionval even to his parents
and his sisters, while the elder, Jean-Baptiste, was
Racine from the cradle up.

"We shall only want a cradle for the baby,"
writes our poet to his sister. "Racine (who was
then eighteen months old) will sleep with us."

When we meet "Racine" next, he is eight years
old. Seated on his father's knee, he traces a line
of his writing across the letter which the poet is
inditing to Mademoiselle Rivière. "Racine vous a
voulu faire ses baisemains, et vous a écrit sur mes
genoux ; mais il écrit mieux que cela ! " sighs the
proud father.

As a schoolboy, the little lad receives some dozen
charming letters from his father, absent at Court or
on the field of battle, which by a happy accident
have come down to us. The first is dated 1691 ;
"Racine" is in his thirteenth year. His father,
in thanking him for a letter recently received, tells
him, in a spirit of gentle teasing, that it is not
necessary to copy into his correspondence the news

he has just read in the newspaper—" we, too, have the Gazette "—neither need he launch out into considerations on the unrest in Ireland (*déjà !*) or in Germany. " Tell me rather about your walks and your outings and if your sisters keep well." And then, to wash down the pill of this good advice, the father gives his boy a grand account of a recent glorious victory—he is writing from the front.

A year later the child is in bed with the small-pox, while our poet is with the armies in camp before Namur. He writes to his son :

How thankful I should be to receive a line of your writing ! But do not dream of sending me a letter till the crisis is past ; for you would have to keep your arms out of the bedclothes and you might catch cold. When I am less anxious about your health, I will tell you all about the siege of Namur. . . . I hear you are very patient in this trial which God has sent us and very good in doing as you are bid. It is most important that you should not give way to impatience. Believe that no one could love you more than I do.

In Racine's next letter the child is convalescent.

Don't hurry back to your lessons just yet. Read what you like, do what tires you least, until the doctors give you leave to resume your usual course of study.

That was in June. In October the poet is on duty with the Court, and his son, in Paris, sends his Latin versions to the Palace of Fontainebleau for a parental revision. Racine, who had urged his son to read Cicero, sees that he has been spurring the child too fast, and sends him back to Livy.

For there is no use in studying what one does not understand. . . . I much approve of your excursions to Auteuil, and you give me an excellent account of them. I hope you understand how grateful you ought to be to M. Despréaux for thus condescending to entertain you. . . . Yes, you may take

Voiture's Letters out of my bookshelf. Some of them will puzzle you, no doubt, and I own I should prefer that you embarked on the translation of Herodotus. It is most amusing, and would teach you the oldest history in the world after the Holy Scriptures. At your age, one should not flit too readily from book to book ; 'tis but a waste of mind and an encumbering of the memory.

In June 1693, from the camp in Flanders, the poet writes in some haste, anxious, flustered even, to see his old dead self reviving in his son.

Let me entreat you not to give so much of your attention to the French poets. They should be just your relaxation, nothing more ; for study read Homer or Quintilian. As for your epigram, I do wish you had not written it ! Not only because it is a very ordinary sort of thing in itself, but because I earnestly recommend you not to be tempted to write French verse. Such things merely distract your mind from your proper studies. And above all never write epigrams—never write verses *against* anyone.

Racine had got thus far when he remembered the immense reputation as a satirist and writer of epigrams of Nicolas Boileau, his dearest friend, the children's fairy godfather, who, they thought, could do no wrong. He, doubtless, was the object of Jean-Baptiste's awkward imitation. The poet dips in his inkpot a more considerate pen, and resumes :

M. Despréaux of course is an exception. He has a peculiar and original talent which neither you nor anyone else could ever hope to copy. Heaven bestowed on him not only a marvellous genius for satire but an excellent judgment, quick to distinguish the true from the insincere. If he be kind enough to amuse himself with the visits of a boy like you, never forget that it is the greatest piece of good luck that could possibly befall you. I should advise you to listen respectfully to all that he has to say and not to be over-prompt with your own opinions in return.

In the next letter " Racine " is called over the

coals. He has ventured to call his father's favourite, Cicero, a poltroon !

You would be wiser not to rail at a man whom all the centuries conspire to honour! It is not decent at your age, or indeed at any age, to call a Cicero by the ugly name of coward. If you wish to express an opinion, merely say that he had not, perhaps, the intrepid courage of a Cato. Yet, if you read his Life, in Plutarch, you will see that he could show himself a fine fellow at a pinch, and I believe he would have cried out less than you did if M. Carmeline, the dentist, had scraped the tartar from his teeth. . . . In your next letter, no need to be so ceremonious, or sign yourself my "most obedient servant." It would be no great matter if you did not sign at all ; I'll warrant I could guess from the handwriting the name of my correspondent.

The most exciting letter of all, written in October 1693, brought young Racine the news of General Catinat's triumphant victory over the Duke of Savoy. What lad of fifteen (for it is a bloodthirsty age) but would be flattered at receiving such a letter from the front, and from his father !

I saw the enemy flags and banners sent into camp by M. de Catinat, and I advise you and your mother to go and look at them when they are displayed in Notre Dame. There are a hundred and two flags, but only two standards, which shows how little resistance was offered by their cavalry. They abandoned the infantry to its fate, and it was almost entirely hacked into pieces. Whole battalions of Spaniards flung themselves on their knees begging for quarter, which sometimes we granted them, but not to the Germans, who had boasted that they would give none to us.

If Racine was utterly devoted to his son, he kept a very warm corner in his heart for his daughters. There was the eldest, Marie-Catherine (always called by her full name as befitted the dignity of Mademoiselle Racine), and four charming little darlings of no importance—Nanette, Babette, Madelon and

Fanchon—the roses of Racine's quinquagenarian years—roses obviously destined for the altar! People in those days had a good many children, but if they had any sort of position to keep up only one or two of them married. The rest drifted into the religious life—into the lax, cheerful convents which so distressed Port-Royal, or, in the case of boys, became priors (often non-resident priors) or abbés; or, if they were of a warlike turn, Chevaliers of Malta or of Saint John of Jerusalem. In some great houses, especially in the south, the custom was enforced with much severity, and it is impossible to read the letters of Madame de Sévigné without feeling a great compassion for that handsome young Chevalier who so loved his beautiful sister-in-law, or for those little girls banished to a convent before they had tasted the faintest flavour of life. But in most families—and certainly in Racine's—there was no forcing a vocation—our poet, indeed, would have given much to have kept his dear girls at home— it was merely taken for granted that one of the sons (perhaps two), one or two of the daughters, should marry, and the others occupy their lives with the varied interests of a religious order. The female supernumeraries of a seventeenth-century family understood their proper place, which was to make life as important as possible for the heir to the name, resigning to him of their dowry all but the slenderest provision for the future, resolved to love his children as dearly as they could have cherished their own offspring.

When little Lionval came into the world, we seem to catch, in one of his father's letters, a sigh that the baby was not this time of that

accommodating gentler sex. He writes to his sister
in November :

> Now that we have a second son, I doubt we must relinquish
> our dream of buying an estate. We are far from rich enough
> to be able to afford such an immense advantage for our eldest
> son—and you are acquainted with the laws of primogeniture
> as to fiefs.

Racine, so anxious to be just, could not foresee
that this late-comer, this disturber of plans, was one
day to be the writer of his father's Life and, on
his own account, a very respectable poet in a minor
walk ; of all his brothers and sisters, the only one
to keep an individual claim on our remembrance.

Marie-Catherine Racine, the eldest daughter, was
a strange girl, with something of her father's nervous,
tender, impulsive disposition. Although, as the first-
born of the daughters, she was more or less entitled
to a dowry, she early declared her predilection
for the religious life. Like her father before her,
she had been a pupil of Port-Royal-des-Champs,
and her dearest wish was to become a postulant of
the Abbey. When the King forbad the reception
of novices (the rebellious sisterhood being already
doomed to death), Marie-Catherine fretted herself
into a fever, until, illuminated by a sudden inspiration, she declared that she would be a Carmelite.
Her father, full of sorrow, writes to his sister on the
10th of January, 1697 :

> I do not know if I have told you already that my dear eldest
> girl has entered a Carmelite nunnery. It is a resolution which
> has cost me many tears, but there is no gainsaying her vocation.
> She has always been the dearest to me of all my children and
> my best comfort. You cannot imagine her pretty, loving ways
> and how much she made of me.

But Marie-Catherine did not stay long in her convent. Her health gave way, she had a bad fall ; and in the following May, Racine writes that he has her back at home again. But now his second girl, Nanette, insists on entering the Convent of the Visitandines at Melun. " We defer as long as may be the moment when she shall pronounce her vows." But that day dawns in due course, and the father (weeping his heart out while his daughter takes the veil, and yet consoled to think she is safe in God's hands, shielded from the griefs and treacheries of this wicked world)—the heart-rent father perceives that it was Nanette, really, who was the flower of all his flock—dear lamb henceforth for ever separated from his private fold. He writes to his Aunt : " I may say without flattery that she is little short of an Angel " ; and to his sister :

She is extremely fond of reading and has always liked good books the best, and she has the most astounding memory. Excuse my tenderness for a child who has never caused me an hour's anxiety and who has given herself to God with such a cheerful wholeheartedness. She was certainly the handsomest of all my children, and it was on her that the world would have lavished its dangerous caresses.

It was in November 1698 that Nanette took the veil ; and this was the first real breaking-up of a happy family circle. If Racine, in the chapel at Melun, melted into a flood of tears, it was doubtless that he realized the sad finality of earthly happiness. Nanette would never come home again, and he himself was very near his end. For some time he had been out of health ; he had recently been laid up by an attack of pain and sickness, and, though

15

these troublesome symptoms were relieved, there still remained (as he writes to his Aunt, the Abbess) " a hardness on the right side, about which, I admit, I had been anxious, but the physicians tell me it will gradually yield to a course of treatment."

Meanwhile Marie-Catherine at home was moody and restless. She would, and she would not, be a nun. She lacked the cheerful serenity of Nanette.

Every ten days or so she has to go to bed with a sick headache " [writes her father to his eldest son, absent at the Hague, where he is attached to the French Embassy]. "Save for these headaches, she is happy and gentle enough, and I am edified by her piety. But if anyone calls, or drops in to a meal, how fierce and sullen she becomes! She nearly fell out the other day with Madame Le Challeux's nephew, who, meaning to be polite, gave her to understand that he admired her figure. When he had gone I was obliged to remonstrate. She would like to sit in her bedroom and see nobody. When we are alone she is bright and cheerful enough, and takes the greatest care of her little sisters and her little brother.

A few weeks later we read :

Your elder sister fills me with compassion. The poor girl cannot make up her mind, fearing to take the last engagements either with God or with the world. Your mother is very pleased with the way she conducts herself in the house. Meanwhile Madelon has caught the chicken-pox. It is no great matter, but I am anxious about little Lionval—at his age it might be serious for him. . . .

Every day at dinner, should any dish a little more dainty than usual appear upon the table, your mother never fails to say : " I am sure Racine would like a helping of that." I never saw such a good mother as you have in her or one more worthy that her children should honour her. . . . Just as I am writing your two little sisters come into the room with a bouquet for my name-day (which is yours as well as mine), since to-morrow is the 24th of June. Do not forget that Saint John the Baptist, who is your patron, is also the protector of all travellers. The Church invokes him in a prayer which is to be found in the Itinerary, and many a time have I said it on behalf of my son.

Your sister continues to ask her various spiritual directors what she ought to do—enter religion, or embrace the common lot. But you can believe that a person in need of so much advice has, all unawares, made up her own mind already and will follow her secret determination. Indeed, your mother and I are quietly on the look-out for a good husband for her—but that is easier sought than found.

The other day I was very near giving in marriage—who do you suppose ?—Why, yourself ! and without your knowing anything at all about it. When it came to the point, I found the affair was less to your advantage than I had at first supposed. No doubt but in twenty years' time you would have been very well off ; but the interval would have been difficult. . . . Of course I should not have entered into any real engagement without consulting your chief, M. l'Ambassadeur, or indeed without making sure of your own approbation. You have never seen the person in question, nor, I think, heard of her, and that is one reason why I went so warily, for, after all, it is only fair that your taste should be consulted. . . . The girl would have had eighty-four thousand francs, and at least as much more at the death of her father and mother ; but these parents are still young ; one might survive the other, marry again and have other children. And meanwhile you might have had to spend a large part of your life with an income not exceeding four thousand francs, and perhaps with eight or ten children before you reached your thirtieth year. And there could have been no question of a horse or carriage : the mere household expenses would have absorbed all your revenue.

Was young Racine indignant at this cavalier disposal of his heart and hand ? Far from it ! Vexed and almost a little indignant that so fine an affair had not come off. In vain did his father repeat that the young lady had worldly tastes. Madame Racine had to come to the rescue, assuring her son that a fortune is far less important to a bridegroom's happiness than his wife's disposition, which may make him the best-contented or most miserable of men. Jean-Baptiste seems to have been impressed by this warning of the risks of matrimony.

He never married. Diplomacy, grammar and Jansenism absorbed him more and more, and finally left no room in his heart for the gentler affections.

Of Racine's daughters, the ex-Carmelite, Marie-Catherine, was the only one to wear a wedding-ring. While she was still consulting her confessor and periodically succumbing to sick headaches, an obliging neighbour—" ce cher M. Vuillard "—discovered an excellent match among his Jansenist acquaintances. The girl had been spending six months with her great-aunt, the Abbess, at Port-Royal-des-Champs, and seemed still as unsettled, while Racine, in Paris, feeling his life-blood ooze away, was morbidly anxious to see his children settled and provided for.

He said to me [writes M. Vuillard, in one of a series of letters to a M. de Prèfontaine, published by Sainte-Beuve in the Appendix to the sixth volume of his *Port-Royal*]—he told me that if he could find a right-thinking young barrister, well-bred, well-educated, with already some promise of success in his profession, provided with a moderate competence honourably acquired, he would prefer such a match to the brilliant proposals made to him by persons of credit and position, and he besought me to give my mind to the matter. I thought at once of M. de Moramber's son—the one who will take the name of M. de Riberpré from a fief his parents possess at Éclaron—who has been spending two months in the country, where he has been reading seven hours a day with his father. He, I know, is all that M. Racine can desire in the way of reason and good feeling, so, after having sounded the parents, I made the proposal to M. Racine, who expressed much satisfaction. We then proceeded to make up the young people's accounts ; they squared exactly, and both parties are alike enchanted. M. Racine can only give his daughter twenty thousand crowns, but they are very well invested. M. de Moramber (but he would not like it to be generally known) gives fifteen thousand to his son, who has, in addition, great expectations, not only from his parents but from an elder sister who proposes not to marry in her brother's interest. Mademoiselle Racine is between eighteen and nineteen years of age ; M. de Riberpré about five-and-twenty. They seem made for each other. M. Racine calls me the Raphael of this alliance.

The wedding took place on the 7th of January—a quiet wedding with only the two families concerned, the " Raphael," and Boileau-Despréaux. Some few days earlier, the great Condé had sent to the bride's parents a mule laden with venison, a whole wild boar, with game of every sort from the woods at Chantilly, which supplied the wedding breakfast. The bridegroom's father put off his banquet until the following evening, " so as not to burden one sole day with two such feasts "; and, on the evening of the wedding day, a short sermon from the Curé of Saint Séverin's Church (who blessed the nuptial bed) was the only festivity. Racine and his wife retired at half-past eight. The young couple attended evening prayer, and all the lights were out before eleven o'clock.

And now a second bird has left the nest. Marie-Catherine is settled close to home. Nanette has carried a slender dowry to her convent at Melun, where she seems well and happy. Babette, just seventeen, has entered the Convent of Variville, near Beauvais, where her mother's sister is Prioress, and will soon pronounce her vows. Little Fanchon is at Port-Royal preparing her first communion, safe under the wing of her great-aunt the Abbess. " Racine " is provided for, with his career in diplomacy and his reversion of his father's post as Gentleman of the Chamber. Madelon, eleven years old, and Lionval, barely seven, will keep their mother company. She has good friends. Racine knows that he can count absolutely on M. Despréaux, on his new son-in-law, on M. Vuillard, on M. and Mme. de Cavoye, and, among the Great, on Condé and his son, and—who knows?—at a pinch, on the King perhaps, and on Madame de Maintenon. They will not let his widow want. He can turn his thoughts to another world. He can look Death in the face.

CHAPTER V

LAST DAYS

ALL his life Racine had been of a nervous disposition, easily startled, courageous on reflection rather than by instinct. " At the first siege of Namur," said the King one day to Boileau, " I remember that you were the bolder of the two." But Boileau had not repeated the experiment, while Racine had dragged his quivering nerves through several campaigns, in trench and under cannon-fire, as intrepid as an old trooper. All his life he had been afraid of death. " The most timorous of men about his own health," writes M. Vuillard, " so that the least scratch set him in a perfect fever." And yet the same witness tells us that, being about to die, he had become the gentlest, the most patient of mortals, with no trace remaining of his passionate and hasty character.

It was in April 1698 that his health, always delicate, had begun to fail. He will take a whole year a-dying. At first he complained of no serious disease but a complication of minor disorders : rheumatism, erysipelas, digestive troubles. He goes no more to Court. He sits at home in his study while his friends imagine him to be chewing the bitter end of unmerited disgrace. But listen to his letters to his son.

You cannot imagine how happy I am in this sort of retreat. You cannot think with what earnestness I pray God that soon you may be able to provide for yourself and do without the modest allowance that I make you, so that at last I may begin to take some rest and lead a life more in conformity with my age and, I may add, with my natural tastes.

Is this the courtier wearying for Royal recognition ? Did Racine go to Court as many a failing paterfamilias goes to the distasteful round of his office, merely because he is the bread-winner ?
And the father resumes his lesson :

Remember that our fortunes are modest. You must count much more on your own exertions than on the little I can leave you. I wish I could have done better ! But now it is your turn to work and earn. I am coming to an age when my principal study must be the salvation of my soul. These reflections will strike you as very serious, but you know that I have entertained them this long while past.

With summer time the poet's health improved ; but in September we note a return of the internal pains. On the 3rd of October the poet can only send a few lines to his son, " being dizzy with the loss of all the blood that the doctors have drawn from me these last few days." Madame Racine, kind, concerned and fussy, takes up the pen.

Your father's cholic has been much worse again with insupportable pain and fever. . . . The doctors say that it is something going about, and that many of their patients are laid up with just this sort of gripes.

She has got this far on the page when Racine puts in a word again—a veiled, cautious hint which shows how ill he feels :

It is not in the least necessary that you should make so long a journey on account of my health. But if your Chief should happen to have some message from the Hague to communicate

to His Majesty—and should he suppose the King would no
take his choice amiss—he might perhaps charge you with it.
Tell him no more than this. Let him act as he thinks best. . . .
You have been constantly in my thoughts these days. I trust
we may meet again, God willing.

Madame Racine evidently thinks the patient is
over-anxious, for she continues the parental anti-
phony in quite another vein :

Do not be surprised to see your father's handwriting so altered.
It is just because he is lying down flat in the middle of his bed.
Were he sitting up, he would write as usual.

Racine has no illusions. The pain is sometimes
intolerable. One day—the 10th of October, 1698—
when he was alone in his study, he decided to make
his will.

In the name of the Father, the Son, and the Holy Ghost.
I desire that after my death my body be carried to Port-
Royal-des-Champs and buried there in the cemetery at the
foot of M. Hamon's grave. I humbly pray the Mother Abbess
and the nuns to grant me this honour, of which I admit myself
to be most unworthy, both on account of the scandals of my
past life and because I have done so little credit to the excellent
education that I received at Port-Royal, and the great examples
of piety and penitence there placed before me. I have been
but a barren enthusiast ! But the more I have offended God
the more I need the prayers of so holy a Community to draw
towards me the Divine Mercy.
And I beg the Mother Abbess and the nuns to kindly accept
a legacy of 800 livres.
Done in my study, this 10 Oct., 1698.

Towards the middle of the month he seemed to
revive.

Thank Goodness [writes Madame Racine to her son] the
doctors say that your father's illness is absolutely devoid of
danger, but it may be a long affair, for all that. He has still
a little fever, especially of an afternoon. The pain in his side
is much relieved.

A few days later Racine is quite in good spirits, but not perhaps in good hopes. *Carpe diem* at present must be his motto.

The fever has quite gone. And your mother is well, thank God, despite all the trouble I gave her when I was so ill. Never was any nurse so vigilant or so clever, with this difference, that *her* cares welled up from the bottom of her heart and brought with them an immediate consolation. I like you to know the worth of such a mother as you have in her, and I trust that, when I shall be no longer here, she may find in you the affection and the gratitude which now she finds in me.

Things go on from better to better, and he writes :

I am well again at last ! My only dread is of those long dinners at Court, which, of late, have afforded me so little satisfaction. Henceforth I shall try to avoid the waste and idleness of that sort of existence.

The late autumn seemed to ripen a promise of recovery. Racine, restored to convalescence, goes with his wife and children to spend a happy day at Boileau's Auteuil cottage.

M. Despréaux treated us famously. He took Lionval and Madelon for a walk in the Bois de Boulogne, pretending that he was going to lose them there in a thicket. Not a blessed word of the children's prattle did the good man hear ! So, after a while, your mother, your sister, and the other guests set out to overtake them.

Racine stayed behind in the quiet garden. It was that little summer of All-Saints which, on the banks of the Seine, is often sweet and sunny. The last flowers bloomed in the beds, the robin chirped and sang. Racine, as a true Jansenist, was a firm believer in present-day miracles, and especially in the cures brought about by faith. He still kept a love of life and a belief in God's power to make him whole, if so He pleased, at any moment.

Then followed the journey to Melun and Nanette's taking of the veil, with, soon after, Marie-Catherine's wedding, which brings young Racine to Paris. By the end of January 1699 the youth is back again at the Hague, and his father writes to him :

" My health is better than when you were here. The tumour has diminished a good deal." This is the first word we have of a tumour, though, two months before, in writing to his Aunt, the Abbess, Racine has mentioned " a hardness."

I went out a walk this afternoon with your mother, thinking that the air would do me good. But we had scarce been half-an-hour in the Tuileries Gardens when I was taken with an intolerable stitch in the back, which forced me to turn back home. . . . Well, well ! I must be patient, go slowly, and wait for fine weather.

That was Racine's last letter to his son.

Henceforth it is through the correspondence of friends and acquaintances that we follow the progress of his singular and cruel illness The doctors were never quite decided by what name to call it : an abscess on the liver, or perhaps on the lungs ? The modern reader will hesitate between a hepatic cancer and a purulent pneumonia. Racine's whole character suggests tuberculosis : that extraordinary sweetness of disposition mixed with a feverish irritability, soon subsided ; that amorous temper— who knows ? perhaps that poetic genius, so strangely assorted with the dour tenets of his doctrine. . . . The doctors came, the great physicians of the Court and the eminent Jansenists too ; they shook their heads together, tried this thing and that, put in a drain (there was much discharge), let blood to relieve the congestion, attempted to allay the violent suffering. The patient bore it so sweetly that, forty years later, his elder son cannot allow Valincour to state that, on one occasion, the poor man cried out for death. Yet, on the Cross, one great cry was sent up to Heaven.

A little abscess pierced his side above the region of the liver. One morning, when Racine had gone into his study to drink his early cup of tea as was his wont, he discovered that the little wound had closed. He was filled with consternation, and cried out that, thenceforth, he was no better than a dead man. He went down into his bedroom, lay down in bed, and never got up again. . . . His pangs became so cruel that once he asked if it would be a crime to put an end to his life.

Again the suffering diminished, again Sisyphus rolled his stone towards the top of the hill. " Ce cher M. Vuillard " writes on the 19th of March :

M. Racine has been desperately ill. He is given back to us from the very gates of death. He is not yet out of danger. All Paris is concerned with his illness and anxious for his preservation—all Paris, and all the Court as well.

On the 15th of March Dangeau writes in his Diary :

Racine is at the last gasp. There is no hope of saving him. He is deeply regretted at Court. Even the King seems affected by his sad state of health and asks for news of his sufferings with much kind feeling.

And the Abbé de Vauban (the brother of Racine's friend the Field-Marshal) writes to a correspondent :

Racine is in a state of high fever with recurrent paroxysms, caused, it is believed, by an abscess on the liver. There is no hope. He lies almost unconscious. You can imagine the feelings of M. de Cavoye !

The King and Madame de Maintenon take the deepest interest in his illness.

The narrow street where Racine had the last of his many residences in Paris—the rue Visconti, as we call it to-day—was encumbered by the coaches of the Court. Great ladies thronged his modest antechamber, where Mary Hamilton, Comtesse de Graumont (as firm a Jansenist as the poet himself), was especially remarked for the abundance of her tears. The Great Condé's son was little less assiduous—that Monsieur le Duc who used to haunt Racine's study, and of whom our hero once said to his children : " Do you think it is my conversation which attracts M. le Duc ? I never open my lips. I let him say his say out, that is all ! . . ." And now the rude, irregular young man deplored his kind listener. The King himself, though he hated all that was ominous or gloomy and strove to ignore it, none the less sent daily to inquire, and was convinced the poet would pull through. As for M. and Mme. de Cavoye, living round the corner, devoted friends and admirers as they were, we can imagine their frequent ministrations.

A narrower circle visited the quiet sick-room. Boileau of course, though too deaf to be of use ; the sick man could no longer make him hear. Young Riberpré and M. Vuillard helped the devoted wife and the elder son to nurse the dying man. Dr. Félix and Dr. Dodart were in constant attendance. No eagles of science they, according to a modern estimate, but men of experience and sense, kindly souls. Dodart was that same eminent Jansenist who had prescribed for Boileau's loss of voice a course of silence, warmth, cheerful occupation—and apricot-syrup.

I was still very young when my father died [wrote the elder Racine, some forty years later to his younger brother, the poet's biographer]. Still I remember that two days before his death —M. Dodart being seated by his bedside—my father told me to go and fetch out of his study a small black box, which I still possess. I brought it, and, having unlocked it, he took out of it a manuscript in small in-folio which he put into M. Dodart's hands. I left the room, and they were a long while in conversation, undisturbed. Then M. Dodart left, taking the manuscript, but saying as he went that he hoped to bring it back again soon. And from that day to this I heard no more about it. I thought it had been lost long ago.

This mysterious and sacred deposit—a dangerous thing for a man to have in his keeping in that last year of the seventeenth century—was that Short History of the Abbey of Port-Royal which was to see the light only after a long interval (the First Part in 1742, the Second Part in 1767), it having been hidden meanwhile, probably in Holland. To give this modest abstract into safe keeping was one of Racine's last acts ; another was to tear up on his death-bed a copy of his plays in which he had corrected the faulty rhymes and vague expressions. The sacrifice must be complete.

Some days before my father's death [continues young Racine] I said to him that the doctors still hoped to save him. He answered me in these noble words :

"Let them say their say ! We are not going to contradict them. But you, my son, would you, too, deceive me ? Are you in their conspiracy ? Believe that God alone is master of the event ! And I can assure you that, did He grant me the option, Living or Dying at choice, I should not know which to choose. I have paid the price of death.

On Tuesday, the 21st of April, we find M. Vuillard in Racine's study, helping his friend's family with that burden of correspondence which presses so heavily on such occasions. And he writes :

After five-and-forty days of the most exemplary patience, God took him from us this morning early, between three and four o'clock. . . . We are going to carry him to Saint-Sulpice, where he will lie to-night, and to-morrow he will be conveyed to Port-Royal in the fields, where he has prayed the Abbess and nuns of the Convent to let him lie at the feet of M. Hamon.

The King has had the kindness to grant his consent.

The family wishes that I should accompany the elder son on this last journey of our friend's.

So Racine had his wish. The prodigal slept at last in his Father's house. But not for long. In 1710 the Abbey-in-the-Fields, so often threatened, dispersed, partially destroyed, was utterly ruined, torn, so to speak, limb from limb. The very graveyard was profaned. The vale of peace became the scene of a desolation beyond words.

But it is to the honour of womanhood that the persecution of tyrants nearly always raises up some Antigone. A noble-hearted woman — a certain Mademoiselle Issali, who had once been a postulant at the Abbey, gathered the remains of Jean Racine and transferred them to the Church of Saint-Etienne-du-Mont, one of the loveliest churches in Paris, where they lie to-day, near to the body of Pascal, beside the rescued ashes of Antoine Lemaistre and M. de Sacy, Racine's old masters at Port-Royal.

May they sleep in peace.

EPILOGUE

THE King had shown a certain magnanimity in granting Racine's last request : that he might be buried at Port-Royal—" a thing the man would never have dared to ask in his lifetime," said one of the wits of Versailles. Magnanimity was inextricably blended with the narrowness and egoism of Louis' disposition. He showed real feeling at the loss of his poet and received his heir with kindness at Versailles ; he allowed the widow and her younger children an annual pension of two thousand livres, which kept them in comfort till at last Madame Racine lost nearly all her money in Law's Bubble. Never was a woman who cared less about being ruined.

The King extended to Boileau the kindness he had felt for Racine. " We have each of us lost a good friend," he said to the satirist with his accustomed grace. And indeed, save his children, Racine had perhaps loved no one else so well as those two. Good Boileau, deafer than ever, had to spend an hour or two one morning at Versailles on a visit of condolence. " Come again often, M. Despréaux ! " cried the King. But Boileau preferred his garden at Auteuil or his winter quarters in the cloisters of Notre Dame. Deaf, gouty, kind, quick-tempered, vain and religious, he survived his younger friend eleven years. M. Vuillard writes of his petulant behaviour at the Academy.

M. Despréaux is not so dead to his own vanity as M. Racine would have been. Rectitude itself in mind and heart, a just man and a generous friend, he has never seriously felt the need of forgiving those that despitefully use us. Perhaps the prayers in Paradise of his incomparable friend, M. Racine, may come to his aid from Heaven, for he at least, so long repentant and contrite, is, we may hope, set by the Grace of God in that place of peace where the Saints intercede for those they loved on earth.

Racine a Saint? a heavenly intercessor? The idea would have confounded Boileau's benevolent admonitory affection for his friend of forty years' standing. He continued to extend a kind protection to the derelict family, and, as we read Louis Racine's *Memoirs*, we feel that " M. Despréaux " was at least as living a figure to the younger children as the father they had lost so young. As time went on, indeed, Boileau's fidelity took a patronizing tone that kept the dead man in his proper place. " Religion taught him virtue," he would say; " Nature made him sarcastic, restless and jealous." And on another occasion, speaking of the great poets who adorned the reign of Louis XIV: " We were three," said Boileau. " There was Corneille, and Molière, and . . . Myself." Some tactless listener asked where he should place Racine. " Ah, Racine!" the great man replied. " Racine was a fine mind, a man of parts! And I showed him how to make, by taking pains, beautiful verses, easy to read." So hard is it to believe in the genius or the saintliness of an intimate! But these old anecdotes, preserved in the *Bolæana*, and elsewhere, are evidence of Boileau's petulant disposition rather than of a tendency to undervalue his friend.

Jean-Baptiste Racine inherited his father's charge

as Gentleman of the Chamber ; he lived to a good old age, a dour, clever old gentleman whose letters to his younger brother are excellent reading. He was not only a Puritan but a purist, and rounds on poor Louis for using such a word as " suicide," " which, at best, can mean but a pork-butcher, the slaughterer of a sow." Fanchon and Madelon never married, nor did they enter a convent like their elder sisters, but lived with their mother, much given to good works. She, good lady, survived her illustrious husband some three-and-thirty years, devoted to the care of her affectionate children (Fanchon had inherited her father's feeble constitution) and to the relief of the poor. Madame de Riberpré lived till the middle of the eighteenth century. Little Lionval grew into M. Louis Racine, Membre de l'Institut, Inspector of Rivers and Forests, an estimable poet, elegant, religious and sincere. His life seemed a career of honest, moderate prosperity until he lost his only son in the earthquake at Lisbon in 1755. It was then that, retired from the world, he published those charming, if occasionally inaccurate, *Memoirs* which, of all his many works, alone survive him to-day.

After Racine's death the subsequent history of " ce cher M. Vuillard " is too characteristic of his times for me to pass it over in silence. On the 2nd of October, 1703, this unfortunate old man was arrested as a secret agent of the Jansenists. He was sent to the Bastille while the affair was examined —and forgotten there ! He remained twelve years in close confinement waiting for his case to come on. After the death of the King he was released, in 1715. He profited by the occasion to die in liberty at the age of seventy-six. The air of the outer world was too strong for him after so long a reclusion.

In the same year, 1715, Madame de Maintenon left the King on his death-bed and retired to Saint-Cyr, where (surely as great an idol as ever was the Living Buddha) she dwelt in an adoring community until she left this world at the age of eighty-four. Perhaps those years of grace were the happiest of her existence. The ladies of the convent used to keep a record of her conversation.

What a martyrdom was mine [she said one day to Madame de Glapion] when I lived at Court! What discomfort and constraint I used to endure while I was supposed to be the most fortunate woman in the world!

Alas! The King said to me with his dying breath: " I could not make you happy, and yet I always loved you! "

And I think he really did love me more than he loved anybody else. . . . But it was not a great deal! Only just as much as he was capable of loving!

She would perhaps have admitted that the King had sincerely loved Racine. But that affection also was no great thing—only as much as the Royal Egoist had to give.

All these persons are long since dust among the dust. Louis Quatorze indeed continues to glitter with the useless beauty of a midnight sun—a magnificent phenomenon that neither warms nor ripens. The mirage of his glory still exists ; but who can slake his thirst in the phantom waters of a mirage ? Of them all, the only one that still can charm, instruct, console and comfort is Racine, and since he continues to act upon living people we may say that he continues to live.

Years ago I cut out of a newspaper (*Écho de Paris*,

18 Avril, 1909) a piquant proof of his influence on all sorts of Frenchmen, even the least polite. A journeyman printer, one Laurent, " dit Coco," had been implicated in an accusation of burglary. Racine helped him to prove an *alibi*.

Juste à cette heure-là, je me trouvais chez un marchand de vin de la rue de Tracy, et je discutais avec un camarade au sujet de la mère de Britannicus dans la tragédie de Racine.[1]

The discussion, having lasted over three-quarters of an hour, had interested several witnesses, so that Laurent, " dit Coco," was able to prove his innocence and the use of the classics.

The journeyman printer had probably seen *Britannicus* at the Théâtre Français, and Racine is always magnificent upon the stage. Yet, for my part, I never appreciate him so much as in the quiet of my study. What a friend I have found in him all through my life ! I see a little girl of fifteen, very homesick at her school in Brussels, who cannot sleep in the moonlight that floods the room, where her companions slumber peacefully. Her bed is in the window ; her eyes are strong and young ; she draws *Esther* from under her pillow, and, learning a chorus by heart in that uncertain light, she forgets all her troubles and is as happy as a queen. Other nights too he has consoled, sadder and still more sleepless nights, when a young widow in her thirties, alone in Paris, would sit hour after hour on a cushion flung at the foot of the tall bookcase, finding an exquisite balm in *Bérénice* and *Andromaque*. Were she ever to be so unhappy again, it is *Athalie*, I think,

[1] " Just at that moment I was in a public-house at the corner of the rue de Tracy, discussing with one of my mates the character of Britannicus's mother in Racine's play."

that she should call to the rescue. A great poet has philtres to suit all ages and all characters.

To ignore Racine as a poet because of a certain superficial pomp and hyper-elegance (only conspicuous in the weaker parts) is as though we should banish Shakespeare because of the redundant metaphors, the puerile conceits, the grossness which occasionally disfigure the language of his time.

If on the principle of Phidias (who took, they say, the brows of such a model, the chin or nape of another, the lips of a third, to compose a type of beauty) I should try to reconstruct for my English readers an image of Racine, composed of more familiar material, how should I proceed? Give me the soul of Cowper—his tender, timid, often tormented piety, and the melancholy dignity of Gray; an echo of Virgil's romantic music; a reflection of Milton's awe and rapture; the emotional quality of Euripides, his pessimism too—but something still escapes me: the flame in the opal, the orient in the pearl—the very quality that *is* Racine.

The poetry of Racine is at the very heart of French literature. " Elle en est le centre incontesté," declared Sainte-Beuve in his *Port-Royal*, while admitting that " elle n'en est pas le centre unique." Rabelais, Montaigne, Molière, Corneille, 'Victor Hugo and the Romantics are not of the filiation of Racine. I hesitate for Rousseau—there is something delicate, tender and corrupt in Rousseau which is akin to that which is tender and remorseful in Racine.

Racine's true sons are few: André Chénier, Gérard de Nerval; there is a strain of him in

Lamartine; a hint of his purity in the style of Anatole France. The greatest geniuses are not the most prolific. Racine was not a garrulous Gaul, splendidly discoursing in his many-coloured plaided mantle ; by some feat of faëry he was a Greek, mysteriously Christian, set down by magic amid the woods and streams, the quivering poplars of the Ile de France.

I wonder if I have given any impression of the grandeur, the sweetness, the grace that I admire in Racine. I was wrong perhaps to make those quotations. It is as though I had taken a stone from that wall of the Acropolis (" celui qui est à gauche quand on monte aux Propylées "), that bare wall which it gave Flaubert so violent a pleasure to contemplate, because of " la précision des assemblages, la rareté des éléments, le poli de la surface, l'harmonie de l'ensemble." It is like handing you a glass of pure water from the Falls of Niagara. The detail here is nothing, and gives no conception of the mass.

And then there is the question of translation. I tried the effect of prose. But some poets cannot be translated into prose. *Vers libre* was a ridiculous failure. These poor formal verses may give, perhaps; the same effect as a blurred photograph may afford of some painting by Raphael. Better than nothing, perhaps, and that is the most we can say. But, in reading M. Maurois' brilliant *Ariel*, I was constantly vexed to find nothing which showed the quality of Shelley's poetry. And what is a poet without his poetry ? Why write about him at all ? My aim was double. I desired to show the gradual building-up, from poor beginnings, of a beautiful character ;

but also I wished to introduce my readers to a poet, one of the great poets of the world, and yet supposed to be peculiarly inaccessible to the English. And how could I do that by mere description and analysis ?

I can see no reason why the English should not love Racine. A few of us do so already—witness Mr. Lytton Strachey. Racine is a very pure and simple poet. At eight years of age, a small French child, if susceptible to poetry, may receive the revelation of beauty from him. In a recent volume M. Charles Maurras assures us that he was not older when, on reading *Athalie* in the schoolroom of a Catholic college, he experienced the mystic, electrical contact of perfection :

Adieu pudeur, scrupules de la vague et profonde sensation musicale ! La poésie parfaite, affranchissant du trouble qu'elle a créé, en retient le plaisir, et mes curiosités portent en couronne ma joie.[1]

Racine would have put the thing more simply, yet we apprehend that a boy under nine may be ravished by the loveliness of *Athalie*. Shall I have been so fortunate as to have attracted any Englishman ? Not I fear among the Romantics or among the Elizabethans ; but lovers of our English eighteenth century should not find it hard to slip a few years backward into the magic circle of Racine.

I do not present him to you as an elemental genius. He added a cubit to his stature by taking pains, both as to his art and as to his moral nature. There are characters, there are talents, like a pearl,

---

[1] Farewell, bashfulness, scruples aroused by the vague and deep sensation of music ! Perfect poetry, liberating my soul from the trouble it had created, retained the delight, and my curiosity wore as a crown my joy.—C. MAURRAS, *La Musique Intérieurs*.

which attain perfection and remain examples of a peculiar beauty, yet whose origin was marked by nothing specially divine. A grain of sand, they say, may be the starting-point of that soft iridescence which, compared with other jewels, seems alive, irradiating a pure serenity. A long patience was the genius of the humble shell-fish, which refused to suffer in ugliness, but hid the thorn in its flesh under gums and glazes, film over film, until the pain became an " orient " imprisoning the gleam of the moonlight on the waves and the first pale beams of dawn. There are poets of this sort, whose initial grain of sand becomes a pearl : born poets, but also made, and, from a sheer love of perfection, made into something richer and rarer than Nature, no doubt, intended ; no lyrical enthusiasts, singing in a fine frenzy, but not less rapt in their interminable attention, weighing every word, calculating every cadence, until they have reproduced exactly the music in their minds. Milton, it may be, was such a nympholept of beauty ; Racine was, undoubtedly. Racine, whose genius stands at the antipodes of Victor Hugo's, yet who is, with him, the greatest of French poets.

PRINCIPAL WORKS CONSULTED

Racine's Plays, Poems, Correspondence, Historical Remains and Classical Translations in M. Paul Mesnard's edition (*Grands Ecrivains de la France*, Hachette), eight volumes ; and in M. Louis Moland's edition (Garnier), eight volumes ; and in Firmin Didot's edition, three volumes ; and Agasse's edition with Laharpe's commentary, five volumes.

Mémoires sur la Vie de Jean Racine, par Louis Racine. Hachette (*Grands Ecrivains de la France*).

Port-Royal, par Sainte-Beuve (Hachette).

Histoire de France, par E. Lavisse (Hachette), t. vi, t. vii.

Histoire religieuse de la France, par George Goyau (Plon Nourrit).

Histoire de Madame Henriette d'Angleterre, par Madame de la Fayette.

Lettres de Madame de Sévigné.

Mémoires du Duc de Saint-Simon.

Journal de la Cour de Louis XIV, par le Marquis de Dangeau.

Mémoires de la Cour de France, Madame de la Fayette.

Correspondance de Madame, Duchesse d'Orléans, Princesse Palatine.

Histoire Amoureuse des Gaules, par le Comte de Bussy-Rabutin.

Lettres de Bussy-Rabutin.

Les Amours de Psyché et de Cupidon, par Jean de la Fontaine.

Œuvres et Lettres à Racine, de Boileau.

Correspondance entre Boileau et Brossette, publiée avec un Appendice par Laverdit. Paris : Techener, 1858. *Bolæana.*

Racine, par Jules Lemaître.

Racine, par Gustave Larroumet.

Les Premières de Jean Racine, par Henry Lyonnet.

Le Drame des Poisons, par Frantz Funck Brentano.

Pascal et son temps, par Fortunat Strowski.

Madame de Maintenon et Saint-Cyr, par Théophile Lavallée.

ANALYTICAL INDEX

Arnauld, a wealthy Jansenist family, the Saints and scholars of Port-Royal, nearly all of them Arnaulds, 17

Arnauld, Antoine, refuses to receive Racine, 137; their reconciliation, 138; the King sends him a monitory message, 140; leaves France, 141; his life and death in exile, 142; his heart is buried at Port-Royal, 142

Arnauld, Angélique, Abbess of Port-Royal-des-Champs, a Jansenist Saint - Theresa, reforms the Order, 17; her intolerance, 24, 72

Arnauld, Mère Angélique de Saint-Jean, Abbess of Port-Royal, niece of the precedent, 142

Arnauld, Anne-Eugénie, a nun at Port-Royal-des-Champs, describes it, 16

Arnauld (Simon, Marquis de Pomponne), in his drawing-room Racine reads his second play to a gifted audience, 57; sent by the King to warn Antoine Arnauld, 140; disgraced by the King, 143; invited, at Racine's request, to see *Esther*, 187

Boileau, Nicolas Seigneur des Préaux, poet and critic, Racine's closest friend, they make acquaintance, 46; his appearance and character, 51; his opinion of Mademoiselle du Parc, 82; his efforts to save *Britannicus*, 86; his opinion of M. and Mademoiselle de Champmeslé, 98, 118; with Racine, he writes a sonnet against the Duc de Nevers, 126; he is best man at Racine's wedding, 131; appointed, with Racine, Historiographer to the King, 132; his comfortable avarice, 135; prepares Racine's reconciliation with Port-Royal, 137-8; Boileau on a battlefield, 145; he suffers from a bad attack of aphonia, 167; takes the waters at Bourbon and corresponds with Racine, 168-72; he rehearses *Esther* with Racine at Saint-Cyr, 184; Racine praises him as satirist and friend, 221; his affection for Racine's children, 221, 234; attends Racine's death-bed, 237; pays a visit of condolence to the King, 240; his petulant behaviour at the French Academy, 241; his death, 241

Bouillon, Duchesse de, her machinations to ruin *Phèdre*, 123; before the Star Chamber, 158

Bussy-Rabutin comments on Mademoiselle du Parc, 80; comments on the beauty of Madame, 92

Cavoye, M. de, one of Racine's friends, his character and courtship, 146-7

Champmeslé, Mademoiselle de, her appearance, 96; Racine makes her acquaintance when she interprets Hermione, 97; her success in Racine's plays, 96, 98; she abandons him, 124

Chevreuse, the Duchy of, passes to the Duc de Luynes, 29

Corneille (Pierre), his fame blocks

the way, 37; sends Racine "back to his gallipots," 58; gloats over the fiasco of *Britannicus*, 86; superseded by Racine, 163; he has his turn, 104; Racine reads his panegyric to the French Academy, 165

Desmoulins, or des Moulins, a Jansenist family, 9
Desmoulins, Claude, Madame Vitart, Racine's great-aunt, 10
Desmoulins, Marie, Madame Racine, Racine's grandmother, 10; settles at Port-Royal-des-Champs, 13; her death, 66
Desmoulins, Suzanne, Madame de Saint-Paul, cellaress of Port-Royal, 10
Dodart, Denis, Dr., an eminent Jansenist physician, attends Boileau, 168; and Racine, 237; receives, on Racine's death-bed, as a sacred deposit, the poet's History of Port-Royal, 238

Fronde, a Liberal revolution that comes to nought, 15

Hamon, Monsieur, a Saint and scholar of Port-Royal, Racine's schoolmaster, 22, 223; was also the master of the Archbishop, M. de Harlay, 140; Racine in his will desires to be buried at the feet of M. Hamon, 233; and is so interred, 239
Henriette d'Angleterre, daughter of Charles I, "Madame," her position at Court, 58. *See* Madame

Jansenism contrasted with Jesuitism, 1, 15; the King's antagonism to, 139, 143, 211
Jesuits are all-powerful at Uzès, 43; Madame de Sévigné gives her opinion on them, 143; Racine has friends among them, 205; he criticizes their methods, *ibid.*

La Fontaine (Jean de), his opinion of Racine, 22; a distant connection of Racine's, their letters, 39-40; his intimacy with Racine, Boileau and Molière, 51; his account of their society in *Psyché*, 52; his portrait of Racine, 54
Lemaistre, Antoine, a hermit of Port-Royal, takes refuge with the Vitarts at La Ferté, 11; his labours at Port-Royal-des-Champs, 16; letter to Racine, 23; dies, 29; Racine mocks his memory, 71
Le Vasseur, François, in later days Prior of Ouchies, a friend of Racine's youth, 32; Racine's letters to, 33-4, 37, 44, 48; attends Racine's wedding, 131
Louis XIV, his troubles with the Fronde, 15; his marriage, 34; bestows a pension on Racine, 35; appoints him Historiographer to the Crown, 133; his dislike of the Jansenists, 139-40; invades the Low Countries, 145; deeply affected by the Poison Case, 160; his taste for praise, 166; he attends the performance of *Esther*, 184-88; his predilection for the play, 186; he appoints Racine Gentleman-in-Ordinary, 207; is offended by Racine's memorandum against excessive taxation, 209; takes a deep interest in Racine's illness, 236; grieves for his death and takes care of the widow and orphans, 240
Luxembourg, Maréchal de, returns victorious from the Netherlands, 148; his person and character, 149; he is implicated in the great poison trial

Madame, Henriette d'Angleterre, first wife of Monsieur, 91; she bids Racine and Corneille each write a play on the theme of Titus and Bérénice, 94, 99; dies, 95

Madame de Maintenon supersedes Madame de Montespan, 161 ; her secret marriage to the King, 161 ; her appearance and character, 177–8, 182 ; she asks Racine to write a pious play for her schoolgirls at Saint-Cyr, and he composes *Esther*, 179 ; her intended likeness to the heroine, 180–83 ; her interest in Saint-Cyr, 181 ; she refuses to let *Athalie* be played with the pomp of *Esther*, 197 ; her ill-considered conduct as to Racine's memorandum, 209 ; her sensitiveness as to any suspicion of heresy, 211 ; she disowns Racine, 213 ; Saint-Simon's appreciation of her, 214

Madame de Montespan, the King's passion for her, 161

Madame, Princess Palatine, her opinion of Louis XIV, 144, 166 ; believes that Madame de Montespan poisoned Fontanges, 158 ; declares the King prefers an Atheist to a Jansenist, 211

Molière meets Racine at the King's Levée, 48 ; offers to produce *La Thébaïde* in his theatre of the Palais Royal, 49 ; his roving career, 50 ; Racine's breach with him, 55, 64 ; applauds *Les Plaideurs*, 85

Nicole, the breach with Racine, 70 *et seq.* ; is reconciled with Racine, 136

Parc (Mademoiselle du), Marquise de Gorle, widow of René Berthelot, appears in Racine's second play, *Le Grand Alexandre*, 59 ; Racine falls in love with her, 60 ; her previous career, 61–2 ; a dancer as well as an actress, 63 ; Racine persuades her to leave Molière's theatre for the Hôtel de Bourgogne, 64 ; where she plays the title part in *Andromaque*, 64 ; her relations with Racine, 74–8 ; the Chevalier de Rohan wishes to marry her, 79, 80 ; her mysterious death, 81 ; his liaison with Mademoiselle de Champmeslé, 96 *et seq.* ; her daughters find a refuge in the house of the Comtesse de Soissons, 122 ; Madame Voisin accuses Racine of having poisoned her, 154–5

Pascal, Blaise, at Port-Royal-des-Champs, 24 ; his *Lettres Provinciales* read by the Huguenots at Uzès, 43 ; his early death, 46 ; Racine compares the *Provinciales* to a comedy, 70

Port-Royal-des-Champs, the Abbey of, a hotbed of Jansenism, 9 ; " the Gentlemen of Port-Royal," 11 ; harbours most of young Racine's relations, 13 ; its situation described, 16–19 ; the schools of Port-Royal, 19–21 ; Racine educated there, 21–9 ; described in verse by the boy Racine, 25–6 ; Port-Royal disowns Racine, 69 *et seq.* ; Racine writes its history, 203–5 ; Port-Royal defended and abetted by Racine, 206–7 ; he begs to be buried there and leaves a legacy to the Abbey, 233

Racine, Agnès, afterwards Mère Agnès de Sainte-Thècle, Racine's aunt, 11, 13 ; her influence on Jean Racine, 21 ; her letter to him, 69 ; prepares Racine's reconciliation with Port-Royal, 136 ; Racine's letters to her, 225, 226 ; Racine writes concerning her to Madame de Maintenon, 212 ; her nieces visit her at Port-Royal, 228

Racine, Jean, a clerk in the Salt Office at La Ferté-Milon, grandfather of the poet, 10 ; dies, 13

Racine, Jean, his son, marries Jeanne Sconin ; they both die young, 13

Racine, Jean, the third, his son, the poet, born at La Ferté, 1639,

12 ; brought up by his grand-parents, 13 ; sent to school at Beauvais, 14 ; joins his family at Port-Royal-des-Champs, 17 ; his education, 19–29 ; his early verses, 25–6 ; enters the land-agent's office of his cousin Nicolas Vitart, 29 ; continues his studies at the Collège d'Har-court, 30 ; his appearance, 31 ; in charge of the repairs to the Chateau de Chevreuse, 33 ; he writes his Ode to the Nymph of the Seine, which wins him a prize and a pension from Louis XIV, 35 ; his life at Chevreuse, 36 ; his journey to Uzès, 38–9 ; his stay there, 38–44 ; he gives up the idea of embracing the life of a monk, 44 ; he leaves Uzès, 45 ; his ecclesiastical sinecures, *ibid.* ; he begins to write for the theatre, 46 ; and produces *La Thébaïde*, 49 ; his meeting with Molière, 48 ; described by La Fontaine, 54 ; his breach with Molière, 55, 59 ; he persuades Made-moiselle du Parc to leave Molière's theatre for the Hôtel de Bour-gogne, where she plays the title part in *Andromaque* with brilliant success, 64 ; his detachment from Port-Royal, 70–2 ; his rela-tions with Mademoiselle du Parc, 78–9 ; his grief at her death, 81 ; he goes to law, loses his suit, and writes *Les Plaideurs*, 83 *et seq.* ; *Britannicus*, 86 *et seq.* ; his liasion with Mademoiselle de Champmeslé, 97 ; he produces *Bérénice*, 100 ; produces *Bajazet*, 105–10; elected a member of the French Academy, 110 ; pro-duces *Mithridate*, 110–13 ; pro-duces *Iphigénie*, 117 *et seq.* ; the fiasco of *Phèdre*, 121–3 ; he composes a sonnet against the Duke of Nevers, 126 ; Racine's religious conversion, 128–9 ; his marriage with Catherine de Romanet, 131 ; he sets up house,

his means, 132 ; appointed, with Boileau, Historiographer to the King, 132 ; his reconciliation with Port-Royal, 136–9 ; meets M. de Harlay at Port-Royal, 140–2 ; accompanies the King to the seat of war, 146–8 ; Racine is accused of having poisoned Mademoiselle du Parc, 152 ; reader to the King, 162 ; asked by Madame de Maintenon to write a play for Saint-Cyr, he composes *Esther*, 178–9 ; rehearses the play at Saint-Cyr, 182 ; its performance a triumph, 184–8 ; he is discouraged by the slight success of *Athalie*, 199 ; he composes his spiritual songs, 200 ; Racine's History of Louis XIV consumed in a fire, 203 ; Racine the constant intercessor between Port-Royal and the King, 206 ; he is accorded the post of Gentleman in-Ordinary to the Chamber, 207 ; he finds it difficult to pay the tax, 208 ; he protests against over-taxation, 208 ; sends a memorandum on the subject to Madame de Main-tenon which the King intercepts, 209 ; Racine falls into a state of semi-disgrace, 210 *et seq.* ; his letter to Madame de Main-tenon, 212 ; he meets her in the Park at Versailles, where she disowns him, 213 ; Racine the kindest father of a family, 215 ; Racine's domestic character, 216 *et seq.* ; his generosity, 216–18 ; his letters to his son, 220–22 ; his second daughter takes the veil, 225 ; his own ill-health, 226 ; he looks out for a husband for his elder daughter, preferring a barrister, 228 ; becomes seri-ously ill, 231 ; he makes his will, 233 ; and asks to be buried at the feet of M. Hamon ; a tumour on the liver or lungs ? 235 ; his last illness, 236–8 ; and death, 239 ; he is buried at Port-Royal, 239.

Racine, Catherine de Romanet, wife of the poet, her marriage, 132; character and tastes, 134, 135; her views on marriage, 227; her letters to her son, 232–3

Racine, Jean-Baptiste, son of the poet: his father's letters to him, 220, 222, 226–7, 232, 235; he is attached to the French Embassy at the Hague, 226; a proposal of marriage, 227; fetches the History of Port-Royal, which his father, dying, entrusts to Dr. Dodart, 238; accompanies his father's remains to Port-Royal, 239; his old age, 242

Racine, Marie-Catherine, the poet's elder daughter, her character, 224; enters a nunnery, 224; returns home ill, 225; her poor health, 226–8; she marries Claude-Pierre Collin de Morambert, Seigneur de Riberpré, 229; she dies in 1751, leaving offspring, 242

Racine, Anne (Nanette), the poet's second daughter, her character, 225; she takes the veil, 225

Racine, Elizabeth (Babet), the poet's third daughter, she takes the veil, 229

Racine, Madeleine (Madelon), the poet's fourth daughter, lives with her widowed mother, 242

Racine, Jeanne Nicole Françoise (Fanchon), the poet's fifth daughter, her visit to Port-Royal, 229, 242

Racine, Louis (Lionval), the poet's second son, his birth, 224; his career: in 1755, being at Cadiz, Louis Racine's only son is engulphed by a tidal wave caused by the Lisbon earthquake, 242; the bereaved father writes the *Memoirs of Jean Racine*, 242; he leaves two daughters, Anne, Madame des Radrets, and Marie-Anne, Madame d'Hariagne

Rohan, Chevalier, proposes to marry Mademoiselle du Parc, 79–80

Saint-Simon, Duc de, recounts the marriage of M. de Cavoye, 147; considers the King's courtesy was acquired in the circle of the Countess of Soissons, 160; his opinion of Racine, 162; his opinion of Madame de Maintenon, 214

Sacy, Isaac Lemaistre, M. de Sacy, tells the boy Racine that his forte is not poetry: Racine gibes at him, 71

Sconin, Antoine, Vicar-General of the diocese of Uzès, Prior of Saint-Maximin, ex-General of the Order of Saint Geneviève, Racine's uncle, born at La Ferté-Milon in 1608, invites Racine to Uzès, 38; his character, 41; Racine's stay with him at Uzès, 38, 45; he procures Racine the benefice of Sainte-Madeleine de l'Epinay in Anjou, 45

Sconin, Jeanne, mother of the poet, 12

Sévigné, Marquise de, her opinion on Mademoiselle de Champmeslé, 96, 98, 106–7; of the Jesuits, 143; she details the circumstances of Luxembourg's imprisonment, 150; her comments on the burning of Madame Voisin, 158; her opinion of *Esther* and of Racine, 187; she attends the play, 187–8

Spanheim, his criticism of Racine's character, 143, 162–3, 202

Uzès, Racine's year-long sojourn there, 38–45

Valincour hears Racine declaiming the end of *Mithridate* in the Tuileries Gardens, 110; Racine's History burned in the fire that consumed Valincour's house at Saint-Cloud, 203; Valincour's praise of the poet's domestic life, 215; attends the poet in his last illness, 236

Vauban, Maréchal de, Racine's description of his fortifications, 169; he pilots Racine through the new redoubts, 173; a friend of Racine's, 210

Vitart, Claude, von Desmoulins, 10

Vitart, Nicolas, the elder, leaves La Ferté for Port-Royal; dies, 13

Vitart, Nicolas, the younger, his son, educated at Port-Royal, brings the banished hermits to La Ferté-Milon, 11; returns to Port-Royal with his parents, 13; one of the earliest pupils there, 17; he becomes land-agent and steward to the Duchess of Chevreuse and her son the Duc de Luynes, 30; and takes Racine into his office; shows Racine's Ode to Colbert, who shows it to the King, 35; best man at Racine's wedding, 131

Vitart, Marguerite Le Mazier, wife of Nicolas Vitart the younger, her affectionate relations with Racine, 30, 32

Voisin, Madame, acquainted with Mademoiselle du Parc, 81; a Parisian celebrity, 152; her arrest, 153; she accuses Racine of having poisoned Mademoiselle du Parc, 154-5; she is burned alive, 157-8

Vuillard, Germain (often spelt Willard), an intimate friend of Racine's, 207; finds a husband for the poet's daughter, 228; attends him in his last illness, 231, 236, 237, 238; and accompanies his body to Port-Royal, 239; sad fate of Vuillard, 242

THE LIFE OF RACINE

Racine.

From an Engraving by Achille Jacquet after Santerre's portrait.

"*Vous pouvez trouver Racine parfumé, alambiqué, et vous ne le lirez même peut-être pas. Peut-être le trouverons-nous même ridicule. Il est pourtant charmant, et, que nous le voulions ou non, c'est un grand poète.*"—Dostoïevsky : *Le Joueur.*

THE LIFE OF RACINE

By MARY DUCLAUX (A. MARY F. ROBINSON)

KENNIKAT PRESS
Port Washington, N. Y./London

THE LIFE OF RACINE

First published in 1925
Reissued in 1972 by Kennikat Press
Library of Congress Catalog Card No: 73-153904
ISBN 0-8046-1595-0

Manufactured by Taylor Publishing Company   Dallas, Texas